"This nuanced, authoritative book shows the diverse approaches to gender variance that Christians can hold with integrity. Scientifically, biblically, and theologically rigorous, *Understanding Gender Identities* confidently leads readers through a field too often fraught with misinformation. Readers who approach the book with a point of view about gender variance—and those who do not know what to make of it at all—will find themselves gently challenged. The authors model robust yet respectful disagreement, challenging and stirring one another. This is a book with love, compassion, and a deep yearning for truth and divine light at its heart."

—**Susannah Cornwall**, senior lecturer in constructive theologies
and director of EXCEPT (Exeter Centre for Ethics
and Practical Theology), University of Exeter

Understanding Transgender Identities

FOUR VIEWS

Edited by James K. Beilby
and Paul Rhodes Eddy

B
Baker Academic
a division of Baker Publishing Group
Grand Rapids, Michigan

© 2019 by James K. Beilby and Paul Rhodes Eddy

Published by Baker Academic
a division of Baker Publishing Group
PO Box 6287, Grand Rapids, MI 49516-6287
www.bakeracademic.com

Printed in the United States of America

Library of Congress Cataloging-in-Publication Data
Names: Beilby, James K., editor.
Title: Understanding transgender identities : four views / edited by James K.
    Beilby and Paul Rhodes Eddy.
Description: Grand Rapids : Baker Academic, a division of Baker Publishing
    Group, 2019. | Includes index.
Identifiers: LCCN 2019007904 | ISBN 9781540960306 (pbk.)
Subjects: LCSH: Sex—Religious aspects—Christianity. | Gender identity—
    Religious aspects—Christianity. | Transgender people—Identity.
Classification: LCC BT708 .U53 2019 | DDC 233/.5—dc23
LC record available at https://lccn.loc.gov/2019007904

ISBN 978-1-5409-6244-7 (casebound)

James K. Beilby and Paul Rhodes Eddy: To our students at Bethel University, particularly those whom it has been our honor to walk alongside as they wrestle with questions of sexual and gender identity

Contents

4. Holy Creation, Wholly Creative: God's Intention
   for Gender Diversity   *Justin Sabia-Tanis*   195

Acknowledgments

We would like to begin by offering our profound thanks to each of our five contributors—Megan DeFranza, Justin Sabia-Tanis, Julia Sadusky, Owen Strachan, and Mark Yarhouse. Together, they made this book into the insightful, challenging, and graciously dialogical volume that it is. Working with them, both individually and as a team, was a joy throughout the entire process. We also want to thank our longtime friend and Baker executive editor extraordinaire, Robert Hosack, for his faith in and guidance throughout this project. And as always, we are thankful for our families—our children and our wives, Michelle Beilby and Kelly Eddy, who have offered their never-ending support of our theological ventures.

I (Jim) would like to thank Bethel University for supporting this project with a sabbatical during the spring semester of 2017 and a course release during interim 2018. I would also like to thank the good people at TreeHouse for an invitation to speak to their staff. As practitioners on the front lines of youth support and outreach, they were invaluable conversation partners.

I (Paul) would like to thank Bethel University for supporting this project in the form of a sabbatical in the fall semester of 2017 and for the ongoing support of the amazing interlibrary loan team. A word of appreciation goes to David and Shirl Romberger for their special friendship and for the gift to my family of the use of 512—and the beauty of Anna Maria—during the sabbatical. Finally, I am deeply thankful to Woodland Hills Church, where I serve as a teaching pastor, for its ongoing encouragement and support of my research and writing.

Finally, we want to offer a special word of thanks to our many Bethel University students over the years who, through their questions and desire to learn, have challenged us to think better and communicate more clearly about important issues. We dedicate this book to them.

Understanding Transgender Experiences and Identities

An Introduction

Paul Rhodes Eddy and James K. Beilby

Since the social ferment of the 1960s, Western culture has become increasingly attuned to matters of **sexuality** and **gender**. Over the last two decades, one way this new sensitivity has manifested is in the increasing awareness of the experiences and identities of **transgender** people. While the contemporary understanding of transgender identity was largely forged in the late twentieth century, it has only been within the last few years that our culture, in the words of *Time* magazine, has reached a "transgender tipping point."[1] Key moments have included Diane Sawyer's *20/20* interview of Caitlyn Jenner in April 2015; the debut in July of that same year of *I Am Jazz*, a reality TV show featuring Jazz Jennings, a transgender teen; and the back-and-forth of the transgender "bathroom debate."

While the church has spent significant energy in recent years engaging certain questions surrounding gender and sexuality—questions about the role of gender in marriage, the place of women in ministry, and an understanding of homosexuality within the context of the Christian life—much less attention has been given thus far to transgender experience. To date, most of what has

---

1. Katy Steinmetz, "The Transgender Tipping Point," *Time*, May 29, 2014. The issue's cover uses the tagline "America's Next Civil Rights Frontier."

been written on this subject comes from the more liberal/progressive quarters of the Christian world.[2] When it comes to more traditional Christian engagement with transgender identity, serious conversation has barely begun.[3]

It is the purpose of this book to further the Christian conversation on transgender experience and identity by bringing a range of perspectives into dialogue. The bulk of the book will be devoted to reflections from our five contributors and their responses to each other's reflections. This introduction will serve to set the context for the dialogue. We will begin by offering a survey of key historical moments over the last century or so (with a focus on the North American context). Next, we will touch on some of the contemporary issues, questions, and debates surrounding transgender experiences and identities. Finally, we will set the stage for the conversation on transgender identity in Christian perspective that follows.

Before we continue, a few words about language and terminology: First, throughout this introduction, we will be using terminology, some of it quite technical, that is specifically related to the contemporary transgender conversation. Some of it may be unfamiliar to the reader. We will, now and then, provide definitions in the text as we proceed, but a more thorough list of terms and their definitions is provided in a glossary at the back of the book. Any term that appears in the glossary will be placed in bold at its first use within the book. Second, as one author of an introductory book on our topic observes, "One of the biggest challenges people face when addressing or talking about trans individuals is the use of pronouns."[4] The issue of pronoun use can be especially challenging for the Christian community, given that significant theological convictions can underlie differences of opinion on this question.[5] No matter one's perspective, every Christian should be able

2. For a small representative sampling, see Vanessa Sheridan, *Crossing Over: Liberating the Transgender Christian* (Cleveland: Pilgrim, 2001); Justin Tanis, *Trans-Gendered: Theology, Ministry, and Communities of Faith* (Cleveland: Pilgrim, 2003); and Christina Beardsley and Michelle O'Brien, eds., *This Is My Body: Hearing the Theology of Transgender Christians* (London: Darton, Longman & Todd, 2016).

3. The short list of books from this sector of Christianity includes Oliver O'Donovan, *Transsexualism and Christian Marriage* (Nottingham: Grove, 1982); Mark A. Yarhouse, *Understanding Gender Dysphoria: Navigating Transgender Issues in a Changing Culture* (Downers Grove, IL: IVP Academic, 2015); and Andrew T. Walker, *God and the Transgender Debate: What Does the Bible Actually Say about Gender Identity?* (Purcellville, VA: Good Book, 2017).

4. Nicholas M. Teich, *Transgender 101: A Simple Guide to a Complex Issue* (New York: Columbia University Press, 2012), 11.

5. E.g., Walker, *Transgender Debate*, 156–57; and Denny Burk, "Bruce or Caitlyn? He or She? Should Christians Accommodate Transgender Naming?," June 4, 2015, http://www.denny burk.com/bruce-or-caitlyn-he-or-she-should-christians-accomodate-transgender-naming/.

to agree with Andrew Walker that our disagreements on this topic must be done charitably.[6]

Transgender Experiences and Identities: A History

One might think that it was only within the last few years—with the fame of transgender people like Chaz Bono, Laverne Cox, Janet Mock, and Caitlyn Jenner—that transgender experience first attracted media attention. Not so. It was December 1, 1952, when the *Daily News* in New York City ran a front-page story with the headline "Ex-GI Becomes Blonde Beauty." And with that, Christine Jorgensen was introduced to America. Transgender histories within the US context commonly begin with Jorgensen (1926–89), the first American to become widely known for having a procedure referred to at the time as a "sex change" but more commonly known today as **sex reassignment surgery (SRS)**, **gender reassignment surgery**, **gender confirmation surgery**, or **gender-affirming surgery**. Jorgensen's surgery was performed in Denmark, and upon returning to the US she became an instant celebrity. She went on to work as an actor and entertainer and became an early transgender advocate.[7]

While Jorgensen was the first **transsexual** person to gain widespread recognition in America, others preceded her in this journey, both in the US and beyond.[8] Certain medical advances were necessary before SRS could become truly viable, including anesthesia, hormone therapy, and plastic surgery. Genital reconstruction surgery initially grew as a response to children with **intersex** conditions and victims of accidents and war injuries.[9] But medical

6. Walker, *Transgender Debate*, 156. It is our view that both charity (*agape*-love) and the church's missional calling are best served by our meeting people wherever they are, regardless of our personal agreement with them (e.g., 1 Cor. 9:19–23). This would include referring to transgender people in the way they prefer. It is in this light that we will approach language issues in this introduction.

7. See Christine Jorgensen, *Christine Jorgensen: A Personal Autobiography* (New York: Bantam, 1967).

8. On transsexuality prior to Jorgensen's transition in the 1950s, see Vern L. Bullough and Bonnie Bullough, *Cross Dressing, Sex, and Gender* (Philadelphia: University of Pennsylvania Press, 1993), pt. 1; Joanne Meyerowitz, *How Sex Changed: A History of Transsexuality in the United States* (Cambridge, MA: Harvard University Press, 2002), chap. 1; and Susan Stryker, *Transgender History* (Berkeley: Seal, 2008), 31–47. For a case of transsexuality in the 1930s, see Lili Elbe, *Man into Woman: An Authentic Record of a Change of Sex* (London: Blue Boat, 1933).

9. On intersex conditions—formerly known as hermaphroditism, and often referred to within medical literature today as **differences/disorders of sex development (DSDs)**—see Alice D. Dreger, *Hermaphrodites and the Medical Intervention of Sex* (Cambridge, MA: Harvard University Press, 1998); and Megan K. DeFranza, *Sex Difference in Christian Theology: Male, Female, and Intersex in the Image of God* (Grand Rapids: Eerdmans, 2015).

advances were not the only necessary condition for SRS to arise. Technological capacity had to be paired with a hospitable theory of sexuality. And just such a theory was in the air in the late nineteenth and early twentieth centuries: the theory of the universal constitutional bisexuality of humanity (i.e., the idea that human sexual differentiation is **nonbinary** in nature). The germ of this idea can be traced back to Charles Darwin, who set the stage for a "new genderless human nature,"[10] and it can be found running through the thought of many of the early leading sexologists (e.g., Magnus Hirschfeld, Havelock Ellis, Sigmund Freud, and James Kiernan). This idea leads to the conclusion that the male and female sexes do not conform to a strict binary but instead reflect something of a continuum. Within this intellectual atmosphere, the idea that a man could become a woman, or vice versa, seemed increasingly plausible.

Prior to the mid-twentieth century—and under the powerful influence of the father of modern sexology, German psychiatrist Richard von Krafft-Ebing, and his magnum opus, *Psychopathia Sexualis*—people who are referred to today as transgender or transsexual were commonly identified as expressing homosexuality, sexual **fetish**, or psychosis.[11] However, in the first decade of the twentieth century, German sexologist Magnus Hirschfeld became the first to clearly distinguish homosexuality and transvestism (from "cross" [*trans*] "dress" [*vestis*])—which in its most "extreme" form today would be called transsexuality.[12] In 1949, David Cauldwell first used the term "transsexualism" to identify people wanting to change their sex.[13]

With new terminology came more nuanced categories and the ability to distinguish between different phenomena. By midcentury, transvestism—or what is more commonly referred to as **cross-dressing** today—was given a clear distinction and public voice by Virginia Charles Prince.[14] For Prince, a self-described transvestite or "femmiphile" (i.e., a lover of the feminine)

10. Lawrence Birken, *Consuming Desire: Sexual Science and the Emergence of a Culture of Abundance, 1871–1914* (Ithaca, NY: Cornell University Press, 1989), 74. See also Meyerowitz, *How Sex Changed*, 22–29.

11. Richard von Krafft-Ebing, *Psychopathia Sexualis: With Especial Reference to the Antipathic Sexual Instinct: A Medico-Forensic Study*, trans. F. J. Rebman, 12th ed. (1906; repr., New York: Physicians and Surgeons Book Co., 1933), 218, 253, 310, 322–24.

12. Magnus Hirschfeld, *The Transvestites: An Investigation of the Erotic Drive to Cross Dress*, trans. M. A. Lombardi-Nash (1910; repr., Buffalo, NY: Prometheus, 1991).

13. David O. Cauldwell, "Psychopathia Transexualis," *Sexology* 16, no. 5 (1949): 274–80.

14. On Virginia Prince, see Richard Ekins and Dave King, eds., *Virginia Prince: Pioneer of Transgendering* (Binghamton, NY: Haworth Medical, 2006); and Bullough and Bullough, *Cross Dressing*, chap. 12. On cross-dressing through history, see Bullough and Bullough, *Cross Dressing*; and Gregory G. Bolich, *Transgender History and Geography* (Raleigh, NC: Psyche's, 2007).

who founded the newsletter *Transvestia* in the 1960s, transvestism was quite distinct from both homosexuality and transsexuality. Prince went on to use the terms "sex" and "gender" to distinguish her transvestism from transsexuality: "I, at least, know the difference between sex and gender and have simply elected to change the latter and not the former."[15]

Through the twentieth century, as transsexuality and cross-dressing were increasingly distinguished both from homosexuality and from each other, another distinction emerged: dressing in drag. "Drag" refers to dressing in clothing associated with the opposite sex, as with cross-dressing, but differs in that it is often for entertainment purposes. Drag has an extensive history within the performing arts, with the performer in drag often enacting exaggerated gender stereotypes associated with that sex. Men who dressed in order to impersonate women became known as **drag queens**, while female impersonators of men became known as **drag kings**.[16]

The 1950s and '60s brought new language and categories that forever transformed how people thought about sexuality and, eventually, **gender identity**. Most importantly, the ideas of **sex** and gender became increasingly distinguished. "Sex" refers to the biological/physical characteristics that identify humans as male and female (i.e., chromosomes, sex hormones, gonads, genitals, etc.). "Gender," on the other hand, refers both to one's gender identity (i.e., one's inner sense of being a man or woman, or what some referred to as one's "psychological sex") and to one's **gender role / expression** (i.e., the outward manifestation of one's gender identity, typically expressed in societal norms associated with masculinity or femininity).[17] These categories were originally formed by doctors and psychologists engaged with the treatment of intersex conditions. It wasn't long, however, before they were being used to explain transsexual persons as well. In this atmosphere, it was increasingly the case that "the mind—the sense of self—was [seen as] less malleable than the body."[18]

In 1966, a landmark book by Harry Benjamin was published: *The Transsexual Phenomenon*.[19] By the time the book was written, Benjamin (who

---

15. Virginia Prince, "Change of Sex or Gender," *Transvestia* 10, no. 60 (1969): 65.

16. See Bullough and Bullough, *Cross Dressing*, chap. 10.

17. As early as 1945, Madison Bentley used the term "gender" to signal "the socialized obverse of sex," while John Money first published on the idea of gender role in 1955. See respectively, Madison Bentley, "Sanity and Hazard in Childhood," *American Journal of Psychology* 58, no. 2 (1945): 228; and John Money, "Hermaphroditism, Gender, and Precocity in Hyperadrenocorticism: Psychologic Findings," *Bulletin of the Johns Hopkins Hospital* 96, no. 6 (1955): 253–64 (esp. 254).

18. Meyerowitz, *How Sex Changed*, 99.

19. Harry Benjamin, *The Transsexual Phenomenon* (New York: Julian, 1966).

served as Christine Jorgensen's endocrinologist) had already been advising transsexual patients regarding the **transition** process—that is, transitioning from living as their **birth sex** (or **assigned sex**) to living in congruence with their gender identity. Along with John Money (who founded the Johns Hopkins Gender Identity Clinic in 1965), Benjamin became a leading resource and advocate for those seeking hormone therapy and SRS.

Throughout the 1960s and '70s, transsexuality slowly grew in terms of public awareness and acceptance.[20] When Money opened the Johns Hopkins clinic in 1965, it became the first major US clinic offering SRS. Others quickly followed. By 1975, over twenty major centers were offering treatment, and around a thousand people had undergone surgery.[21] Despite the growing availability of medical centers able and willing to guide people through the stages of transition, most transsexuals were not able to afford such an expensive procedure. In the mid-1960s, the Erickson Educational Foundation (EEF)—founded and run by Reed Erickson, a female-to-male (**FtM**) **transman**—stepped in to aid in the funding of transsexual research.[22]

During this period, transgender activism grew. The 1966 riot at the Compton Café in San Francisco—a response by drag queens and transvestites to police raids—has been deemed the first significant act of transgender-focused protest in America.[23] The 1970s saw the formation of new transgender-related organizations.[24] An important public figure at this time was Renée Richards, a **transwoman** who underwent a male-to-female (**MtF**) transition in 1975. The next year, she was denied entrance to the women's US Open tennis tournament. Richards fought the decision, and in 1977 the New York Supreme Court ruled in her favor. The incident became a landmark moment for transgender rights.

While the 1960s and '70s brought increasing awareness and acceptance of transgender people, this time period also brought new challenges and critiques. One area of challenge was largely the result of a medical "turf

20. Meyerowitz, *How Sex Changed*, 188–254; Stryker, *Transgender History*, chaps. 3–4; and Barry Reay, "The Transsexual Phenomenon: A Counter-History," *Journal of Social History* 47, no. 4 (2014): 1042–70.

21. Meyerowitz, *How Sex Changed*, 217–22. As Reay notes in "Transsexual Phenomenon," this doesn't mean things were anything like smooth sailing for the transgender community during these years.

22. Aaron H. Devor and Nicholas Matte, "ONE Inc. and Reed Erickson: The Uneasy Alliance of Gay and Trans Activism, 1964–2003," *GLQ* 10, no. 2 (2004): 179–209.

23. The 2005 film *Screaming Queens: The Riot at Compton's Cafeteria*, written and directed by Susan Stryker and Victor Silverman, documents this event.

24. Jordy Jones, "Transgender Organizations and Periodicals," in *Encyclopedia of Lesbian, Gay, Bisexual, and Transgender History in America*, ed. Marc Stein (New York: Thomson Gale, 2004), 3:196–99.

war."[25] As the number of medical doctors willing to assist people in transitioning grew, pushback came from the psychiatric and psychological fields, where psychotherapeutic interventions were encouraged instead. From the beginning, many psychoanalysts working within the Freudian tradition were particularly critical of so-called sex-change interventions.[26] In the early 1960s, UCLA's department of psychiatry opened its Gender Identity Research Clinic. In contrast to Money's clinic, the UCLA clinic would neither assist in nor recommend transitioning for transsexuals. Instead, psychotherapeutic protocols were developed with the intention of enabling gender-variant children to eventually embrace their birth sex and its gender identity correlates.[27]

To close out the decade, 1979 brought a year of conflicting episodes in America. On the one hand, a Standards of Care (SoC)—a milestone in medical care protocol for transsexual persons—was released for the first time. This SoC was designed for several purposes, including advising the health care world on appropriate treatment protocols, protecting transgender patients from less-than-appropriate treatment methods, and safeguarding medical professionals from accusations of malpractice. Originally known as the Harry Benjamin Standards of Care, it was produced by the Harry Benjamin International Gender Dysphoria Association (HBIGDA), which was launched that same year. In 2007, HBIGDA changed its name to the World Professional Association for Transgender Health (WPATH), and the SoC was renamed Standards of Care for the Health of Transsexual, Transgender, and Gender Nonconforming People. This document is regularly revised by WPATH and is the most common protocol document for professionals working with the transgender community today.[28]

On the other hand, 1979 also marked the year in which Paul McHugh, the new director of the department of psychiatry at Johns Hopkins, put an end to performing SRS at the very clinic where John Money had begun it all. McHugh has gone on to become a leading voice among those warning that transitioning

25. Meyerowitz, *How Sex Changed*, 107. One can get a sense of the range of views in this skirmish in Richard Green and John Money, eds., *Transsexualism and Sex Reassignment* (Baltimore: Johns Hopkins University Press, 1969). On the fraught relationship between the psychoanalytic movement and transsexuals, see Patricia Elliot, "Psychoanalysis," *Transgender Studies Quarterly* 1, nos. 1–2 (2014): 165–68; and Reay, "Transsexual Phenomenon."

26. See Reay, "Transsexual Phenomenon."

27. Robert J. Stoller, *Sex and Gender: On the Development of Masculinity and Femininity* (New York: Science House, 1968); and Richard Green, *Sexual Identity Conflict in Children and Adults* (New York: Basic Books, 1974).

28. The current (seventh) version was published in 2011 and is available at https://www.wpath.org/publications/soc.

is not the best response to **gender dysphoria**.[29] The year 1979 also saw the publication of Janice Raymond's *The Transsexual Empire*, the most well-known feminist critique of transsexuality.[30] Raymond challenged both the medical/psychiatric approach to transsexualism as a disease and transitioning as its cure.

There is broad agreement that the 1980s saw a significant conservative cultural adjustment to America. This cultural shift, which began in the late '70s and extended through the '80s, brought both a conservative political impulse, marked by the Reagan presidency, and the emergence of a number of new socially conservative, often explicitly Christian organizations such as Focus on the Family, the National Federation for Decency, and the Moral Majority. The 1980s served as the immediate context for what James Davison Hunter identified as the "culture wars."[31]

According to transgender historian Susan Stryker, during this time things became increasingly difficult for the transgender community. "All across the political spectrum, from reactionary to progressive, and all points in between, the only options presented to [transgender people] were to be considered bad, sick or wrong."[32] The decade opened with the term "transsexualism" being included for the first time in the American Psychiatric Association's *Diagnostic and Statistical Manual of Mental Disorders* (*DSM*). Its inclusion as a diagnosable mental disorder within the *DSM*—which fosters the notion that transgender experience is a form of pathology—has continued to be a point of contention between the transgender and psychiatric communities ever since. Stryker reports that, throughout the 1980s, antitransgender cultural sentiments continued to "proliferate" and that the "level of vitriol directed against transgender people actually increased."[33] As a result, the transgender community tended to circle the wagons and focus on offering each other mutual support, rather than moving outward in political activism. Meyerowitz notes that as the 1980s came to a close, bringing the deaths of both Harry Benjamin and Christine Jorgensen, in an important sense an "era had ended" for the transgender experience in America.[34]

29. Paul R. McHugh, "Surgical Sex: Why We Stopped Doing Sex Change Operations," *First Things*, November 2004, http://www.firstthings.com/article/2004/11/surgical-sex; and McHugh, "Transgender Surgery Isn't the Solution," *Wall Street Journal*, June 12, 2014, http://www.wsj.com/articles/paul-mchugh-transgender-surgery-isnt-the-solution-1402615120.

30. Janice Raymond, *The Transsexual Empire: The Making of the Shemale* (1979; repr., New York: Teachers College Press, 1994).

31. James Davison Hunter, *Culture Wars: The Struggle to Define America* (New York: Basic Books, 1991).

32. Stryker, *Transgender History*, 113.

33. Stryker, *Transgender History*, 110.

34. Meyerowitz, *How Sex Changed*, 256.

In a number of respects, the 1990s brought a new day for the transgender community. Catalysts for this shift ranged from the effects of the HIV/AIDS crisis to the rise of postmodernism and the advent of the internet. By the 1990s, the public visibility and cultural acceptance of transgender identity was slowly on the increase. Despite the fact that transgender people played a role in the 1969 Stonewall riots that inaugurated the contemporary gay liberation movement, they often experienced rejection from the gay and lesbian communities throughout the late 1970s and '80s. But this trend began to reverse significantly in the 1990s.[35] It became increasingly common during this decade for the "T" to be included alongside "LGB." Transgender activism also increased significantly during this decade.[36]

By the early '90s, a growing number of academics were using "transgender" as an umbrella term that included any and all **gender minority** people who exhibited **gender variance** or **gender nonconformity** (i.e., **TGNC**), including transsexuals, cross-dressers/transvestites/**femmes**, drag kings and queens, intersex persons, and those who understand their gender as something beyond the male/masculine–female/feminine binary (e.g., **genderqueer, bigender, pangender, postgender, agender, third gender/sex**, Two-Spirit, etc.).[37] With this contemporary usage came an increased emphasis that transgender identity had to do with one's sense of gender identity, not **sexual orientation**. As the transgender community has continued to grow and develop, language and terminology have evolved as well.[38] Seeking to foster more inclusivity, some have begun to substitute "**trans**" (sometimes "**trans-**" or "**trans***") for "transgender."[39] In the '90s, transgender activists also coined the term "**cisgender**" (now sometimes "**cissexual**" or simply "**cis**") to refer to nontransgender people (i.e., people whose sense of gender identity matches their birth sex

35. Amy L. Stone, "More Than Adding a T: American Lesbian and Gay Activists' Attitudes towards Transgender Inclusion," *Sexualities* 12 (2009): 334–54.

36. Jones, "Transgender Organizations," 198–99; and Stryker, *Transgender History*, 135–47.

37. Leslie Feinberg's 1992 pamphlet, *Transgender Liberation: A Movement Whose Time Has Come*, is regularly credited with originating this umbrella use of the term "transgender." One recent study of specific self-identities within the wider transgender community found that the most commonly endorsed gender identity was "genderqueer." See L. E. Kuper, R. Nussbaum, and B. Mustanski, "Exploring the Diversity of Gender and Sexual Orientation Identities in an Online Sample of Transgender Individuals," *Journal of Sex Research* 49 (2012): 244–54.

38. Cristan Williams, "Transgender," *Transgender Studies Quarterly* 1, nos. 1–2 (2014): 232–34; and K. J. Rawson and Cristan Williams, "Transgender*: The Rhetorical Landscape of a Term," *Present Tense* 3, no. 2 (2014): 1–9.

39. Gwynn Kessler, "Transgender/Third Sex/Transsexualism," in *Oxford Encyclopedia of the Bible and Gender Studies*, ed. Julia M. O'Brien (New York: Oxford University Press, 2014), 2:427; and Ruth Pearce, Deborah Lynn Steinberg, and Igi Moon, "Introduction: The Emergence of 'Trans,'" *Sexualities* 22, nos. 1–2 (2019): 3–12.

and/or cultural gender norms).[40] The concept of **cisnormativity** eventually arose as well.

The decade of the 1990s also brought the emergence of the interdisciplinary field of **transgender studies**.[41] A major impetus for the rise of this new academic field was Sandy Stone's essay "The Empire Strikes Back: A Posttranssexual Manifesto."[42] In this essay, Stone, a transwoman, presses a new transgender vision that, in her words, is characterized by "postmodernism, postfeminism, and (dare I say it) posttranssexualism."[43] A key to understanding Stone's essay—and the wider transgender studies movement that followed—is its connection to **queer theory**, which also arose in the '90s.

The moniker **"queer"**—originally a derogatory slur—came to be embraced by the gay and lesbian communities of the '90s as a term of pride, one that "encompassed defiance, celebration and refusal."[44] Queer theory itself emerged from the confluence of several academic streams, including poststructuralist/deconstructionist literary theory, feminist thought, and gay and lesbian studies.[45] The work of Michel Foucault, especially his three-volume *The History of Sexuality*, was highly influential.[46] Early shapers of queer theory include Judith Butler and Eve Kosofsky Sedgwick.[47] Noreen Giffney captures the theoretical gist—along with the philosophical-aesthetic proclivities—of queer theory.

> Queer theory is an exercise in discourse analysis. . . . Queer is all about excess, pushing the boundaries of the possible, showing up language and discursive categories more specifically for their inadequacies. . . . There is an unremitting emphasis in queer theoretical work on fluidity, über-inclusivity, indeterminacy,

40. A. Finn Enke, "The Education of Little Cis: Cisgender and the Discipline of Opposing Bodies," in *The Transgender Studies Reader 2*, ed. Susan Stryker and Aren Z. Aizura (New York: Routledge, 2013), 234–47.

41. Kristen Schilt and Danya Lagos, "The Development of Transgender Studies in Sociology," *Annual Review of Sociology* 43 (2017): 425–43.

42. Stone's essay, originally written in 1987, was published in 1991. Citations below are from its reprint: Sandy Stone, "The Empire Strikes Back: A Posttranssexual Manifesto," in *The Transgender Studies Reader*, ed. Susan Stryker and Stephen Whittle (New York: Routledge, 2006), 221–35.

43. Stone, "Empire Strikes Back," 224.

44. Noreen Giffney, "Introduction: The 'q' Word," in *Ashgate Research Companion to Queer Theory*, ed. Noreen Giffney and Michael O'Rourke (Burlington, VT: Ashgate, 2009), 2.

45. On queer theory, see Nikki Sullivan, *A Critical Introduction to Queer Theory* (New York: New York University Press, 2003).

46. Michel Foucault, *The History of Sexuality*, 3 vols., trans. Robert Hurley (1976–84; repr., New York: Random House, 1978–86). See Lynne Huffer, *Mad for Foucault: Rethinking the Foundations of Queer Theory* (New York: Columbia University Press, 2010).

47. Judith Butler, *Gender Trouble: Feminism and the Subversion of Identity* (New York: Routledge, 1990); and Eve Kosofsky Sedgwick, *Epistemology of the Closet* (Berkeley: University of California Press, 1990).

indefinability, unknowability, the preposterous, impossibility, unthinkability, unintelligibility, meaninglessness and that which is unrepresentable or incommunicable. . . . The erotics of thinking, speaking, writing, listening and reading is a chief concern.[48]

It is evident from this description that queer theory is located within the wider postmodern cultural impulse. In terms of religio-philosophical moorings, queer theory, similar to the poststructuralism/deconstructionism that inspired it, is most comfortably at home in a nontheistic, or religiously nonrealist, conceptual environment. That being said, religious appropriations of it are, to one degree or another, increasingly being made, often under the rubric of "queer theology."[49] Queer theory aligns with those quarters of the social sciences that embrace a vision of reality guided by **social constructionism**. It sets itself against the tendency within the hard sciences to understand phenomena, including sexual phenomena, in terms of definable essences (**essentialism**) with a "nature," often rooted in biology, that preexists and transcends language.[50] In this, it resonates with twentieth-century feminism's emphasis on the socially constructed nature of gender and gender differences. But it presses further to suggest that even the supposed sex differences associated with male and female are primarily a factor of sociolinguistic construction, not objective biological facts. To think otherwise is to fall victim to the "phallocentric straightjacket of biological reductionism."[51] A key idea within queer theory—one that resonates with the field of transgender studies—is that identity is fluid and malleable and thus that gender is not an "essence" human beings possess but rather a "performance" they engage in.[52] Gender is understood as "potentially porous and permeable spatial territories (arguably numbering more than two) each capable of supporting rich and rapidly proliferating ecologies of embodied difference."[53]

48. Giffney, "Introduction," 7–9.

49. On queer theology, see Marcella Althaus-Reid, *Indecent Theology* (New York: Routledge, 2001); and Patrick S. Cheng, *Radical Love: Introduction to Queer Theology* (New York: Seabury, 2011).

50. See Butler, *Gender Trouble*; Jeffrey Weeks, "Essentialism," in *The Languages of Sexuality* (New York: Routledge, 2011), 43–45; Weeks, "Social Constructionism," in *Languages of Sexuality*, 204–8; and Deborah F. Sawyer, "Gender," in O'Brien, *Oxford Encyclopedia*, 1:264–73.

51. Leonore Tiefer, quoted in Jane M. Ussher, "Unraveling the Mystery of 'The Specificity of Women's Sexual Response and Its Relationship with Sexual Orientations': The Social Construction of Sex and Sexual Identities," *Archives of Sexual Behavior* 46, no. 5 (2017): 1207.

52. The concept of performativity is central to Butler's landmark work, *Gender Trouble*.

53. Susan Stryker, Paisley Currah, and Lisa Jean Moore, "Introduction: Trans-, Trans, or Transgender?," *WSQ: Women's Studies Quarterly* 36, nos. 3–4 (2008): 12.

With the turn of the century and the coming of age of the millennial generation, cultural acceptance of transgender identity was on the rise. Similar to other sexual minority communities, transgender people from around the globe were able to connect and organize because of the internet's revolutionary transformation of our communication modes.[54] Along with other expressions of the LGBT community, transgender people began to experience a higher profile within the media and entertainment worlds. In April 2007, for example, Barbara Walters introduced Jazz Jennings, a seven-year-old transgender girl, to the nation.[55] In 2009, President Barack Obama declared June to be Lesbian, Gay, Bisexual, and Transgender Pride Month. In 2011, Chaz Bono's transition was the subject of the documentary film "Becoming Chaz," and Bono's book *Transition: Becoming Who I Was Always Meant to Be* was released.[56] By June 2014, *Time* magazine could proclaim that our culture had reached a "transgender tipping point."

In recent years, much of the international attention on the transgender community has focused on things like appropriate medical protocols for the process of transitioning and legal protection for transgender persons.[57] On the legal front, issues being addressed include legal guidelines regarding medical/surgical intervention, legal recognition of a new sex status, policies for governmental and/or health insurance provider coverage for medical treatments, minimum legal age for transitioning processes, legal effects of transitioning on marital status, and, of course, legislative enactment of equal access and antidiscrimination laws.[58]

Certain European countries led the way in terms of legislation related to transgender persons, with Switzerland being the first to grant individuals the ability to change their legal sex status in the 1930s.[59] In the US, a few states began to include transgender people within their antidiscrimination laws in the 1990s. At present, this number has grown to seventeen states and

54. Andre Cavalcante, "'I Did It All Online': Transgender Identity and the Management of Everyday Life," *Critical Studies in Mass Communication* 33 (2016): 109–22; and Eve Shapiro, "'Trans' cending Barriers: Transgender Organizing on the Internet," *Journal of Gay and Lesbian Social Services* 16, nos. 3–4 (December 2004): 165–79.

55. Jazz Jennings, *Being Jazz: My Life as a (Transgender) Teen* (New York: Random House, 2016).

56. Chaz Bono with Billie Fitzpatrick, *Transition: Becoming Who I Was Always Meant to Be* (New York: Dutton, 2011).

57. On the former topic, see Randi Ettner, Stan Monstrey, and Eli Coleman, eds., *Principles of Transgender Medicine and Surgery*, 2nd ed. (New York: Routledge, 2016).

58. Jens M. Scherpe, ed., *The Legal Status of Transsexual and Transgender Persons* (Portland, OR: Intersentia, 2015).

59. Friedemann Pfäfflin, "Transgenderism and Transsexuality: Medical and Psychological Viewpoints," in Scherpe, *Legal Status*, 17.

the District of Columbia. Japan, Singapore, and Taiwan have also enacted legislation. The Yogyakarta Principles were eventually formulated and released in 2006–7, a key moment for international transgender human rights.[60] A few predominantly Muslim Middle Eastern countries have also enacted protective legislation for transgender people. Turkey, for example, did so in 1988. And, interestingly, more sex reassignment surgeries are performed annually in Iran than in any other country in the world, with the exception of Thailand.[61]

Alongside the growing cultural awareness and acceptance of the transgender community have come countertendencies that serve to raise critical questions regarding transgender identity, particularly transsexuality. For example, the feminist critique that began in the 1970s has continued within certain sectors of contemporary feminist thought. Referred to as radical feminism or gender-critical feminism—or, alternatively, as trans-exclusionary radical feminism or TERF by its critics—this feminist perspective proposes that the presence of MtF transsexuals can threaten (natal) women-only safe spaces, and poses just one more way in which men are able to co-opt and "erase" women.[62]

Transgender Experiences and Identities Today: Some Issues and Controversies

"Sex" and "Gender": Academic Terminology and Its Challenges

Inherent within the term "transgender" itself is the idea of gender. As noted earlier, the contemporary notion of gender is relatively new, having emerged in the mid-twentieth century.[63] Within second-wave feminism, the sex/gender divide was widely adopted during the 1970s and '80s. As used today

60. *The Yogyakarta Principles: The Application of International Human Rights Law in Relation to Sexual Orientation and Gender Identity*, 2007, http://www.yogyakartaprinciples.org/.

61. Vanessa Barford, "Iran's 'Diagnosed Transsexuals,'" *BBC News*, February 25, 2008, http://news.bbc.co.uk/2/hi/7259057.stm. This fact is a direct result of a 1987 fatwa issued by Ayatollah Ruhollah Khomeini. See M. Alipour, "Islamic Shari'a Law, Neotraditionalist Muslim Scholars and Transgender Sex-Reassignment Surgery: A Case Study of Ayatollah Khomeini's and Sheikh al-Tantawi's Fatwas," *International Journal of Transgenderism* 18, no. 1 (2017): 91–103.

62. Sheila Jeffreys, *Gender Hurts: A Feminist Analysis of the Politics of Transgenderism* (New York: Routledge, 2014); and Ruth Barrett, ed., *Female Erasure: What You Need to Know about Gender Politics' War on Women, the Female Sex and Human Rights* (Pacific Palisades, CA: Tidal Time, 2016).

63. On the history of the use of "sex" and/or "gender," see Diederik F. Janssen, "Know Thy Gender: Etymological Primer," *Archives of Sexual Behavior* 47, no. 8 (2018): 2149–54, https://doi.org/10.1007/s10508-018-1300-x; and David Haig, "The Inexorable Rise of Gender and the Decline of Sex: Social Change in Academic Titles, 1945–2001," *Archives of Sexual Behavior* 33, no. 2 (2004): 87–96.

in most contexts, the distinction is understood as follows: "sex" refers to the biological/physiological characteristics that identify humans as male, female, or intersex (i.e., chromosomes, sex hormones, gonads, genitals, secondary sex characteristics, etc.), while "gender" signals the common traits associated with being a man/masculine, a woman/feminine, or some gender-variant alternative within any given sociocultural context. Seen in this light, gender came to be understood as "a social construction that arises from biological sex."[64] Over the last few decades of the twentieth century, these two terms—along with the concept of "sexuality" as referring to one's preferred object of desire (i.e., sexual orientation)—came to form the three-part schema of sex-gender-sexuality that is now widely used within the social sciences and beyond.[65]

Increasingly, however, there are signs that this commonly shared schema—particularly the ideas of sex and gender—has problems, both conceptual and practical. First, there is widespread equivocal use of the term "gender" such that it is sometimes used in contradistinction from the term "sex," while at other times the two are used as virtual synonyms. This has led a number of researchers to call for a moment of interdisciplinary reassessment and reclarification of terminology.[66] Milton Diamond, for example, has argued that, given the most common academic definitions of sex and gender today, conceptual consistency should lead us to refer to "the way one views him- or herself as a male or female" as one's *sexual* identity, not *gender* identity, as is most common today.[67] In light of the terminological equivocations and inconsistencies associated with the terms "sex" and "gender," others have gone so far as to question whether this distinction is any longer meaningful.[68]

A second problem is tied to the disciplinary turf wars between the biological and social sciences of the last several decades.[69] Under the pressure of

64. Kimberly Tauches, "Transgendering: Challenging the 'Normal,'" in *Handbook of the New Sexuality Studies*, ed. Steven Seidman, Nancy Fischer, and Chet Meeks (New York: Routledge, 2006), 174.

65. E.g., American Psychiatric Association, "Gender Dysphoria," in *The Diagnostic and Statistical Manual of Mental Disorders*, 5th ed. (Washington, DC: American Psychiatric Association, 2013), 451 (hereafter *DSM-5*).

66. E.g., D. A. Gentile, "Just What Are Sex and Gender, Anyway? A Call for a New Terminological Standard," *Psychological Science* 4 (1993): 120–22; and Milton Diamond, "Sex and Gender Are Different: Sexual Identity and Gender Identity Are Different," *Clinical Child Psychology and Psychiatry* 7, no. 3 (2002): 320–34.

67. Diamond, "Sex and Gender," 323.

68. Charlene L. Muehlenhard and Zoe D. Peterson, "Distinguishing between Sex and Gender: History, Current Conceptualizations, and Implications," *Sex Roles* 64 (2011): 791–803.

69. On this unfortunate state of interdisciplinary affairs within contemporary sexuality studies, see Roy F. Baumeister, Jon K. Maner, and C. Nathan DeWall, "Theories of Human Sexuality," in *Sex and Sexuality*, vol. 1, *Sexuality Today: Trends and Controversies*, ed. Richard D. McAnulty and M. Michele Burnette (Westport, CT: Praeger, 2006), esp. 17–23.

this tension, the social sciences have witnessed the ascendency of a social constructionist approach to human sexuality, and with it a strong rejection of anything that tends toward biological "essentialism."[70] In fact, by the late 1970s and into the '80s, some within the social sciences and feminist studies had begun to treat the category of sex—the specific category of the sex/gender binary that was originally reserved for the biological side of things—as virtually fully accounted for by social/cultural construction of gender.[71]

Throughout the 1980s and onward, the postmodern trajectory of thought within the Western academy served to further anchor and intensify this perspective.[72] In the 1990s, the rise of queer theory reinforced the idea that the category of sex was as much a social construction as gender, with the former arising out of the latter. As noted previously, an important voice here was Judith Butler in her landmark book *Gender Trouble*. Butler's thesis is succinctly captured in the opening chapter: "If the immutable character of sex is contested, perhaps this construct called 'sex' is as culturally constructed as gender; indeed, perhaps it was always already gender, with the consequence that the distinction between sex and gender turns out to be no distinction at all."[73] The social constructionist impulse within the social sciences has led many to the point of functionally deconstructing any significant difference between sex and gender by effectively casting all things sexual as merely sociolinguistically constructed gender all the way down.

Finally, the fallout of the academic turf wars over the configuration of sex, gender, and sexuality has had implications for the wider society, particularly for the transgender community and its political and legal concerns. For example, with the rights movement serving as an initial model, sexual minority communities have found that one effective way of anchoring themselves within a legal paradigm of human rights, analogous to that which protects people from racism or sexism, is to appeal to biology as a basis for the community's

70. E.g., Jennifer Harding, "Investigating Sex: Essentialism and Constructionism," in *Constructing Sexualities: Readings in Sexuality, Gender, and Culture*, ed. Suzanne LaFont (Upper Saddle River, NJ: Prentice Hall, 2003), 6–17; Weeks, "Essentialism"; and Weeks, "Social Constructionism." As applied to transgender experience, see Boby Ho-Hong Ching and Jason Teng Xu, "The Effects of Neuroessentialism on Transprejudice: An Experimental Study," *Sex Roles* 78 (2018): 228–41.

71. E.g., Suzanne J. Kessler and Wendy McKenna, *Gender: An Ethnomethodological Approach* (New York: Wiley, 1978); and Sherry B. Ortner and Harriet Whitehead, *Sexual Meanings: The Cultural Construction of Gender and Sexuality* (New York: Cambridge University Press, 1981).

72. William Simon, "The Postmodernization of Sex," in *Sexualities and Society: A Reader*, ed. Jeffrey Weeks, Janet Holland, and Matthew Waites (Cambridge: Polity, 2003), 22, 29.

73. Butler, *Gender Trouble*, 9–10. See also Judith Butler, *Bodies That Matter: On the Discursive Limits of "Sex"* (New York: Routledge, 1993), 5.

identity. From this perspective, defending a biological etiology for transgender experience—for example, the brain-sex theory (discussed below under "Biological Theories")—makes good sense.

On the other hand, the transgender community has also seen the way in which the appeal to a biological etiology easily lends itself to being co-opted by a disease model of transgender experience, which naturally leads to pathologization and stigma and, moreover, to a biological determinism that undercuts human "agency." Seen from this perspective, the rejection of "biological essentialism" seems to offer the most politically advantageous path. However, here another potential risk emerges. In rejecting biological causation by emphasizing sociocultural forces, as, for example, queer theorists and many within trans activist circles tend to do today, transgender experience is left open to being understood as primarily a psychosocial phenomenon, and thus as something possibly to be approached from a psychological therapeutic model. This raises the possibility of a new pathologizing interpretation from a different direction.[74] In all of this, the categories of sex, gender, and sexuality are found to be mired in another level of controversy and debate.

Implications for Understanding the Human Sexes

In most people's estimations there are two sexes, and they are expressed in the binary of male and female. With the increasing awareness of the various experiences and identities expressed within the transgender community, especially when viewed through the lens of queer theory, the idea that the category of human sex is better understood as a continuum is receiving increasing attention. A significant factor here has been the proposal by some to include intersex persons within the transgender umbrella. As a category, intersex includes over forty different conditions, such as Klinefelter Syndrome, Turner Syndrome, Androgen Insensitivity Syndrome (AIS), and Congenital Adrenal Hyperplasia (CAH).[75] In varying ways, intersex leads to a situation where the physical/biological characteristics that typically identify a person's sex (e.g., chromosomes, hormones, gonads, genitals) are such that the person, at one biological level or another, is neither unambiguously female nor unambiguously male.

Many activists press the point that the seemingly clear, biologically based sex binary of male versus female is fundamentally destabilized and disrupted

---

74. We will return to these sorts of questions below in the section "The Causal Question."

75. Amy B. Wisniewski, Steven D. Chernausek, and Bradley P. Kropp, *Disorders of Sex Development: A Guide for Parents and Physicians* (Baltimore: Johns Hopkins University Press, 2012), chap. 2.

by the phenomena of intersex. According to Cheryl Chase, founder of the Intersex Society of North America (ISNA), intersex offers "clear evidence" that "the male/female binary is not 'immutable.'" Furthermore, it "furnishes an opportunity to deploy 'nature' strategically to disrupt heteronormative systems of sex, gender, and sexuality."[76]

Beyond intersex, scholars working within queer theory and transgender studies frequently cite other sources that appear to call into question the traditional male/female sex binary. These include the following: (1) Neurofeminist studies that deconstruct claims of biologically based sex differences, which are seen as often fed by the biases of "neurosexism."[77] (2) Thomas Laqueur's argument that, from ancient times until about 1750, the dominant model of human sexuality held that there was only one sex (i.e., women were essentially seen as inferior males) and that the current two-sex model is a modern innovation.[78] (3) Various cross-cultural examples of gender variance that can be construed as something like a "third sex"—for example, the Hijra of India, the Two-Spirit people (formerly **berdache**) of certain First Nations groups, and the Xanith of Oman.[79]

Of course, each of these lines of argument has been challenged in one way or another. For example, with regard to the appeal to intersex conditions in order to deconstruct the male/female binary, Emi Koyama, founder of the Portland-based Intersex Initiative, points out that "most people born with intersex conditions do view themselves as belonging to one binary sex or another. They simply see themselves as a man (or a woman) with a birth condition like any other."[80]

Koyama's observation points to an increasingly common area of criticism leveled against queer theory—namely, that it frequently disregards the lived experiences of the very people it appeals to in its theoretical arguments. More specifically, from early on queer theorists tended to cast a skeptical eye on the

76. Cheryl Chase, "Hermaphrodites with Attitude: Mapping the Emergence of Intersex Political Activism," in Stryker and Whittle, *Transgender Studies Reader*, 301. See also Suzanne J. Kessler, *Lessons from the Intersexed* (Piscataway, NJ: Rutgers University Press, 1998).

77. Robyn Bluhm, Anne Jaap Jacobson, and Heidi Lene Maibom, eds., *Neurofeminism: Issues at the Intersection of Feminist Theory and Cognitive Science* (New York: Palgrave Macmillan, 2012).

78. Thomas W. Laqueur, *Making Sex: Body and Gender from the Greeks to Freud* (Cambridge, MA: Harvard University Press, 1990).

79. Thomas E. Bevan, *The Psychobiology of Transsexualism and Transgenderism: A New View Based on Scientific Evidence* (Santa Barbara, CA: Praeger, 2014), chap. 4; Bolich, *Transgender History and Geography*; and Gilbert Herdt, ed., *Third Sex, Third Gender: Beyond Sexual Dimorphism in Culture and History* (New York: Zone, 1994).

80. Emi Koyama, "From 'Intersex' to 'DSD': Toward a Queer Disability Politics of Gender," http://www.intersexinitiative.org/articles/intersextodsd.html.

transsexual sector of the transgender community. The reason for this is simple. The reported experience of many transsexuals is that their true self, which they often describe in terms of an innate and unchanging gender identity, is trapped in the "wrong body" (i.e., the wrong **biological sex**). But this sort of claim appears to depend on something like a fixed, essentialist identity and the male/female sex binary, which runs afoul of the central convictions of queer theory.[81] This explains why many trans activists who embrace queer theory have often expressed attitudes toward SRS ranging from ambivalence to outright disdain.[82]

In light of this common sentiment among queer theorists—including those trans activists who have embraced a queer theoretical approach—a number of advocates for transsexual people have voiced concerns regarding queer theory's "erasure" of the transsexual experience from the ranks of the wider transgender community.[83] All too often, it is said, queer theory and its political vision do not "leave space for trans people who don't self-identity as beyond the binary. Many trans people see themselves as men and women. Taken to its most extreme, the beyond-the-binary model suggests these people are mistaken (i.e., it invalidates their self-identities). At best, it accepts such self-identifications while recognizing them as politically problematic since they disavow the resistant force of trans lives lived in opposition to the oppressive binary."[84]

Criticisms have also been voiced in regard to the other aforementioned lines of argument against the male/female sex binary. While neurofeminists strive to deconstruct biologically based arguments for significant sex differences, many within the biological sciences see indisputable evidence of just such differences.[85] Frequently, these biologically based sex differences focus on sex hormones—particularly testosterone—and their effect on the early sexual

81. This queer-based critique of the transsexual experience is articulated in Sandy Stone's essay, "The Empire Strikes Back" (222), the very essay that inaugurated the discipline of transgender studies. See also Ulrica Engdahl, "Wrong Body," *Transgender Studies Quarterly* 1, nos. 1–2 (2014): 267–69.

82. A recent issue of *Transgender Studies Quarterly* was devoted to this contested question. See the guest editors' opening essay: Eric Plemons and Chris Straayer, "Introduction: Reframing the Surgical," *Transgender Studies Quarterly* 5, no. 2 (2018): 164–73.

83. E.g., Viviane K. Namaste, *Invisible Lives: The Erasure of Transsexual and Transgendered People* (Chicago: University of Chicago Press, 2000); and Henry Rubin, *Self-Made Men: Identity and Embodiment among Transsexual Men* (Nashville: Vanderbilt University Press, 2003).

84. Talia Mae Bettcher, "Trapped in the Wrong Theory: Rethinking Trans Oppression and Resistance," *Signs* 39, no. 2 (2014): 385.

85. E.g., Jill B. Becker, Arthur P. Arnold, Karen J. Berkley, et al., "Strategies and Methods for Research on Sex Differences in Brain and Behavior," *Endocrinology* 146 (2005): 1650–73; and Akira Matsumoto, ed., *Sexual Differentiation of the Brain* (New York: CRC, 1999).

differentiation of the brain.[86] Moreover, some within feminist quarters have called into question the common feminist assumption that granting innate, biologically based sex differences will inevitably lead to negative consequences for women.[87]

Thomas Laqueur's one-sex model has also come under attack.[88] Methodologically, some have chastised Laqueur for his uncritical employment of a radical postmodern philosophy of science.[89] He has also been critiqued at the level of historical argument—namely, by those who say that, contrary to his thesis, there are clear examples of "two-sexes" models in various pre-1700 sources.[90] Finally, the use of cross-cultural instances of gender variance as examples of the widespread occurrence of transgender experience—or as evidence of a "third gender"—has been called into question.[91]

Transgender Population Frequencies

With the growing scholarly focus on transgender experience has come increasing attention to population and demographic questions. But with this growing body of research has come divergent methodologies and differing results. For example, the *DSM-5* (the most recent edition of the *DSM*, published in 2013) estimates that between 0.005 percent and 0.014 percent of adult males, and between 0.002 percent and 0.003 percent of adult females, experience gender dysphoria.[92] This set of estimates is based on data regarding people seeking treatment in clinical settings. Others have criticized this approach, pointing out that "most transsexuals and transgender people are never treated . . . by a mental health professional."[93] When we turn to self-reporting sur-

---

86. E.g., Sheri A. Berenbaum and Adriene M. Beltz, "Sexual Differentiation in Human Behavior: Effects of Prenatal and Pubertal Organizational Hormones," *Frontiers in Neuroendocrinology* 32 (2011): 183–200.

87. Mary Midgley, "On Not Being Afraid of Natural Sex Differences," in *Feminist Perspectives in Philosophy*, ed. M. Griffiths and M. Whitford (New York: Palgrave Macmillan, 1988), 29–41.

88. E.g., Helen King, *The One-Sex Body on Trial: The Early and Modern Evidence* (Burlington, VT: Ashgate, 2014); and Heinz-Jürgen Voss, *Making Sex Revisited: Dekonstruktion des Geschlechts aus biologisch-medizinischer Perspektive* (Bielefeld: Transcript, 2010).

89. Alan G. Soble, "The History of Sexual Anatomy and Self-Referential Philosophy of Science," http://philpapers.org/archive/alatho.pdf.

90. E.g., the ancient Hippocratic treatise *Diseases of Women*, which proposes that women have a very different physiology than men.

91. E.g., Evan B. Towle and Lynn M. Morgan, "Romancing the Transgender Native: Rethinking the Use of the 'Third Gender' Concept," in Stryker and Whittle, *Transgender Studies Reader*, 666–84.

92. *DSM-5*, 454.

93. Bevan, *Psychobiology*, 47.

veys, the frequency numbers increase significantly.[94] For example, from this perspective, Thomas Bevan concludes that MtF transsexuals represent roughly 0.1 percent (or higher) of the male population, while the broader MtF transgender population (i.e., those who identify in some way with another gender, while stopping short of extensive transitioning procedures) represents 1 percent of the male population.[95] Regarding population frequency estimates for FtM transsexuals, Bevan offers 0.05 percent as a "conservative" rule of thumb and proposes a 0.5 percent estimate for the wider FtM transgender population.[96] In terms of actual numbers, the Williams Institute of the UCLA School of Law estimates that, as of 2016, around 1.4 million American adults "identify as transgender."[97] Interestingly, the American Society of Plastic Surgeons (ASPS) reported that the US saw an increase of nearly 20 percent in the number of gender confirmation surgeries performed in 2016 compared to 2015.[98]

The Question of Comparisons

As public awareness of the range of transgender experience and identity has grown, the question of relevant comparisons to other phenomena has been raised. One set of comparative experiences is related to transability, which refers to the experience of an able-bodied person sensing that their authentic identity is reflected in having a particular physical impairment or disability.[99] This has been tied to the phenomenon of **body integrity identity disorder (BIID)**.[100] Comparisons have also been made with transracialism—that is, the

---

94. E.g., L. Kuyper and C. Wijsen, "Gender Identities and Gender Dysphoria in the Netherlands," *Archives of Sexual Behavior* 43 (2014): 377–85; and E. Van Caenegem, K. Wierckx, E. Elaut, et al., "Prevalence of Gender Nonconformity in Flanders, Belgium," *Archives of Sexual Behavior* 44 (2015): 1281–87.

95. Bevan, *Psychobiology*, 49.

96. Bevan, *Psychobiology*, 50. On transgender/transsexual population frequencies, see also Yarhouse, *Understanding Gender Dysphoria*, 92–95; and Francisco J. Sánchez and Eric Vilain, "Transgender Identities: Research and Controversies," in *Handbook of Psychology and Sexual Orientation*, ed. C. J. Patterson and A. R. D'Augelli (New York: Oxford University Press, 2013), 43.

97. Andrew R. Flores, Jody L. Herman, Gary J. Gates, and Taylor N. T. Brown, "How Many Adults Identify as Transgender in the United States," June 2016, https://williamsinstitute.law.ucla.edu/research/how-many-adults-identify-as-transgender-in-the-united-states/.

98. American Society of Plastic Surgeons, "Gender Confirmation Surgeries Rise 20% in First Ever Report," May 22, 2017, https://www.plasticsurgery.org/news/press-releases/gender-confirmation-surgeries-rise-20-percent-in-first-ever-report.

99. E.g., Alexandre Baril, "Needing to Acquire a Physical Impairment/Disability: (Re)Thinking the Connections between Trans and Disability Studies through Transability," *Hypatia* 30, no. 1 (2015): 30–48.

100. Antonia Ostgathe, Thomas Schnell, and Erich Kasten, "Body Integrity Identity Disorder and Gender Dysphoria: A Pilot Study to Investigate Similarities and Differences," *American*

experience of sensing that one's authentic racial/ethnic identity is other than that of one's genetic ancestry.[101] Such comparisons have quickly become sites of controversy as critics of transgender identities have used them within the context of polemical reductio ad absurdum and slippery-slope arguments.[102] In response, many trans activists and allies have, not surprisingly, rejected not only the comparisons but the very idea of these other trans phenomena as worthy of serious consideration.[103] In an all-too-rare example of a measured consideration of such comparisons—one calling for open-mindedness and dialogue—Stryker concludes,

> To say that *transracial* is not "like" *transgender* merely highlights how impoverished our conceptual vocabulary truly is, for specifying modes of resemblance and dissimilarity—for clearly there are underlying similarities as well as divergences which we have yet to adequately map. It is not time to settle the question of their identities once and for all—and after all, who are we to assume that we properly occupy the position of the decider?—but rather to keep the conversation going, at increasingly fine levels of nuance and detail.[104]

The Causal Question

As Vern and Bonnie Bullough have observed, "The struggle of the professional therapeutic community to find causality for a cross-gendered identity has been a long and difficult one."[105] Indeed, the question of what causes the

---

Journal of Applied Psychology 3, no. 6 (2014): 18–43. The experiences of both gender dysphoria and BIID must be distinguished from that of **body dysmorphic disorder (BDD)**.

101. E.g., Roger Brubaker, *Trans: Gender and Race in an Age of Unsettled Identities* (Princeton: Princeton University Press, 2016). Additional comparisons have been made with the phenomena of transpecies (species dysphoria) and age dysphoria/age identity disorder. See respectively, S. E. Roberts, C. N. Plante, K. C. Gerbasi, and S. Reysen, "The Anthrozoomorphic Identity: Furry Fandom Members' Connections to Non-human Animals," *Anthrozoos* 28, no. 4 (2015): 533–48 (esp. 540 and 543); James Gile, "Age Dysphoria: A Case Study," in *Sexual Essays: Gender, Desire, and Nakedness* (Lanham, MD: Hamilton, 2017), 81–93.

102. E.g., Michelle A. Cretella, "Gender Dysphoria in Children and Suppression of Debate," *Journal of American Physicians and Surgeons* 21, no. 2 (2016): 51; and Jeffreys, *Gender Hurts*, 34–35, 187.

103. E.g., note the outrage expressed by many within the academic community toward the article by Rebecca Tuvel, "In Defense of Transracialism," *Hypatia* 32 (2017): 263–78. See Jennifer Schuessler, "A Defense of 'Transracial' Identity Roils Philosophy World," *New York Times*, May 19, 2017, https://www.nytimes.com/2017/05/19/arts/a-defense-of-transracial-identity-roils-philosophy-world.html?mcubz=0.

104. Susan Stryker, "Caitlyn Jenner and Rachel Dolezal: Identification, Embodiment, and Bodily Transformation," *AHA Today: A Blog of the American Historical Association*, July 13, 2015, http://blog.historians.org/2015/07/caitlyn-jenner-and-rachel-dolezal-identification-embodiment-bodily-transformation/.

105. Bullough and Bullough, *Cross Dressing*, 268.

transgender experience in its various forms has been surrounded by controversy for many years. Not surprisingly, the academic debates on this question often reflect interdisciplinary turf wars and their respective methodological biases. While many call for a balanced approach, often under the moniker of an "integrationist" model, far fewer actually go on to demonstrate it.

Another complicating factor here is that the transgender community now includes such a wide array of gender-variant people. This means that to ask the question of what lies behind the "transgender experience" is actually to ask the question of what lies behind cross-dressing, drag expression, genderfluidity, transsexuality, and a host of other gender-variant expressions. Several approaches to the causal question—most of them focusing on transsexuality—have come to dominate the scholarly discussion over the last number of decades. We will now survey some of these leading etiological theories.

Psychological Theories

To begin, those who hold that psychological phenomena offer the best explanatory pathways for understanding transgender phenomena often point to the many studies that show a significantly higher degree of mental health problems among the trans population compared with the general populace.[106] Specifically, researchers have found that conditions including ADHD, autism, affective and anxiety disorders, depression, and schizophrenia occur at significantly higher-than-usual rates among transgender people.[107] Those advocating a psychological approach to treatment, as opposed to hormone and/or surgery-based transitioning protocols, can point to research showing that, while SRS appears to alleviate mental health problems for some, for a sizable group of others psychological morbidity is unaffected by—or actually increases after—surgical transitioning.[108]

106. E.g., Cecilia Dhejne, Roy Van Vlerken, Gunter Heylens, and Jon Arcelus, "Mental Health and Gender Dysphoria: A Review of the Literature," *International Review of Psychiatry* 28, no. 1 (2016): 44–57; and Melanie Bechard, Doug P. VanderLaan, Hayley Wood, Lori Wasserman, and Kenneth J. Zucker, "Psychosocial and Psychological Vulnerability in Adolescents with Gender Dysphoria: A 'Proof of Principle' Study," *Journal of Sex and Marital Therapy* 43, no. 7 (2017): 678–88.

107. E.g., R. P. Rajkumar, "Gender Identity Disorder and Schizophrenia: Neurodevelopmental Disorders with Common Causal Mechanisms?," *Schizophrenia Research and Treatment*, 2014, http://dx.doi.org/10.1155/2014/463757; and J. F. Strang, L. Kenworthy, A. Dominska, et al., "Increased Gender Variance in Autism Spectrum Disorders and Attention Deficit Hyperactivity Disorder," *Archives of Sexual Behavior* 43, no. 8 (2014): 1525–33.

108. R. K. Simonsen, A. Giraldi, E. Kristensen, and G. M. Hald, "Long-Term Follow-Up of Individuals Undergoing Sex Reassignment Surgery: Psychiatric Morbidity and Mortality," *Nordic Journal of Psychiatry* 70, no. 4 (2016): 241–47.

A common rebuttal to this line of evidence is the claim that these increased rates of mental health problems are due to the stress and stigma caused by the ubiquitous transprejudice and transphobia at work within our culture (more on this below). But proponents of psychological approaches have countered with the observation that "anxiety has been found to be relatively common in individuals with gender dysphoria, even in cultures with accepting attitudes toward gender-variant behavior."[109] In this vein, J. Michael Bailey and Ray Blanchard write, "The idea that mental health problems—including suicidality—are caused by gender dysphoria rather than the other way around (i.e., mental health and personality issues cause a vulnerability to experience gender dysphoria) is currently popular and politically correct. It is, however, unproven and as likely to be false as true."[110]

With regard to the question of specific causes, psychological explanations of transsexuality have often focused on factors related to psychosexual maladjustment during childhood. For example, some have argued that gender dysphoria can develop in a child as a result of an overly enmeshed relationship with the parent of the opposite sex and/or a distant relationship with the parent of the same sex.[111] Some refer to insecure parental attachment in terms of being a risk factor rather than a cause.[112] A related proposal traces the roots of gender dysphoria or cross-dressing to being encouraged, or even forced, to adopt cross-sex behavior as a child. It is theorized that this can happen when, for example, a parent wishes that their baby boy had been a girl (or vice versa), or when a mother takes revenge on her son for being masculine.[113] For researchers who take this sort of perspective, it is not surprising to find that therapeutic treatments of gender-variant children often focus as much on the parents as they do the child.[114]

109. *DSM-5*, 459.

110. J. Michael Bailey and Ray Blanchard, "Suicide or Transition: The Only Options for Gender Dysphoric Kids?," *4th Wave Now*, September 8, 2017, https://4thwavenow.com/2017/09/08/suicide-or-transition-the-only-options-for-gender-dysphoric-kids/.

111. E.g., Robert J. Stoller, "Fathers of Transsexual Children," *Journal of the American Psychoanalytic Association* 27 (1979): 837–66; and Domenico Di Ceglie, "Reflections on the Nature of the 'Atypical Gender Identity Organization,'" in *A Stranger in My Own Body: Atypical Gender Identity Development and Mental Health*, ed. D. Di Ceglie and D. Freedman (London: Karnac, 1998), 9–25.

112. Kenneth J. Zucker and Susan J. Bradley, *Gender Identity Disorder and Psychosexual Problems in Children and Adolescents* (New York: Guilford, 1995), 119.

113. Robert J. Stoller, "The Term 'Transvestism,'" *Archives of General Psychiatry* 24 (1971): 230–37; and Kenneth J. Zucker, Hayley Wood, Devita Singh, and Susan J. Bradley, "A Developmental, Biopsychosocial Model for the Treatment of Children with Gender Identity Disorder," *Journal of Homosexuality* 59, no. 3 (2012): 376–77.

114. Kenneth J. Zucker and Peggy T. Cohen-Kettenis, "Gender Identity Disorder in Children and Adolescents," in *Handbook of Sexual and Gender Identity Disorders*, ed. David L. Rowland

Others have proposed a link between gender dysphoria and childhood sexual abuse. Here, gender dysphoria can be seen as tied to a coping mechanism that allows the person to disassociate from the painful experience of abuse.[115] Those who hold this theory point to studies demonstrating that the transgender population reports experiencing higher levels of various types of abuse as children than does the general population.[116]

Other psychological theories offer different explanations. Some scholars have proposed that transsexualism is a personality disorder or, alternatively, a disorder that commonly co-occurs with a personality disorder. Others have tied transgender identity to identity defense mechanisms, such as repression or fantasy.[117] Finally, some who embrace the psychological paradigm critique transition-affirmative approaches by pointing to studies showing that a statistically significant number of people who have undergone transition—one 2009 study suggests up to 8 percent—have later expressed regrets, with some even deciding to retransition back to their birth sex.[118]

It is important to note here that many who propose some form of a psychological causation theory hold that it is merely one piece of the puzzle. Increasingly today, psychological theories are combined with biological and/ or sociological theories to create more complex multifactorial or interactionist models that identify a wide range of possible causative factors and/ or pathways.[119] Regardless of the specifics, what unites those who offer psychological explanations is the conviction that, in terms of both etiological

---

and Luca Incrocci (Hoboken, NJ: Wiley & Sons, 2008), 395–400; and Zucker, Wood, Singh, and Bradley, "Developmental, Biopsychosocial Model," 388–89.

115. D. P. Wailing, J. M. Goodwin, and C. M. Cole, "Dissociation in a Transsexual Population," *Journal of Sex Education and Therapy* 23 (1998): 121–23. Related to this, see Judith Trowell, "Child Sexual Abuse and Gender Identity Development: Some Understanding from Work with Girls Who Have Been Sexually Abused," in Di Ceglie and Freedman, *Stranger in My Own Body*, 154–72.

116. Darlynne Gehring and Gail Knudson, "Prevalence of Childhood Trauma in a Clinical Population of Transsexual People," *International Journal of Transgenderism* 8, no. 1 (2005): 23–30.

117. E.g., J. F. Veale, T. C. Lomax, and D. E. Clarke, "The Identity-Defense Model of Gender-Variant Development," *International Journal of Transgenderism* 12, no. 3 (2010): 125–38.

118. A. Baranyi, D. Piber, and H.-B. Rothenhäusler, "Mann-zu-Frau-Transsexualismus. Ergebnisse geschlechtsangleichender Operationen in einer biopsychosozialen Perspektive," *Wiener Medizinische Wochenschrift* 159, nos. 21–22 (2009): 548. See also M. L. Djordjevic, M. R. Bizic, D. Duisin, M. B. Bouman, and M. Buncamper, "Reversal Surgery in Regretful Male-to-Female Transsexuals after Sex Reassignment Surgery," *Journal of Sexual Medicine* 13 (2016): 1000–1007. For autobiographical accounts of transition regret, see Walt Heyer, *Gender, Lies and Suicide: A Whistleblower Speaks Out* (n.p.: Create Space, 2013), and the website sexchangeregret.com.

119. E.g., Veale, Lomax, and Clarke, "Identity-Defense Model"; and Zucker, Wood, Singh, and Bradley, "Developmental, Biopsychosocial Model."

understanding and treatment approach, the transgender population is best served by focusing on the realm of psychological factors.[120]

In our culture today, those who hold that transgender experience is tied to psychopathologies are commonly criticized by trans activists and allies as stigmatizing and transphobic. In response, it appears that these professionals have either quietly backed away from the public conversation and chosen to avoid working with the trans population or else, less commonly, have risked public scorn and openly expressed their concerns nonetheless. In this regard, Stephen Levine and Anna Solomon voice the concern that contemporary social forces "conspire to create a gender identity problem that is not a psychopathology and has no significant associated psychopathologies. This political correctness can easily befuddle or drive away professionals who are aware that the concepts of psychopathology and civil rights are separate matters."[121]

Critics of psychological explanations for transgender experience deploy a range of arguments against them. For example, with regard to parent-focused theories, critics cite alternative studies that suggest such linkages are inconclusive, if not flatly wrong.[122] Another criticism is that psychologically focused studies show, at best, evidence of correlation, not causation. An increasingly common response from transgender advocates to associations made between transgender identity and various psychological disorders is to propose a reversal of the causal arrow. The claim is this: rather than equating transgender experience with, or attributing it to, psychopathology, we should recognize co-occurring psychological problems as the unsurprising result of the stigmatization and oppression, and frequently even violence, that are commonly suffered by transgender people.[123] Moreover, studies can be found that deny any significant correlation between the transgender population and certain

120. Paul McHugh has become one of the leading voices for this perspective. See McHugh, "Psychiatric Misadventures," *American Scholar* 61 (1992): 501–4; and Lawrence S. Mayer and Paul R. McHugh, "Sexuality and Gender: Findings from the Biological, Psychological, and Social Sciences," *New Atlantis* 50 (Fall 2016): 10–143. See also Richard P. Fitzgibbons, Philip M. Sutton, and Dale O'Leary, "The Psychopathology of 'Sex Reassignment' Surgery: Assessing Its Medical, Psychological, and Ethical Appropriateness," *National Catholic Bioethics Quarterly* 9, no. 1 (2009): 97–125.

121. S. B. Levine and A. Solomon, "Meanings and Political Implications of 'Psychopathology' in a Gender Identity Clinic: A Report of 10 Cases," *Journal of Sex and Marital Therapy* 35 (2009): 45.

122. V. Prince and P. M. Bentler, "A Survey of 504 Cases of Transvestism," *Psychological Reports* 31 (1972): 903–17; Sánchez and Vilain, "Transgender Identities," 46; and Bevan, *Psychobiology,* chap. 8.

123. M. L. Hendricks and R. J. Testa, "A Conceptual Framework for Clinical Work with Transgender and Gender Nonconforming Clients: An Adaptation of the Minority Stress Model," *Professional Psychology: Research and Practice* 43, no. 5 (2012): 460–67.

mental illnesses.[124] Finally, when it comes to the issue of **transition regret**, advocates point to studies arguing that regret is a statistically rare outcome for those who pursue **gender-affirming hormone therapy** and SRS.[125]

Increasingly, it is the very foundational assumption of many psychological explanations that is coming under attack—namely, the belief that transgender experience represents a disorder or pathology requiring diagnosis and treatment. For some time now, transgender activists have been pressing the psychological establishment to depathologize transgender experience in its various forms.[126] Instead, it is proposed that transgender experience represents a natural variation within the broad human experience of gender. Here, the transgender community is following in the wake of the lesbian and gay communities who, in the early 1970s, successfully pressured the American Psychiatric Association to remove homosexuality from the *DSM*.[127] With the 2013 publication of the manual's fifth edition came a shift toward depathologization when it dropped the previous edition's diagnosis of gender identity disorder and replaced it with gender dysphoria.[128] Here, the pathology only lies with the distress—or dysphoria—that can accompany transgender experience, not with that experience per se.

While some have hailed the *DSM-5*'s shift to gender dysphoria as a step in the right direction, many transgender activists have criticized it as too little, too late—with some even arguing that it represents a step backward toward increased stigmatization.[129] For an increasing number of transgender advocates, the mere inclusion of transgender experience within the reigning US manual of mental disorders represents the continued regulation, surveillance, and stigmatization of the transgender community by the medical-psychiatric profession. For many activists, nothing short of complete depathologization can ensure that transitioning will be treated as "a human right within a health

124. P. P. Miach, E. F. Berah, J. N. Butcher, and S. Rouse, "Utility of the MMPI-2 in Assessing Gender Dysphoric Patients," *Journal of Personality Assessment* 75 (2000): 268–79.

125. Anne A. Lawrence, "Factors Associated with Satisfaction or Regret Following Male-to-Female Sex Reassignment Surgery," *Archives of Sexual Behavior* 32, no. 4 (2003): 299–315; and Brynn Tannehill, "Myths about Transition Regrets," *Huffington Post*, February 2, 2016, http://www.huffingtonpost.com/brynn-tannehill/myths-about-transition-regrets_b_6160626.html.

126. Amets Suess, Karine Espineira, and Pau Crego Walters, "Depathologization," *Transgender Studies Quarterly* 1, nos. 1–2 (2014): 73–77.

127. For an account of this process, see Ronald Bayer, *Homosexuality and American Psychiatry: The Politics of Diagnosis* (Princeton: Princeton University Press, 1981). On the parallels between the lesbian/gay and transgender communities in their quest for depathologization, see Jemma Tosh, *Perverse Psychology: The Pathologization of Sexual Violence and Transgenderism* (New York: Routledge, 2015), chap. 4.

128. *DSM-5*, 454.

129. Tosh, *Perverse Psychology*, chap. 5; and Zowie Davy, "The DSM-5 and the Politics of Diagnosing Transpeople," *Archives of Sexual Behavior* 44 (2015): 1165–76.

framework" and thus a decision based solely on a transgender person's own "rational self-determination and agency."[130] From such a perspective, gender-variant children should never be saddled with a pathologizing label such as "gender identity disorder" or "gender dysphoria," but rather should be seen, for example, simply as engaging in "gender identity creativity" as they come to express their "true gender self."[131]

Others, however, push back on this line of thought wherein transgender experience is seen merely as a natural variation of human gender. Levine and Solomon, for example, raise concerns:

> The alternative to designating [transgender experiences] as psychopathologies is to understand them as simply variations in the range of the patterns of gender expression among humans. . . . They are, of course. . . . It would be illogical to remove these disorders based on the existence of a range of gender expressions, however. All psychopathologies are arbitrary designations that separate extreme ends of large spectra of behavioral, subjective, and adaptive patterns. . . . Gender disorders are one end of a pattern of acceptance and comfort with the anatomic self. All diagnoses arbitrarily draw lines between the ordinary and the extraordinary, the common and the rare, the adaptive and the maladaptive.[132]

Heino Meyer-Bahlburg similarly avers: "It is difficult to justify the term 'natural' variation for a condition that compels the respective individual to severely alter a healthy body by gonadectomy with attendant infertility and the replacement of intact primary and secondary sex characteristics with those of the other gender."[133]

These concerns serve to raise the question of whether contemporary arguments in support of the complete depathologization of transgender experience have fallen victim to the naturalistic fallacy—that is, the fallacy of assuming that simply because some phenomenon occurs in nature, it must therefore be good or desirable.

Biological Theories

Among most researchers today, there appears to be a trend toward explaining transgender-related phenomena with biologically based etiologies

130. Davy, "DSM-5," 1173.

131. Diane Ehrensaft, "From Gender Identity Disorder to Gender Identity Creativity: True Gender Self Child Therapy," *Journal of Homosexuality* 59, no. 3 (2012): 337–56.

132. Levine and Solomon, "Meanings," 45–46.

133. Heino F. L. Meyer-Bahlburg, "From Mental Disorder to Iatrogenic Hypogonadism: Dilemmas in Conceptualizing Gender Identity Variants as Psychiatric Conditions," *Archives of Sexual Behavior* 39, no. 2 (2010): 467.

—what Thomas Bevan favorably refers to as a "biological imperative."[134] To date, several different lines of evidence have been offered. One common type of argument generally follows a clear three-step approach. First, fundamental male/female brain differences are established by identifying specific sex-dimorphic (i.e., male vs. female) features of the human brain. Second, the brains of transgender persons are studied in order to detect similarities with brains associated with their gender identity (and thus differences from brains associated with their **natal sex**). Finally, a plausible, biologically based causal mechanism is offered to explain this phenomenon.

The first step of this argument is widely recognized as having been accomplished with the rise and dominance of the brain-sex theory. This theory is based on a wide range of studies, both animal and human, demonstrating differences in brain structures between males and females. Commonly cited differences include gray-/white-matter volume and density (e.g., aspects of the hypothalamus [INAH-3] and the bed nucleus of the stria terminalis [BSTc]), neurochemical differences (e.g., oxytocin and vasopressin effects), and so forth.[135] Such findings have led to the development of the neurohormonal theory, which claims that the presence or absence of in-utero sex hormones during gestation—particularly testosterone—is a key factor in sexual differentiation of the brain.[136]

The second step involves demonstrating similarities between the brains of transgender persons and those of people whose biological sex matches the trans person's gender identity rather than their natal sex. Beginning with a key 1995 article in the journal *Nature*, a number of studies have proposed just such similarities.[137] For example, in one widely cited study, FtM transsexuals were found to have a similar number of neurons in the BSTc to males in the control group, while, conversely, MtF transsexuals had roughly the same number as did control-group females.[138]

The third and final step involves proposing biological mechanisms to explain these trans-related brain phenomena. One avenue has been to return to

134. Bevan, *Psychobiology*, 180.

135. Matsumoto, *Sexual Differentiation*.

136. D. F. Swaab, "Sexual Differentiation of the Brain and Behavior," *Best Practice and Research: Clinical Endocrinology and Metabolism* 21 (2007): 431–44.

137. J. N. Zhou, M. A. Hoffman, L. J. G. Gooren, and D. F. Swaab, "A Sex Difference in the Human Brain and Its Relation to Transsexuality," *Nature* 378 (1995): 68–70; E. S. Smith, J. Junger, B. Derntl, and U. Habel, "The Transsexual Brain—A Review of Findings on the Neural Basis of Transsexualism," *Neuroscience and Biobehavioral Reviews* 59 (2015): 251–66; and A. Guillamon, C. Junque, and E. Gómez-Gil, "A Review of the Status of Brain Structure Research in Transsexualism," *Archives of Sexual Behavior* 45 (2016): 1615–48.

138. F. P. M. Kruijver, J. N. Zhou, C. W. Pool, M. A. Hofman, L. J. Gooren, and D. F. Swaab, "Male-to-Female Transsexuals Have Female Neuron Numbers in a Limbic Nucleus," *Journal of Clinical Endocrinology and Metabolism* 85, no. 5 (2000): 2034–41.

the neurohormonal theory and the proposal that it is possible for a discrepancy to emerge during gestation between the (early) genital/gonadal development, on the one hand, and (later) brain differentiation, on the other. This theory suggests that an infant could be born male according to genitals and gonads, yet (more or less) female according to brain structure.[139] For those persuaded by the prenatal hormone theory, transsexuality can effectively be seen as "an intersex condition" of the brain.[140]

More recently, two additional explanatory biological mechanisms have gained ground: genetic and epigenetic pathways.[141] Central to establishing evidence for a genetic mechanism is the use of twin studies. In one recent study, for example, 39.1 percent of the monozygotic (i.e., identical) twins shared the experience of gender incongruence, while none of the same-sex dizygotic (i.e., fraternal) twins did so.[142] Proposals have been offered regarding specific gene abnormalities associated with transgender persons.[143] As our understanding of the inherent complexity of human genetics has grown, some researchers have proposed that only a complex polygenic model can account for things like human variation in gender identity.[144] Epigenetic factors have also been proposed as potential biological pathways for transgender experience, specifically in-utero exposure to certain drugs such as the antimiscarriage drug Diethylstilbestrol (DES) and anticonvulsants (AEDs).[145]

A final line of argument, one that is tied to genetics, appeals to studies of the experiences of genetic males (XY) or females (XX) who are raised as

139. Gender Identity Research and Education Society (GIRES), "Atypical Gender Development—A Review," *International Journal of Transgenderism* 9, no. 1 (2006): 29–44. Some studies based on finger-length ratios have come to a similar conclusion. See M. Leinung and C. Wu, "The Biologic Basis of Transgender Identity: 2D:4D Finger Ratios Implicate a Role for Prenatal Androgen Activity," *Endocrine Practice* 23, no. 6 (2017): 669–71.

140. Milton Diamond, "Transsexualism as an Intersex Condition," in *Transsexuality in Theology and Neuroscience: Findings, Controversies, and Perspectives*, ed. Gerhard Schreiber (Boston: de Gruyter, 2016), 43–53.

141. Bevan, *Psychobiology*, esp. chaps. 5–7.

142. G. Heylens, G. De Cuypere, K. J. Zucker, et al., "Gender Identity Disorder in Twins: A Review of the Case Report Literature," *Journal of Sexual Medicine* 9, no. 3 (2012): 751–57.

143. E. Bentz, L. Hefler, U. Kaufmann, J. Huber, A. Kolbus, and C. Tempfer, "A Polymorphism of the CYP17 Gene Related to Sex Steroid Metabolism Is Associated with Female-to-Male but Not Male-to-Female Transsexualism," *Fertility and Sterility* 90, no. 1 (2008): 56–59; and F. Yang, X. H. Zhu, Q. Zhang, et al., "Genomic Characteristics of Gender Dysphoria Patients and Identification of Rare Mutations in RYR3 Gene," *Scientific Reports* 7, no. 1 (2017): 8339.

144. T. J. C. Polderman, B. P. C. Kreukels, M. S. Irwig, et al., "The Biological Contributions to Gender Identity and Gender Diversity: Bringing Data to the Table," *Behavior Genetics* 48, no. 2 (2018): 95–108.

145. Bevan, *Psychobiology*, chap. 6.

the opposite sex because of either intersex conditions or irreversible genital damage. The most infamous example of the latter situation is known in the annals as the "John/Joan" case. Briefly, a natal male, born in 1965, suffered a botched circumcision that effectively destroyed his penis. In 1967, under the guidance of John Money of Johns Hopkins Hospital, the parents agreed to sexually reassign the infant as a female through surgery and raise the child as a girl. Money continued to report on this case over the years, claiming a successful reassignment and offering it as evidence that gender identity is socially learned, not biologically innate.[146] In 1997 it was revealed that Money had failed to tell the full story. In fact, the child had, from early on, regularly rejected his female-assigned gender identity. By the age of fourteen, he had decided to live as a boy rather than a girl, taking the name David. He went on to marry a woman and adopt three children. David Reimer's story was brought to international attention when he agreed to go public so that others would not have to suffer the same fate at the hands of the medical establishment.[147] At the age of thirty-eight, after suffering a series of painful incidents, Reimer took his own life. For many, the Reimer case offers a clear example of gender identity being biologically fixed and resilient, rather than socially constructed and malleable. In fact, one recent meta-analysis of biologically based arguments for gender identity concluded that studies focusing on the experiences of intersex persons are among "the strongest evidence for the organic basis of transgender identity."[148]

It will not surprise anyone to hear that every line of evidence just offered for a biological basis to transgender experience has been contested by critics. With regard to the three-step argument for the brain-sex theory: (1) A number of scholars, including those associated with neurofeminism and what some are calling queer biology, have argued that the evidence of biologically based sex differences in the human brain is highly questionable.[149] In particular, studies are cited that seem to directly contradict those on which the sex-dimorphic brain paradigm is built.[150]

146. E.g., John Money, "Ablatio Penis: Normal Male Infant Sex-Reassignment as a Girl," *Archives of Sexual Behavior* 4, no. 1 (1975): 65–71.

147. John Colapinto, *As Nature Made Him: The Boy Who Was Raised as a Girl* (New York: Harper Perennial, 2000).

148. Aruna Saraswat, Jamie Weinand, and Joshua Safer, "Evidence Supporting the Biologic Nature of Gender Identity," *Endocrine Practice* 21, no. 2 (2015): 202. See also Heino F. L. Meyer-Bahlburg, "Gender Identity Outcome in Female-Raised 46,XY Persons with Penile Agenesis, Cloacal Exstrophy of the Bladder, or Penile Ablation," *Archives of Sexual Behavior* 34 (2005): 423–38.

149. Bluhm, Jacobson, and Maibom, *Neurofeminism*.

150. D. Marwha, M. Halari, and L. Eliot, "Meta-analysis Reveals a Lack of Sexual Dimorphism in Human Amygdala Volume," *NeuroImage* 147 (2017): 282–94.

(2) Studies purporting to demonstrate similarities between the brains of trans persons and those of people whose biological sex matches the trans person's gender identity rather than their natal sex have also been challenged. For example, while much has been made of the studies involving comparisons of the BSTc (noted above), critics point out that other studies have concluded otherwise, and that this brain structure does not even become sexually dimorphic in humans until adulthood, which leaves it unable to explain the transgender experience in children.[151] A study focusing on brain functioning, rather than structure, found that the brains of the FtM subjects functioned similarly to control females.[152] Other common criticisms include the problem of small sample sizes, and the fact that many of these studies are done on trans persons who have already undergone cross-sex hormone therapy, thus rendering the results immediately suspect.

(3) Finally, critics have challenged the plausibility of each of the proposed causal mechanisms. With regard to the prenatal hormone theory, detractors point to the fact that numerous studies have raised serious problems for it. For example, Louis Gooren points to studies showing that "prenatal androgenization of 46,XX fetuses leads to marked masculinization of later gender-related behavior but does not lead to gender confusion/dysphoria."[153]

With regard to genetic theories, other problems have been posed. For example, while twin studies are offered as evidence for a genetic basis for transgender experience, critics claim these very studies count *against* it in that, for the vast majority of monozygotic twins, when one of them grows up to experience transgender phenomena, the other one does not.[154] And with respect to epigenetic theories, even advocates of epigenetic mechanisms admit the evidence is exceedingly sparse.[155] In sum, critics have concluded that this range of current biologically oriented research shows "inconclusive evidence and mixed findings regarding the brains of transgender adults" and is "correlational rather than causal in character."[156]

151. E.g., I. Savic and S. Arver, "Sex Dimorphism of the Brain in Male-to-Female Transsexuals," *Cerebral Cortex* 21, no. 11 (2011): 2525–33.

152. E. Santarnecchi, G. Vatti, D. Déttore, and A. Rossi, "Intrinsic Cerebral Connectivity Analysis in an Untreated Female-to-Male Transsexual Subject: A First Attempt Using Resting-State fMRI," *Neuroendocrinology* 96, no. 3 (2012): 188–93.

153. Louis Gooren, "The Biology of Human Psychosexual Differentiation," *Hormones and Behavior* 50 (2006): 589. See also Bevan, *Psychobiology*, 111–15.

154. E.g., Nancy L. Segal, "Two Monozygotic Twin Pairs Discordant for Female-to-Male Transsexualism," *Archives of Sexual Behavior* 35, no. 3 (2006): 346–57.

155. E.g., Bevan, *Psychobiology*, 115.

156. See, respectively, Mayer and McHugh, "Sexuality and Gender," 102; and Heino F. L. Meyer-Bahlburg, "Gender Identity Disorder in Young Boys: A Parent- and Peer-Based Treatment Protocol," *Clinical Child Psychology and Psychiatry* 7, no. 3 (2002): 363.

Some critics argue against biologically based theories in the course of proposing an alternative etiological approach, such as a psychological explanation. But queer theorists critique biological and psychological theories alike. In their deployment of strong social constructionism and their critique of all "regulatory" discourses, queer theorists tend to reject biologically based arguments as "essentialism," and psychologically based explanations as fostering pathologizing discourses and troubling forms of "biopower."[157] Far from being a "biological imperative," gender, according to queer theorists, is socioculturally constructed and thus is fundamentally fluid and "free-floating," not innate and fixed.[158]

The Blanchard Typology and the Autogynephilia Theory

With the Blanchard proposal, we come to a particularly controversial perspective on the roots of transsexualism. This theory originally took shape in 1985 when Ray Blanchard, a noted sexologist connected with the University of Toronto, proposed a two-part typology of MtF transsexuals based on their *sexual orientation*.[159] The first type, referred to as "androphilic" (or homosexual) transsexuals, includes all transsexual men who experience **androphilia**—i.e., a sexual attraction toward men.[160] According to the typology, this group of transsexuals is a subgroup of gay men who typically come out as transsexual quite early in life and who are primarily motivated toward transitioning by their attraction to the idea of heterosexual men being attracted to them as a woman. The second type, termed "autogynephilic," is composed of heterosexual men who commonly come out later in life and whose primary motivation toward transitioning is that they are sexually aroused by the image of themselves as a woman. In Blanchard's view, **autogynephilia** is a type of **paraphilia** (i.e., an unusual pattern of sexual arousal involving atypical behaviors, objects of desire, etc.).[161] According to the typology, there are additional differences between these two groups. Specifically, the claim is that, compared to the androphilic/homosexual type, autogynephilic transsexuals

157. The term "biopower" was coined by Michel Foucault in *History of Sexuality*, vol. 1, *The Will to Knowledge*, 140.

158. Butler, *Gender Trouble*, 6.

159. Ray Blanchard, "Typology of Male-to-Female Transsexualism," *Archives of Sexual Behavior* 14, no. 3 (1985): 247–61; and Blanchard, "The Concept of Autogynephilia and the Typology of Male Gender Dysphoria," *Journal of Nervous and Mental Disease* 177 (1989): 616–23.

160. Increasingly today sex researchers refer to androphilia and **gynephilia** (i.e., sexual attraction to women) rather than hetero- and homosexuality.

161. Anne A. Lawrence, "Autogynephilia: A Paraphilic Model of Gender Identity Disorder," *Journal of Lesbian and Gay Psychotherapy* 8, nos. 1–2 (2008): 69–87.

are less feminine as children, are likelier to have a history of engaging in erotic cross-dressing, have a more difficult time passing as women, and have a greater likelihood of postoperative dissatisfaction or regret.[162]

Not surprisingly, Blanchard's theory has become highly controversial within both the transgender and academic communities. Some have found it to be enlightening and have gone on to develop and defend it.[163] Two of its most forceful advocates are Michael Bailey[164] and Anne Lawrence.[165] One sign of this theory's influence is the addition of "autogynephilia" as a subcategory under the diagnosis of transvestic disorder in the *DSM-5*.[166]

At the same time, Blanchard's typology has come under severe critique, especially by some within the trans community. Common criticisms include (1) it does not fit the actual reported experience of many transsexuals; (2) its binary typology is too restrictive; (3) it confuses gender identity with sexual orientation; (4) it does not account for the experiences of FtM transsexuals; (5) it is scientifically unfalsifiable; (6) it is socially and politically damaging in that it pathologizes much of the transgender community; and (7) particularly in Bailey's articulation of it, the language used is often insensitive and arrogant.[167]

In conclusion, when all of the research and the differing perspectives are taken into account, it seems that many scholars today are concluding that the specific causal mechanisms of transgender experience are exceedingly complex, are probably multidimensional, and, at this point in time, are simply something that we cannot be certain about.[168]

162. Ray Blanchard, "Deconstructing the Feminine Essence Narrative," *Archives of Sexual Behavior* 37 (2008): 435; and Ray Blanchard, Betty W. Steiner, Leonard H. Clemmensen, and Robert Dickey, "Prediction of Regrets in Postoperative Transsexuals," *Canadian Journal of Psychiatry* 34 (1989): 43–45. It should be noted that Blanchard does not see his theory as necessarily in conflict with other etiological theories. In fact, Blanchard's own view is that androphilic transsexualism probably does involve biologically based "sex-dimorphic structures" in the brain ("Deconstructing," 437).

163. In addition to Bailey and Lawrence (see next two notes), others who embrace Blanchard's theory to one degree or another include such recognized sexuality scholars as James Cantor, Peggy Cohen-Kettenis, Alice Dreger, and Kevin Hsu.

164. J. Michael Bailey, *The Man Who Would Be Queen: The Science of Gender Bending and Transsexualism* (Washington, DC: Joseph Henry, 2003). This book brought a firestorm of criticism from certain transgender activists.

165. Anne A. Lawrence, *Men Trapped in Men's Bodies: Narratives of Autogynephilic Transsexualism* (New York: Springer, 2013). Lawrence self-identifies as an autogynephilic transsexual.

166. *DSM-5*, 457, 685–705.

167. Julia Serano, "The Case against Autogynephilia," *International Journal of Transgenderism* 12, no. 3 (2010): 176–87; Charles Moser, "Blanchard's Autogynephilia Theory: A Critique," *Journal of Homosexuality* 57, no. 6 (2010): 790–809; and Bevan, *Psychobiology*, 191–94.

168. Bullough and Bullough, *Cross Dressing*, 271, 275; Gooren, "Biology," 589; Heino F. L. Meyer-Bahlburg, "'Diagnosing' Gender? Categorizing Gender-Identity Variants in the

Transgender Children and Treatment Approaches

One increasingly controversial issue—referred to recently as the "Transgender Battle Line"—concerns the growing prevalence of transgender children.[169] As Tey Meadow, a researcher focusing on the first generation of families raising transgender kids, has pointed out, the concept of the transgender child is a "relatively new social form. . . . We see no references to transgender children prior to the mid-1990s."[170] One can gauge something of the direction of the cultural trend on this issue by comparing a *Time* magazine article appearing in 2000 with a spate of articles appearing in various periodicals since 2015. In September 2000, *Time* reported on an Ohio family who, in light of their son Zachary's insistent protestations that he was not really a boy, decided to begin raising the child as a girl. The state of Ohio eventually took the parents to court in a custody battle, removed the child from their home, and found foster placement where Zachary could be raised as a boy.[171] Fast-forward fifteen years, and one finds that the cultural default setting regarding transgender kids has dramatically shifted.[172] In many sectors of our culture, the debate is not *whether* parents should support the transitioning of a gender dysphoric child, but rather *how*—that is, what the nature and timing of that support should look like.

Since the 1990s, there has been an explosion of research on gender nonconforming/dysphoric children. Several studies suggest that children experiencing gender dysphoria typically recognize it between the ages of seven and ten, although reports of even younger children—one as young as eighteen months—are growing.[173] A 2012 report of an American Psychiatric Association task

Anthropocene," *Archives of Sexual Behavior* (2019), https://doi.org/10.1007/s10508-018-1349-6 (epub prior to printing); and Yarhouse, *Understanding Gender Dysphoria*, 80.

169. Debra W. Soh, "The Transgender Battle Line: Childhood," *Wall Street Journal*, January 4, 2016, https://www.wsj.com/articles/the-transgender-battle-line-childhood-1451952794. A recent UK study notes the "unprecedented increase in referrals of gender-diverse young people seeking professional help" (p. 1302). In terms of sex ratio, this study also notes a "steep increase" of birth-assigned females seeking help from gender services (p. 1304). See Nastasja M. De Graaf, Guido Giovanardi, Claudia Zitz, and Polly Carmichael, "Sex Ratio in Children and Adolescents Referred to the Gender Identity Development Service in the UK (2009–2016)," *Archives of Sexual Behavior* 47, no. 5 (2018): 1301–4, https://doi.org/10.1007/s10508-018-1204-9.

170. Tey Meadow, "Child," *Transgender Studies Quarterly* 1, nos. 1–2 (2014): 57.

171. John Cloud, "His Name Is Aurora," *Time*, September 25, 2000, http://content.time.com/time/magazine/article/0,9171,998007,00.html.

172. E.g., Gail O'Conner, "Transparenthood: Raising a Transgender Child," *Parents Magazine*, September 2015, http://www.parents.com/parenting/dynamics/raising-a-transgender-child/; and Francine Russo, "Debate Is Growing about How to Meet the Urgent Need of Transgender Kids," *Scientific American Mind*, January/February 2016, 27–35.

173. Stephanie Brill and Rachel Pepper, *The Transgender Child: A Handbook for Families and Professionals* (San Francisco: Cleis, 2008), 2, 16–22.

force on treating gender dysphoria in children captures the challenging and controversial nature of this endeavor: "Opinions vary widely among experts, and are influenced by theoretical orientation, as well as assumptions and beliefs (including religious) regarding the origins, meanings, and perceived fixity or malleability of gender identity. Primary caregivers may, therefore, seek out providers for their children who mirror their own world views, believing that goals consistent with their views are in the best interest of their children."[174]

At the writing of this introduction, a skirmish has recently broken out on this front. It has to do with a published study involving a subset of transgender adolescents and the controversial thesis of *rapid onset gender dysphoria* (ROGD).[175] Specifically, the question raised by this study is whether some children might be adopting a transgender identity at least in part through the effects of social conditioning within a peer-group context. As happens regularly now in our culture with issues related to transgender experience, the question of ROGD has been quickly and ruthlessly politicized. In the hands of cultural conservatives, it has been adopted and deployed as yet another weapon within the arsenal trained against transgender "ideology."[176] In response, trans activists and allies have just as quickly pronounced the very idea of ROGD to be a "hoax diagnosis" based on "biased junk science" that offers just one more sign of the pervasive transphobia at work in our culture.[177] Sadly, both sides within this cultural war seem more interested in quickly and effectively neutralizing the political opposition than in engaging

---

174. William Byne, Susan Bradley, Eli Coleman, et al., "Report of the American Psychiatric Association Task Force on Treatment of Gender Identity Disorder," *Archives of Sexual Behavior* 41, no. 4 (2012): 762–63.

175. Lisa Littman, "Rapid-Onset Gender Dysphoria in Adolescents and Young Adults: A Study of Parental Reports," *PLoS One* 13, no. 8 (2018), https://doi.org/10.1371/journal.pone .0202330.

176. E.g., Barbara Kay, "A New Report Sounds the Alarm on Rapid Onset Gender Dysphoria," *National Post*, August 22, 2018, https://nationalpost.com/opinion/barbara-kay-a-new -report-sounds-the-alarm-on-rapid-onset-gender-dysphoria; and Jillian Kay Melchior, "Peer Pressure and 'Transgender' Teens: Ideologues Try to Suppress a Study on the Increasing Prevalence of 'Rapid Onset Gender Dysphoria,'" *Wall Street Journal*, September 9, 2018, https://www .wsj.com/articles/peer-pressure-and-transgender-teens-1536524718?ref=gazelle.popsugar .com.

177. Zinnia Jones, "'Rapid Onset Gender Dysphoria': What a Hoax Diagnosis Looks Like," *Gender Analysis*, February 1, 2018, https://genderanalysis.net/2018/02/rapid-onset-gender-dysph oria-what-a-hoax-diagnosis-looks-like; and Brynn Tannehill, "'Rapid Onset Gender Dysphoria' Is Biased Junk Science," *Advocate*, February 20, 2018, https://www.advocate.com/commentary /2018/2/20/rapid-onset-gender-dysphoria-biased-junk-science. See also Arjee Javellana Restar, "Methodological Critique of Littman's (2018) Parental-Respondents Accounts of 'Rapid-Onset Gender Dysphoria,'" *Archives of Sexual Behavior* (2019), https://doi.org/10.1007/s10508-019 -1453-2 (epub prior to printing).

in measured, critical (including self-critical) reflection and respectful, bridge-building dialogue.[178]

In an attempt to map the current landscape on this contested issue, a number of researchers have proposed a typology of three basic approaches being used today to understand, support, and treat gender dysphoric children.[179]

Gender Realignment

The first approach, which was the dominant response to gender noncon-forming/dysphoric children throughout the twentieth century, focuses on encouraging the child to decrease cross-gender behavior and identification so as to facilitate a realignment of their sense of gender identity with their embodied/natal sex. This approach has been commonly adopted by psycho-analytically trained professionals and tends to focus on behavioral and psy-chologically based treatment plans.[180]

Specific treatment avenues include (1) behavioral therapy (e.g., fostering such things as building a healthy relationship with the same-gender parental figure, encouraging parents to ignore cross-gender behavior while redirecting the child toward same-gender alternatives, etc.),[181] (2) psychodynamic thera-pies focusing on direct therapeutic sessions with the child and/or parents (e.g., play therapy, etc.),[182] (3) assisting with parent-guided interventions in the child's naturalistic environment, and (4) in the case of co-occurring psychiatric issues, the use of psychotropic medications. These therapeutic options are commonly combined.[183]

---

178. Questions concerning ROGD had been raised prior to this current fracas. But, again, they were largely framed within a polemical (culture war) context. E.g., David French, "The Tragic Transgender Contagion," *National Review*, August 18, 2016, https://www.nationalreview.com/2016/08/transgender-teens-parents-rapid-onset-gender-dysphoria-doctors.

179. E.g., Byne, Bradley, Coleman, et al., "Report," 763; and J. Drescher, "Controversies in Gender Diagnoses," *LGBT Health* 1 (2013): 10–14. Yarhouse (*Understanding Gender Dysphoria*, 107–9) adds a fourth approach—puberty suppression—and points out that, while this treatment is often seen as merely one aspect in the process of transitioning, the two are in fact separable.

180. E.g., Marina Bonfatto and Eva Crasnow, "Gender/ed Identities: An Overview of Our Current Work as Child Psychotherapists in the Gender Identity Development Service," *Journal of Child Psychotherapy* 44, no. 1 (2018): 29–46.

181. G. A. Rekers, M. Kilgus, and A. C. Rosen, "Long-Term Effects of Treatment for Gender Identity Disorder of Childhood," *Journal of Psychology and Human Sexuality* 3 (1990): 121–53; and Zucker and Cohen-Kettenis, "Gender Identity," 395–97.

182. Domenico Di Ceglie, "Management and Therapeutic Aims in Working with Children and Adolescents with Gender Identity Disorders and Their Families," in Di Ceglie and Freed-man, *Stranger in My Own Body*, 185–97; and Zucker and Cohen-Kettenis, "Gender Identity," 395, 397–98.

183. E.g., Meyer-Bahlburg, "Gender Identity"; S. W. Coates, "Intervention with Preschool Boys with Gender Identity Issues," *Neuropsychiatrie de l'Enfance et de l'Adolescence* 56, no. 6

Several rationales are given for such therapeutic approaches, including "(1) reduction in social ostracism, (2) treatment of underlying psychopathology, (3) treatment of the underlying distress, [and] (4) prevention of transsexualism in adulthood."[184] Another factor that can fuel the psychological approach is the concern that when children or adolescents move toward the path of cross-sex hormone therapy, "they or their parents are consenting to lifelong infertility."[185] A final defense of the psychological model emerges from the conclusion, drawn by a number of studies, that for the vast majority of children who experience gender dysphoria—current statistics seem to suggest around 80 percent—it will eventually desist, and they will end up identifying with their natal sex by the time they have moved out of puberty.[186] Seen in this light, proponents of this approach see therapeutic intervention as simply helping to "speed up the fading of the cross-gender identity which will typically happen in any case."[187]

Again, this approach was the dominant response throughout the twentieth century.[188] In one of the very few studies of the long-term effectiveness of such treatments, researchers observed that "subjects who completed treatment improved about twice as much as those who did not complete treatment" and concluded that "treatment intervention does result in significant improvement over the long-term."[189] They also found that the younger the child was at the time of treatment, the greater the improvement.[190] These researchers, guided by the conviction that gender is not innate and biologically based but rather is a malleable phenomenon, concluded that "treatment focused on gender behavior was found to significantly improve gender identity."[191]

(2008): 386–91; and Zucker, Wood, Singh, and Bradley, "Developmental, Biopsychosocial Model."

184. Zucker and Cohen-Kettenis, "Gender Identity," 394.

185. Russo, "Debate," 35.

186. Thomas Steensma, Roeline Biemond, Fijgjie de Boer, and Peggy T. Cohen-Kettenis, "Desisting and Persisting Gender Dysphoria after Childhood: A Qualitative Follow-Up Study," *Clinical Child Psychology and Psychiatry* (2011): 499–516. A recent article reports the persistence rate ranges as follows: "6 to 23 percent of boys and 12 to 27 percent of girls treated in gender clinics showed persistence of their gender dysphoria into adulthood." Jack Drescher and Jack Pula, "Ethical Issues Raised by the Treatment of Gender-Variant Prepubescent Children," *Hastings Center Report* 44 (September 2014 supp.), S17.

187. Meyer-Bahlburg, "Gender Identity," 361.

188. Earlier case studies that conclude for the effectiveness of psychotherapeutic treatment include D. H. Barlow, G. G. Abel, and E. B. Blanchard, "Gender Identity Change in Transsexuals: Follow-Up and Replications," *Archives of General Psychiatry* 36 (1979): 1001–7; and Robert J. Edelmann, "Adaptive Training for Existing Male Transsexual Gender Role: A Case History," *Journal of Sex Research* 22, no. 4 (1986): 514–19.

189. Rekers, Kilgus, and Rosen, "Long-Term," 137.

190. Rekers, Kilgus, and Rosen, "Long-Term," 146, 149–50.

191. Rekers, Kilgus, and Rosen, "Long-Term," 130.

Those who hold to the gender affirmation approach (see below) tend to be highly critical of this gender realignment paradigm. A common critique is that, similar to reparative therapy for homosexuality, treatments focused on gender realignment are, in fact, unethical, stigmatizing, and generally ineffective.[192] They point out that, over the last decade or so, there has been a widespread tendency for gender clinics to abandon this approach in favor of a gender affirmative paradigm.[193] Critics have also challenged a number of the supporting arguments offered in defense of the gender realignment model. For example, one recent study has called into question the common claim that gender dysphoric children exhibit a high rate of desistence by the time they reach young adulthood.[194]

Gender Affirmation

The second approach—the gender affirmative model—seeks to affirm and support the transgender child's inner sense of gender identity by helping them facilitate a social transition to their expressed gender.[195] Social transition typically involves making gender appropriate adjustments to things like clothing, hairstyle, personal name, pronoun preference, and so forth. Advocates of prepubertal social transitioning remind their critics that a child can always "revert to their originally assigned gender if nec-

192. E.g., Stewart L. Adelson, "Practice Parameter on Gay, Lesbian, or Bisexual Sexual Orientation, Gender Nonconformity, and Gender Discordance in Children and Adolescents," *Journal of the American Academy of Child and Adolescent Psychiatry* 51 (2012): 957–74.

193. A particularly high-profile example of this involved Kenneth Zucker, a leading researcher of childhood gender dysphoria and for many years the director of the Child, Youth, and Family Gender Identity Clinic in Toronto. Apparently as a consequence for continuing to embrace a predominantly gender realignment approach rather than a fully gender affirmative one, he was terminated from his position in 2015 and the clinic was closed. See Jesse Singal, "How the Fight over Transgender Kids Got a Leading Sex Researcher Fired," *The Cut*, February 7, 2016, https://www.thecut.com/2016/02/fight-over-trans-kids-got-a-researcher-fired .html.

194. Julia Temple Newhook, Jake Pyne, Kelley Winters, et al., "A Critical Commentary on Follow-Up Studies and 'Desistance' Theories about Transgender and Gender-Nonconforming Children," *International Journal of Transgenderism* 19, no. 2 (2018): 212–24. This article is followed by responses, including Kenneth J. Zucker, "The Myth of Persistence: Response to 'A Critical Commentary on Follow-Up Studies and "Desistance" Theories about Transgender and Gender Nonconforming Children' by Temple Newhook et al. (2018)," *International Journal of Transgenderism* 19, no. 2 (2018): 231–45.

195. E.g., Marco A. Hidalgo, Diane Ehrensaft, Amy C. Tishelman, et al., "The Gender Affirmative Model: What We Know and What We Aim to Learn," *Human Development* 56 (2013): 285–90; and Diane Ehrensaft, Shawn V. Giammattei, Kelly Storck, Amy C. Tishelman, and Colton Keo-Meier, "Prepubertal Social Gender Transitions: What We Know; What We Can Learn—A View from a Gender Affirmative Lens," *International Journal of Transgenderism* 19, no. 2 (2018): 251–68.

essary since the transition is solely at a social level and without medical intervention."[196]

This approach has been gaining in acceptance in recent years, sometimes with children as young as three or four.[197] Its popularity has been fueled by a number of factors. Trans activism has made the recognition and support of transgender children a central concern, catalyzed by reports of high levels of depression and suicide among gender-variant young people.[198] Various forms of media—from more traditional modes such as television, film, and books, to newer social media formats such as Facebook and YouTube—have brought increased visibility and social acceptance to the experience of childhood gender variance.[199] Many within the medical and psychological communities—for example, the American Academy of Pediatrics—have responded by embracing a gender affirmative stance and developing clear transition protocols for children and adolescents.[200] Along with this, the number of child and adolescent gender affirmative clinics designed to assist children and their families through the transitioning process has grown significantly. Critics of gender affirmative clinics have voiced concerns that this approach can lead to the transitioning of children who are merely going through a temporary phase of gender nonconformity. But advocates respond by noting the strict protocols in place to prevent just such things from happening, including the fact that only children who are "insistent, persistent, and consistent" in their gender nonconformity are eventually supported through transition.[201]

196. Jiska Ristori and Thomas D. Steensma, "Gender Dysphoria in Childhood," *International Review of Psychiatry* 28, no. 1 (2016): 17. See also Byne, Bradley, Coleman, et al., "Report," 763.

197. For a study of thirty-six socially transitioned children between the ages of three and five, see A. A. Fast and K. R. Olson, "Gender Development in Transgender Preschool Children," *Child Development*, April 25, 2017, https://doi.org/10.1111/cdev.12758 (epub prior to printing).

198. On suicide risk among LGBT youth, see Effie Malley, Marc Posner, and Lloyd Potter, *Suicide Risk and Prevention for Lesbian, Gay, Bisexual and Transgender Youth* (Newton, MA: Suicide Prevention Resource Center, 2008).

199. E.g., Diane Ehrensaft, *Gender Born, Gender Made: Raising Healthy Gender-Nonconforming Children* (New York: Experiment, 2011); Susan Kuklin, *Beyond Magenta: Transgender Teens Speak Out* (Somerville, MA: Candlewick, 2014); Ryan J. Testa, Deborah Coolhart, and Jayme Peta, *The Gender Quest Workbook: A Guide for Teens and Young Adults Exploring Gender Identity* (Oakland: New Harbinger, 2015); Jennings, *Being Jazz*; and Ann Travers, *The Trans Generation: How Trans Kids (and Their Parents) Are Creating a Gender Revolution* (New York: New York University Press, 2018).

200. American Academy of Pediatrics Committee on Adolescence, "Policy Statement: Office-Based Care for Lesbian, Gay, Bisexual, Transgender, and Questioning Youth," *Pediatrics* 132, no. 1 (2013): e198–203, www.pediatrics.org/cgi/doi/10.1542/peds.2013-1282.

201. Hidalgo, Ehrensaft, Tishelman, et al., "Gender Affirmative Model," 286.

Those holding to a gender affirmative view propose that by helping the child to make a social transition to living as the experienced gender, transgender kids can avoid "the severe depression that accompanies the onset of an unwanted puberty and . . . the physically and psychologically painful procedures required to reverse puberty's physical manifestations."[202] Advocates of the gender affirmative paradigm point out that the increasing acceptance of transgender identity within our culture has made it easier for gender nonconforming children and their parents to approach transgender experience from a perspective of *pride* rather than pathology.[203] In essence, the gender affirmative approach sees the transitioning process as simply helping a transgender child realign with their original gender identity, one from which they were alienated at birth by their well-meaning but uninformed parents and doctors. From this perspective, it is understandable why children are assigned at birth as a male (**AMAB**) or as a female (**AFAB**) based on genitalia, but in the end it is the child's own inner sense of gender identity that must be acknowledged as having final authority on the matter. As a gender nonconforming child nears puberty, one intervention that often accompanies this approach is the use of puberty suppression drugs to prevent the development of unwanted secondary sex characteristics, which, among other things, would make transitioning more difficult going forward.[204]

Critics of this approach—from professionals to parents—have posed difficult questions about the ethics of transitioning children.[205] Interestingly, critics of the gender affirmative paradigm can be found within both "conservative" (gender-traditionalist) and "radical left" (gender-constructionist) circles.[206]

202. Norman Spack, "Transgenderism," *Medical Ethics* 12 (Fall 2005), http://www.imatyfa .org/assets/spack-article.pdf.

203. Cory Silverberg, "From Pathology to Pride: Supporting Gender Non-conforming Children," *Contemporary Sexuality* 47, no. 8 (2013): 1, 3–6.

204. Annelou L. C. de Vries, Jenifer K. McGuire, Thomas D. Steensma, Eva C. F. Wagenaar, Theo A. H. Doreleijers, and Peggy T. Cohen-Kettenis, "Young Adult Psychological Outcome after Puberty Suppression and Gender Reassignment," *Pediatrics* 134, no. 4 (2014): 696–704.

205. E.g., Heather Brunskell-Evans and Michele Moore, eds., *Transgender Children and Young People: Born in Your Own Body* (Newcastle upon Tyne, UK: Cambridge Scholars, 2018); A. Korte, U. Lehmkuhl, D. Goecker, K. M. Beier, H. Krude, and A. Grüters-Kieslich, "Gender Identity Disorders in Childhood and Adolescence: Currently Debated Concepts and Treatment Strategies," *Deutsches Ärzteblatt International* 105, no. 48 (2008): 834–41; and American College of Pediatricians, "Gender Ideology Harms Children," March 2016 (updated September 2017), https://www.acpeds.org/wordpress/wp-content/uploads/9.14.17-Gender-Ideology-Harms-Chil dren_updated-MC.pdf. Both parent and professional websites devoted to warning others about the dangers of childhood transitioning have arisen. See 4thwavenow.com; transgendertrend .com; and First, Do No Harm: Youth Gender Professionals, youthtranscriticalprofessionals.org.

206. E.g., see, respectively, Focus on the Family, "Helping Children with Gender Identity Confusion," 2017, http://media.focusonthefamily.com/topicinfo/helping-children-with-gen

Among other things, concerns about health risks, both short- and long-term, related to puberty blockers and hormonal drug treatments have been raised (e.g., infertility, poor bone health, and neurodevelopmental issues).[207] Given that most studies have concluded that the majority of children will not persist in their cross-gender expression on into adulthood, the psychological and interpersonal distress associated with "having to make a social transition twice" has also been voiced.[208]

Watchful Waiting

The third and final approach attempts to chart a course somewhere between the first two. Commonly referred to as "watchful waiting," those who advocate this approach tend to take a stance of neutrality with regard to the child's expressions of gender nonconformity.[209] That is, on the one hand, "there is no active effort to lessen the gender dysphoria or cross-gender behavior."[210] On the other hand, neither is there "an a priori assumption in place that functions as a goal for the child's gender identity."[211] In essence, this model takes something of a "wait and see" stance, while focusing on helping the family, both the parents and the child, adjust to the situation in as healthy and positive a way as possible.[212] This approach has come to be identified with the "Dutch protocol," with some of its advocates arguing

der-identity-confusion.pdf; and Heather Brunskell-Evans, "Gendered Mis-intelligence: The Fabrication of 'The Transgender Child,'" in Brunskell-Evans and Moore, *Transgender Children*, 41–63.

207. Eva Moore, Amy Wisniewski, and Adrian Dobs, "Endocrine Treatment of Transsexual People: A Review of Treatment Regimens, Outcomes, and Adverse Effects," *Journal of Endocrinology and Metabolism* 88, no. 9 (2003): 3467–73; Thomas D. Steensma, S. Annelijn Wensing-Kruger, and Daniel T. Klink, "How Should Physicians Help Gender-Transitioning Adolescents Consider Potential Iatrogenic Harms of Hormone Therapy?," *AMA Journal of Ethics* 19, no. 8 (2017): 762–70; and Rebecca M. Harris, Amy C. Tishelman, Gwendolyn P. Quinn, and Leena Nahata, "Decision Making and the Long-Term Impact of Puberty Blockade in Transgender Children," *American Journal of Bioethics* 19, no. 2 (2019): 67–69.

208. Thomas D. Steensma and Peggy T. Cohen-Kettenis, "Gender Transitioning before Puberty?," *Archives of Sexual Behavior* 40, no. 4 (2011): 649. See also Cretella, "Gender Dysphoria," 50–54; and Mayer and McHugh, "Sexuality and Gender," 9.

209. Drescher, "Controversies"; Kenneth J. Zucker, "On the 'Natural History' of Gender Identity Disorder in Children," *Child and Adolescent Psychiatry* 47, no. 12 (2008): 1362; and A. L. de Vries and P. T. Cohen-Kettenis, "Clinical Management of Gender Dysphoria in Children and Adolescents: The Dutch Approach," *Journal of Homosexuality* 59, no. 3 (2012): 301–20.

210. Zucker, "'Natural History,'" 1362.

211. Yarhouse, *Understanding Gender Dysphoria*, 106.

212. Christine Aramburu Alegria, "Gender Nonconforming and Transgender Children/Youth: Family, Community, and Implications for Practice," *Journal of the American Association of Nurse Practitioners* 28, no. 10 (2016): 521–27.

that, globally considered, the "watchful waiting" approach is the "current standard of care worldwide."[213]

Critics of this middle-way perspective can be found on either side. Those from the gender affirmative side, for example, can see it as encouraging "delayed transition," which only serves to prolong the child's experience of dysphoria.[214] Critics from the gender realignment side can view this approach as withholding the type of therapeutic resources that can assist the child in recovering an integrated, holistic sense of their embodied self. The conflict between these three views represents more than simply a practical disagreement on treatment options. As Kenneth Zucker has noted, these three approaches are "informed by a variety of distinct conceptual and philosophical assumptions regarding psychosexual differentiation."[215]

Moving beyond the Controversies to Real People

Beyond the celebrities and media sensations, beyond the controversies, the legal battles, and the culture wars, a significant number of people find themselves or their loved ones experiencing some form of gender variance or dysphoria. A growing number of books, many of them self-published, offer autobiographical insights into the lives of transgender people:[216] from those who feel the occasional need to cross-dress to those who pursue a complete social and medical transition; from surprisingly young children to adolescents, middle-aged folks, and on up to senior citizens; from parents attempting to walk with their gender dysphoric children to spouses and significant others trying to navigate life after the "coming out" of their transgender partner;[217]

213. Michael Laidlaw, Michelle Cretella, and G. Kevin Donovan, "The Right to Best Care for Children Does Not Include the Right to Medical Transition," *American Journal of Bioethics* 19, no. 2 (2019): 75. On the Dutch protocol, see de Vries and Cohen-Kettenis, "Clinical Management."

214. Gabe Murchison, *Supporting and Caring for Transgender Children* (Washington, DC: Human Rights Campaign, 2016), 13–14, https://www.aap.org/en-us/Documents/solgbt_resource_transgenderchildren.pdf.

215. Zucker, "'Natural History,'" 1362. Others offer alternative models with nuances of their own. For example, Melina Sevlever and Heino Meyer-Bahlburg propose a "gender exploration" approach that appears to fall somewhere between the "watchful waiting" and the gender affirmative models. See Melina Sevlever and Heino F. L. Meyer-Bahlburg, "Late-Onset Transgender Identity Development of Adolescents in Psychotherapy for Mood and Anxiety Problems: Approach to Assessment and Treatment," *Archives of Sexual Behavior* (2019), https://doi.org/10.1007/s10508-018-1362-9 (epub prior to printing).

216. E.g., Jennifer Finney Boylan, *She's Not There: A Life in Two Genders* (New York: Broadway, 2013); and Kenna Dixon, *I'm Not the Man I Used to Be* (n.p.: Kenna Dixon, 2012).

217. E.g., Janna Barkin, *He's Always Been My Son: A Mother's Story about Raising Her Transgender Son* (Philadelphia: Kingsley, 2017); and Virginia Erhardt, *Head over Heels: Wives Who Stay with Cross-Dressers and Transsexuals* (New York: Routledge, 2007).

from medical professionals, therapists, teachers, and clergy striving to support and guide their transgender patients, clients, students, and congregants to siblings, in-laws, employers, and neighbors seeking to understand, embrace, and journey with their transgender relatives, coworkers, and friends. Beyond the glare of the television camera lights and the gloss of the magazine cover—this is where most transgender people, and those who know and love them, live their daily lives.

Among the common realities faced by many transgender people is the experience of mistreatment by others. One transgender resource describes it in this way: "As members of the trans community, we may experience high levels of violence, victimization, and trauma, which puts us at an increased risk of mental health issues. The violence and trauma many of us experience includes emotional, psychological, verbal, physical, and sexual abuse. It can occur at home, at school, or in the community, and it can come from family members, friends, peers, or strangers."[218] A range of studies has documented the types of mistreatment and abuse that many transgender people face. School settings and the workplace are commonly cited as contexts where transgender people regularly experience indignity, bullying, and torment—from being the brunt of jokes to being on the receiving end of outright violence.[219] A recent survey found that, while 40 percent of US adults know someone who is transgender, 27 percent are not open to being friends with anyone who personally identifies as such.[220] The outright rejection of transgender people, particularly youth, by their immediate families has been directly tied to increased rates of homelessness, substance abuse, violence, and suicide.[221] A groundbreaking survey of 6,450 transgender people in America (one of the lead authors of which is Justin Sabia-Tanis, a contributor to the present volume) found that "a staggering 41% of respondents reported attempting suicide compared to 1.6% of the general population, with rates rising for those who lost a job due to bias (55%), were harassed/

218. Tamar Carmel, Ruben Hopwood, and lore m. dickey, "Mental Health Concerns," in *Trans Bodies, Trans Selves: A Resource for the Transgender Community*, ed. Laura Erickson-Schroth (New York: Oxford University Press, 2014), 310.

219. S. Wyss, "'This Was My Hell': The Violence Experienced by Gender Non-conforming Youth in US High Schools," *International Journal of Qualitative Studies in Education* 17, no. 5 (2004): 709–30; and Christine Michelle Duffy, *Gender Identity and Sexual Orientation Discrimination in the Workplace: A Practical Guide* (Edison, NJ: Bloomberg BNA, 2014).

220. "Transgender Issues," *YouGov*, February 9, 2017, https://d25d2506sfb94s.cloudfront .net/cumulus_uploads/document/537rxhcloa/US%20Results%20(Transgender%20Issues)%20 025%2002.10.2017.pdf.

221. Augustus Klein and Sarit A. Golub, "Family Rejection as a Predictor of Suicide Attempts and Substance Misuse among Transgender and Gender Nonconforming Adults," *LGBT Health* 3, no. 3 (2016): 193–99.

bullied in school (51%), had low household income, or were the victim of physical assault (61%) or sexual assault (64%)."[222] Not surprisingly, studies regularly report that the prevalence rates of mental health issues are significantly higher among the transgender population than the general populace.[223] It is within this context that the church of Jesus Christ is called to engage transgender people—people loved by the God who created them in the very "image of God."

Transgender Experiences and Identities in Christian Perspective

This final section will serve to set the stage for the topic that will occupy the rest of this book: Christian perspectives on transgender experiences and identities. At the outset, some might be inclined to think that this conversation is destined to be something less than fruitful. On the one hand, some researchers have suggested that transgender people, along with others in the LGBT community, generally show a "relative disinterest" in things religious.[224] On the other hand, many have pointed out that Christian— especially conservative Christian—responses to transgender experiences have often come across as demeaning and even hateful.[225] Beyond this, Christian infighting about sexuality in general—and about aspects like homosexuality and transgender experience in particular—often dominates the media today. In light of these dynamics, one might wonder what good can really come from a consideration of transgender experience in light of a Christian worldview.

222. Jaime M. Grant, Lisa A. Mottet, and Justin Tanis, with Jack Harrison, Jody L. Herman, and Mara Keisling, *Injustice at Every Turn: A Report of the National Transgender Discrimination Survey* (Washington, DC: National Center for Transgender Equality and National Gay and Lesbian Task Force, 2011), 2. See also Justin Tanis, "The Power of 41%: A Glimpse into the Life of a Statistic," *Journal of Orthopsychiatry* 86, no. 4 (2016): 373–77. For a more recent analysis of this question, see Noah Adams, Maaya Hitomi, and Cherie Moody, "Varied Reports of Adult Transgender Suicidality: Synthesizing and Describing the Peer-Reviewed and Gray Literature," *Transgender Health* 2, no. 1 (2017), https://doi.org/10.1089/trgh.2016.0036.

223. E.g., Jacob C. Warren, K. Bryant Smalley, and K. Nikki Barefoot, "Psychological Well-Being among Transgender and Genderqueer Individuals," *International Journal of Transgenderism* 17, nos. 3–4 (2016): 114–23.

224. Esther D. Rothblum, "Lesbian, Gay, Bisexual, and Transgender Communities," in Patterson and D'Augelli, *Handbook of Psychology and Sexual Orientation*, 305.

225. Jonathan Merritt has argued that one of the chief reasons conservative Christians will "lose the transgender debate" is their lack of focus on "real transgender people with real struggles who experience real oppression." "3 Reasons Conservative Christians Will Lose the Transgender Debate," *Religion News Service*, May 14, 2016, http://religionnews.com/2016/05/14/3-reasons-conservative-christians-will-lose-the-transgender-debate/.

Christian Dialogue on Transgender Experience: Hopes and Challenges

Contrary to common sentiments, we want to suggest that there is good reason to be hopeful about the possibility of a fruitful engagement between differing Christian perspectives on transgender experience. While it is no doubt the case that many within the transgender community have become disenchanted with religion, it is also true that a significant sector of this community takes religion—including Christianity—very seriously.[226] For these folks, there is often a struggle to make sense of their transgender experience in light of their religious faith, a process that therapists and clergy are often called on to assist with.[227] And yet, even as religious faith can pose a challenge, it can also bring great insight, strength, and comfort. Using data from a large-scale Pew Research Center survey of US LGBT adults, a 2017 study found that "religious affiliation is a significant predictor of LGBT individuals' happiness."[228] And, again, while there are certainly instances of bitter controversy between Christians about matters of sexuality, there are also wonderful examples of respectful dialogue even in the midst of serious disagreement.[229]

Given the current state of the culture war, one could easily assume that, while there may be a place of welcome for transgender people within the liberal or progressive quarters of the church, no such place exists within more conservative traditional forms of Christianity. But even here, things are more complex than one might expect. It is true that religiosity and conservatism have often been correlated with more negative attitudes toward transgender identity.[230] Conservative Christians—Protestant, Catholic, and Eastern Orthodox

---

226. Delfin bautista and Quince Mountain, with Heath Mackenzie Reynolds, "Religion and Spirituality," in Erickson-Schroth, *Trans Bodies, Trans Selves*, 62–79; Beardsley and O'Brien, *This Is My Body*; and Malcolm Himschoot, Carla Robinson, Andrew Tobias Nelson, et al., "How Do You Hold Together Your Trans Identity and Your Life of Faith?," *Christian Century* 134, no. 2 (January 18, 2017): 22–27.

227. R. Lewis Bozard and Cody J. Sanders, "Helping Christian Lesbian, Gay, and Bisexual Clients Recover Religion as a Source of Strength," *Journal of LGBT Issues in Counseling* 5, no. 1 (2011): 47–74; and Mark A. Yarhouse and Trista L. Carr, "MTF Transgender Christians' Experiences: A Qualitative Study," *Journal of LGBT Issues in Counseling* 6, no. 1 (2012): 18–33.

228. M. N. Barringer and David A. Gay, "Happily Religious: The Surprising Sources of Happiness among Lesbian, Gay, Bisexual, and Transgender Adults," *Sociological Inquiry* 87, no. 1 (2017): 75–96.

229. E.g., Preston Sprinkle, ed., *Two Views on Homosexuality, the Bible, and the Church* (Grand Rapids: Zondervan, 2016).

230. A. T. Norton and G. M. Herek, "Heterosexuals' Attitudes toward Transgender People: Findings from a National Probability Sample of US Adults," *Sex Roles* 68 (2013): 738–53; and A. P. Makwana, K. Dhont, J. De keersmaecker, P. Akhlaghi-Ghaffarokh, M. Masure, and A. Roets, "The Motivated Cognitive Basis of Transphobia: The Roles of Right-Wing Ideologies and Gender Role Beliefs," *Sex Roles* 79 (2018): 206–17.

alike—have raised many critical questions and concerns about the way contemporary Western culture approaches issues of sexuality, including transgender experience.[231] For this sector of Christianity, voicing these questions and criticisms is a matter of pursuing faithfulness to the divinely inspired biblical vision of sexuality and to the centuries of wisdom contained in the Christian tradition. It is important to note here that the critiques of transgender identity put forward by a number of conservative Christians are explicitly not directed at transgender persons. Rather, they are focused on *particular interpretations* of the transgender experience and the *philosophical assumptions* that fuel them. That is to say, conservative Christian critiques are often calling into question what some have referred to as a "transgender ideology," an interpretation of transgender experience forged among elite intelligentsia of the Western academy and fueled by the fires of late twentieth-century postmodern philosophy, particularly queer theory. It is this particular interpretation of transgender experience—not necessarily transgender persons themselves—that many perceive to be fundamentally at odds with traditional Christian understandings of God, humanity, and sexuality.[232] It is also worth noting that Christians who critique queer theory's role in the contemporary transgender narrative are raising some of the same probing questions that the queer-critical sector of the transgender activist community has, albeit for different reasons.

With regard to evangelical Christians in particular, a 2016 survey found that self-identified evangelicals are "almost twice as likely (61%) as non-evangelicals (32%) to say using surgery or hormones to change birth gender is morally wrong."[233] At the same time, however, another recent study found that evangelicals generally "displayed overwhelming endorsement of the fundamental value of transgender persons."[234]

231. Pope Francis's 2016 exhortation *Amoris Laetitia*, http://w2.vatican.va/content/dam/fran cesco/pdf/apost_exhortations/documents/papa-francesco_esortazione-ap_20160319_amoris -laetitia_en.pdf; and Southern Baptist Convention, "On Transgender Identity" (Baltimore, MD, June 10–11, 2014), http://www.sbc.net/resolutions/2250/on-transgender-identity.

232. Katherine Kersten, "Transgender Conformity," *First Things*, December 2016, 25–31; John Milbank, "Long Read: What Liberal Intellectuals Get Wrong about Transgenderism," *Catholic Herald*, January 13, 2017, http://www.catholicherald.co.uk/commentandblogs/20 17/01/13/long-read-what-liberal-intellectuals-get-wrong-about-transgenderism/; and R. Albert Mohler Jr., "The Transgender Challenge: An Evangelical Response," *Billy Graham Evangelistic Association*, January 3, 2017, https://billygraham.org/decision-magazine/january-2017/trans gender-challenge-evangelical-response/.

233. Lisa Cannon Green, "Where Evangelicals Stand on Transgender Morality," *Christianity Today*, July 14, 2016, http://www.christianitytoday.com/news/2016/july/where-evangelicals -stand-on-transgender-morality-lifeway.html.

234. Yasuko Kanamori, Jeffrey H. D. Cornelius-White, Teresa K. Pegors, Todd Daniel, and Joseph Hulgus, "Development and Validation of the Transgender Attitudes and Beliefs Scale," *Archives of Sexual Behavior* 46, no. 5 (2017): 1513. See also Yasuko Kanamori, Teresa K. Pegors,

In turning to the question of the perception of evangelical Christians among those within the transgender community, they are commonly seen as a prime source of hatred and attack.[235] This observation makes all the more surprising the results of the 2017 study, mentioned above, on religiosity and LGBT persons' happiness. One of its unexpected findings is that the highest levels of happiness were reported by LGBT persons within evangelical and mainline Protestant churches (there were "no significant differences" between these two groups), while lower reported happiness was found among LGBT persons identifying as Catholic, agnostic, atheist, and religiously unaffiliated.[236]

John Kilner has recently commented on "the huge importance of many ethical debates today, together with the seeming impossibility of resolving those disputes." But he goes on to make a significant observation: "Opposing 'sides' in so many disagreements argue that people matter—that how people are viewed and treated is crucially important. . . . If people have that much in common, then the opportunity for fruitful discussion is great."[237] If any worldview *should* place the conviction that people truly do matter at the center of its value system, it should be the Christian faith—the founder of which placed other-oriented, self-sacrificial *agape*-love as his first and foremost commandment (e.g., Matt. 5:38–48; 22:36–40).

Sources of Disagreement

In the quest for respectful, mutually enriching dialogue, one element of authentic engagement between differing perspectives will be the ability to express one's own convictions openly and within a context where they will be listened to and taken seriously. As Christians of different persuasions engage questions related to transgender experiences together, differences of perspective and conviction will emerge at almost every level of the conversation. Many of these sources of disagreement can be categorized as follows: (1) biblical and theological, (2) scientific, and (3) practical and pastoral.

Joseph F. Hulgus, and Jeffrey H. D. Cornelius-White, "A Comparison between Self-Identified Evangelical Christians' and Nonreligious Persons' Attitudes toward Transgender," *Psychology of Sexual Orientation and Gender Diversity* 4, no. 1 (2017): 75–86.

235. Tommie Smith, "When Evangelicals Attack: Christian Evangelical Leaders Viciously Attack the LGBTQ+ Community," *Transgender Forum*, September 25, 2017, http://www.tg forum.com/wordpress/index.php/when-evangelicals-attack/.

236. Barringer and Gay, "Happily Religious," 75.

237. E.g., John F. Kilner, "Why This Book Matters: The Need for Common Ground in Debates Today," in *Why People Matter: Christian Engagement with Rival Views of Human Significance*, ed. J. F. Kilner (Grand Rapids: Baker Academic, 2017), 3, 11.

Biblical and Theological Disagreements

One central reason why Christians arrive at significantly different convictions about transgender experience and identity is that they hold to different interpretations and contemporary applications of specific biblical passages, some of the key ones being Genesis 1–3; Deuteronomy 22:5; 23:1; Isaiah 56:1–5; Jeremiah 31:22; Matthew 19:3–12; Acts 8:25–39; 1 Corinthians 6:9–11; 11:2–16; and Galatians 3:27–28.[238]

One leading site of interpretive controversy is Genesis 1–3. What are the implications for our understanding of transgender experience that God created humanity "male and female"? In particular, what are we to make of the fact that, even if God's creation included a prelapsarian ideal of male and female, we are most certainly not, at present, living in a Genesis 1 world? Our post–Genesis 3 world has obscured and marred the human ideal in myriad ways. For some, the experience of transgender identity is understood as a product of the fall and, as such, something to be brought back into alignment with God's ideal. Others see the experience of transgender persons as part of the fall but emphasize that in a post–Genesis 3 world we are all broken, and ultimately our "fixing" is not likely to be experienced this side of the eschaton. Still others see the diversity of gender identities as part of the unfolding of God's beautifully diverse creation, not something to be feared or seen as fallen and certainly not something to be fixed.

In addition to Genesis 1–3, the statements in Matthew 19 about eunuchs comprise an important, if controversial, data point in this conversation. Christians are left to wrestle with the fact that Jesus affirmed the Genesis creation account—that at the beginning the Creator "made them male and female"— and then went on to hold up the eunuch as a model for life in the kingdom (Matt. 19:4, 12). Was Jesus validating a choice to live outside the typical gender norms and expressions of the day? Or was he defending a genderless expression of humanity? Or was he only highlighting the willingness of the kingdom-centered eunuch to sacrifice that which was deemed by many to be an essential part of human expression in the service of a higher cause?

Of course, as important as these scriptural texts are to Christians, when taken by themselves they do not clearly or straightforwardly "teach" any particular position on transgender experience. The difficulty represented by scriptural texts is that, by their very nature, they tend to underdetermine the

---

238. For a few examples of differing interpretive approaches to some of these key texts, see G. G. Bolich, *Transgender and Religion* (Raleigh, NC: Psyche's Press, 2009), 21–62; Tanis, *Trans-Gendered*, chap. 3; Walker, *Transgender Debate*, 47–91; and Yarhouse, *Understanding Gender Dysphoria*, 30–46.

theological views they are used in support of. Scriptural interpretations are complex things that are influenced by many factors: interpretations of other texts, theological and philosophical beliefs, cultural commitments, and polemical or apologetic purposes.

Also crucially important is one's stance on the scriptural teaching about gender roles. Even apart from the question of transgender experience, the gender role question is highly controversial and continues to split churches and denominations. Complementarians hold that males and females are equal in nature, worth, and dignity but are given different roles, one implication of which is that leadership in church and family is reserved for men.[239] For complementarians, key differentiating expressions of gender are not determined by the particular culture in which people find themselves but are divinely ordained. Egalitarians, on the other hand, reject any necessary, transcultural gender hierarchy and, as such, are more open to cultural differences in how gender is expressed.[240] The implications of one's perspective on gender roles on questions related to transgender experience are complex and are affected by other variables. But two lines of influence seem clear: First and most obviously, the more one sees gender roles and their expression as divinely ordained, the more one is likely to see gender dysphoria as an unhealthy symptom of the fall, and the less likely one is to allow for, or encourage, any sort of transitioning. Second, the more narrowly the expression of gender is defined the more likely that such definitions will increase the gender dysphoria experienced by individuals who do not align easily with those highly specified gender roles or who do not match that particular ideal of gender expression.

In addition to interpretation of particular passages of Scripture, one's approach to hermeneutics will powerfully shape one's perspective on transgender experience and identity. Particularly important is the contested question of how much hermeneutical weight should be given to human experience when interpreting Scripture and doing theology. More specifically, a crucial question is whether—and/or to what extent—the experience of transgender persons should shape our theological grids and biblical interpretation. Most Christians would allow that experience must play some role in our biblical

---

239. John Piper and Wayne Grudem, eds., *Recovering Biblical Manhood and Womanhood: A Response to Evangelical Feminism*, 2nd ed. (Wheaton: Crossway, 2006).

240. John G. Stackhouse, *Partners in Christ: A Conservative Case for Egalitarianism* (Downers Grove, IL: InterVarsity, 2015); and Ronald W. Pierce, Rebecca Merrill Groothuis, and Gordon D. Fee, eds., *Discovering Biblical Equality: Complementarity without Hierarchy* (Downers Grove, IL: InterVarsity, 2004). Feminism would be an egalitarian position but would develop broader, more systemic arguments against complementarianism in a variety of ways. For a classic presentation of Christian feminism, see Rosemary Radford Ruether, *Sexism and God Talk: Toward a Feminist Theology* (Boston: Beacon, 1983).

and theological work—as evidenced by the popularity of John Wesley's quadrilateral, in which Scripture is interpreted not only by tradition and reason but also by experience. Similarly, most Christians are uncomfortable allowing personal experience completely free rein in the definition and articulation of biblical interpretations and theological commitments. However, while these agreements are important, there remains a lot of room for disagreement on how and in what ways experience might shape our theological commitments.

Finally, lying behind these exegetical and hermeneutical questions are beliefs about the nature and authority of Scripture. Is Scripture divinely inspired and truthful/infallible/inerrant? If so, what is meant by those claims? The implications of these theological beliefs are seen most clearly in the felt need (or lack thereof) to reconcile apparent contradictions between scriptural texts. Those who are committed to the plenary inspiration and the inerrancy of Scripture will see apparent contradictions in Scripture as just that—merely *apparent*—and will seek various strategies for harmonizing the texts. Those who reject the inerrancy of Scripture have the option of denying one or both of the scriptural texts that create the contradiction. In other words, one who denies inerrancy is afforded the ability to say, for example, "The apostle Paul was simply wrong about women in 1 Corinthians 11."

Scientific Disagreements

A second broad category of disagreement among Christians regarding transgender experience and identity concerns the interpretation and implications of relevant findings in the fields of biology, psychology, and the social sciences. Crucially important in this respect are questions regarding sex and gender. Are human sex and gender binary realities—that is, male and female, woman and man—or are they best understood as a range of phenomena on a continuum? While the nature of human reproduction suggests that sex is a binary reality, the existence of intersex persons constitutes a challenge to that belief. Similarly, the experiences of persons with gender dysphoria or who are gender nonconforming challenge the belief that gender is a simple binary. On the other hand, there are a number of avenues for interpreting these challenges in ways that preserve the binary nature of sex and gender as normative.

Beneath debates over whether sex and gender are binary are more fundamental questions about what constitutes biological sex (is it merely genetic coding, hormones, genitalia—or something more complex?) and gender (does it map onto one's sex, or is it psychologically or socially constructed?). And finally, on top of these debates is the question of whether gender is fixed or fluid. Whatever gender is, can it change over time, perhaps tracking psychological changes or sociological context, or is it a relatively stable reality?

As discussed previously, one of the contested questions is the assessment of the etiology of transgender experience and identity. When it comes to the causal question, should we consider spiritual approaches, psychological approaches, sociological approaches, biological approaches, some sort of multifactorial integrationist approach, or something else entirely?[241] This question, of course, necessarily involves understandable, but unfortunate, interdisciplinary turf wars over which discipline or set of methodological assumptions is most fit to explain transgender experience. Moreover, these turf wars are often intractable because different disciplines have different and mildly incommensurate standards for what constitutes adequate explanation or theory confirmation. For Christians, each of these questions must inevitably intersect with the previously mentioned questions concerning biblical interpretation and theological coherence.

Practical and Pastoral Disagreements

As difficult as the above questions are, the practical and pastoral disagreements can be even more intense, in part because they assume or build on the potentially divisive issues discussed above. One of the most pressing practical areas of disagreement concerns the best and most appropriate ways of assisting people who experience gender dysphoria. In particular, there is a fundamental disagreement on whether the diagnosis of gender dysphoria calls for treatments that mitigate the dysphoria through the realignment of one's sense of gender identity or whether it calls for treatments that respond to the dysphoria by affirming one's sense of gender identity and instead re-aligning one's gender expression and sometimes one's body. Moreover, it is possible that such issues will need to be handled on a case-by-case basis. As we have already seen, most pressing in this respect are cases where children experience gender dysphoria. Should our desire to help children deal with the psychological consequences of gender dysphoria lead us to encourage them to transition to living in accord with their inner sense of gender? Or should the fact that children's personalities, values, and even brain structures are still being formed cause us to urge restraint regarding any sort of transitioning?

241. For a small sampling of the different ways that Christians have approached this issue, see Sheridan, *Crossing Over*; Tanis, *Trans-Gendered*; Walker, *Transgender Debate*; Yarhouse, *Understanding Gender Dysphoria*; and David H. Barlow, Gene G. Abel, and Edward B. Blanchard, "Gender Identity Change in a Transsexual: An Exorcism," *Archives of Sexual Behavior* 6, no. 5 (1977): 387–95.

Moreover, if one believes that transitioning is acceptable for adults but that restraint is required for children, a salient question is, At what age or level of maturity does the decision to transition become reasonable?

A second set of practical and pastoral questions concerns how Christians should think about and respond to transgender individuals. As the local church welcomes transgender people and invites them to walk in the ways of Jesus, what does this mean, practically speaking, for discipleship, for church membership, for marriage and family life, for church leadership and ordination?[242] What does it look like for the local church to love and support gender-variant children, as well as their parents, other family members, and friends?[243] And as the church seeks to engage the world in faithful missional witness and service, what does this mean for ministry to transgender people (churched and unchurched), as well as for Christian involvement in the wider public conversations on transgender experience and identity that are taking place within civic and political spheres today?

One of the barriers to practical engagement with the questions surrounding transgender experience is the fact that for many Christians this is a very new and unfamiliar issue, perhaps especially for those in rural or middle America or those from an older generation, who may have never really had the opportunity to reflectively engage the questions that the experiences of transgender people pose. As such, there is a wide ideological, conceptual, and even cultural gap between the simple assumption that God "made them male and female," on the one hand, and on the other hand, Facebook's fifty-one different ways of identifying one's gender[244] and the ten different pronouns offered as options in some university diversity trainings.[245]

The relative newness of this issue for many people raises the question of how to respond and show love to those Christians who sincerely desire to love their neighbor as themselves but who are utterly befuddled by the blooming, buzzing confusion that the transgender issue represents for them. Our desire

---

242. Fraser Watts, "Transsexualism and the Church," *Theology and Sexuality* 9, no. 1 (2002): 63–85.

243. Mark A. Yarhouse and Dara Houp, "Transgender Christians: Gender Identity, Family Relationships, and Religious Faith," in *Transgender Youth: Perceptions, Media Influences and Social Challenges*, ed. Shemya Vaughn (New York: Nova Science, 2016), 51–65; and Mark A. Yarhouse and Dara Houp, "Christian Parents' Experiences of Transgender Youth during the Coming Out Process," in Vaughn, *Transgender Youth*, 193–208.

244. Debby Herbenick and Aleta Baldwin, "What Each of Facebook's 51 New Gender Options Means," *Daily Beast*, February 15, 2014, https://www.thedailybeast.com/what-each-of-facebooks-51-new-gender-options-means.

245. "Pronouns," UC Davis, LGBTQIA Resource Center, https://lgbtqia.ucdavis.edu/educated/pronouns.

to treat them with respect and not dismiss their questions (even ones that others see as ignorant or insensitive) should not be seen as an alternative to caring for, showing God's love to, and including persons with transgender identity. We need a robust "both/and" here.

Introducing Our Conversation

As we transition (no pun intended) to the conversation between our contributors, a few points of clarification are in order. Multiview books such as this often come with a clear taxonomy and set of labels for individual views that fall on a continuum. For instance, a multiview book on election includes "Calvinist" and "Arminian" views. However, when it comes to the question of transgender experience, there are as yet no clear, widely embraced labels in this debate.[246] Perhaps clearly defined positions on this matter will eventually emerge and labels will be appended to those positions, but we are certainly not there yet.

In lieu of a well-defined taxonomy of clearly labeled positions, we have sought to find contributors who have some fundamental differences on the important issues within this debate. In particular, we have focused on finding contributors who hold differing perspectives on such questions as whether sex is binary; whether gender is binary; whether there are stable, transcultural, or divinely ordained gender expressions/roles; and whether social and/or medical/surgical transitioning is appropriate or advantageous for transgender individuals.

One other difference between our contributors is also important to mention—namely, that of firsthand experience. Justin Sabia-Tanis transitioned from female to male more than twenty years ago and, as such, brings his unique, firsthand experience to our conversation. His contribution to this volume is not only valuable; it is courageous, given how difficult it is to engage in a controversial conversation that requires speaking so directly out of one's own personal experiences and identity.

We also sought to find contributors who can engage this difficult and polarizing issue in clear and respectful dialogue. For Christians, this should be nonnegotiable. This does not mean that there are no difficult questions raised or that everyone in the conversation will remain comfortable. Rather,

---

246. One recent survey of Christian perspectives on transgender experience uses the monikers "conservative," "moderate," and "radical." See Duncan Dormor, "Transgenderism and the Christian Church: An Overview," in Scherpe, *Legal Status*, 27–76. While we understand the reasoning, we do not find this schema particularly compelling.

it means that when we disagree, it must be with an acknowledgment of the full humanity and dignity of our interlocutor. We believe that the conversation in this volume has met this high bar, and we hope that it serves both to clarify this important topic and to provide a model of substantive engagement of difficult issues.

1

Transition or Transformation?

A Moral-Theological Exploration of Christianity and Gender Dysphoria

Owen Strachan

The first thing—the very first thing—that must be said about individuals who experience gender dysphoria at any level is that they are fully, substantially, immovably *human*. Whether they embrace a transgender identity or not, whether they go through a surgical or pharmacological transition or not, whether they receive any vestige of biblical truth and Christian teaching or not, they are inexorably image-bearers made by God.

The individual who experiences gender dysphoria is not a different class of human than any other; such persons are not freaks, misfits, subhuman, superhuman, inhuman, irredeemable, hopeless. They are *people*. Men or women. Fashioned by God. Formed for his glory. As C. S. Lewis once wrote, capturing the heaven-tinged nature of the human race, "You have never talked to a mere mortal."[1]

More than any other worldview, any other belief system, Christian theology champions the dignity of humanity, all humanity, every person, without exception. There is no one—friend or foe, loved one or mortal enemy—whom we class beneath us, whose dignity we deny, whose worth we play down. Before we dive into disagreements and debates, let us confess this freely and

1. C. S. Lewis, *The Weight of Glory* (San Francisco: HarperOne, 2001), 45–46.

happily: there is no ennobler of the human person like biblical Christianity.[2] Humankind continually drives downward, seeking the mud and the muck like a heaving beast, but the faith once for all delivered to the saints enchants this besotted race and lifts it into the skies, where it flies just a bit below Icarus. Christian preaching to sinners is, in one sense, little more than the pleading of one person to others to recover their humanity, to refire their existential imagination and dare them to leave the pagan wilderness for the city on the hill.[3]

This we must continually do, on one issue after another. That baby spinning and gleefully kicking in response to Mom's laughter is not a clump of cells, but a baby, a child. The person with different skin color than yours is not an abstraction, a stereotype whose value you can flick aside, but a human being. Those women featured in horrifically compromising poses, unveiling themselves before hungry eyes, are not objects, but God-made image-bearers. At issue in each of these and many other instances of prejudice, objectification, and outright abuse is denial of humanity, full humanity.

The Christian does not merely shake his or her head at these wrongs. To the person objectified and the objectifier alike, we plead: you were made for more than this. You *are* more than this. In repentance and faith, you will find all the happiness and Godward fullness you can imagine, and more. The Christian preacher, known today as "intolerant" and a charter member of a "hate group," is in point of fact the figure most poised to affirm the full humanity of every person, including those who hate him. So we gladly and unflinchingly say to the man or woman who experiences gender dysphoria: you are not your confusion. You are not "damaged goods." You are the God-made one, and the gospel of divine grace is fitted for your deepest failings and strongest needs. As we will see, understanding the gospel—and specifically the significance of conversion—is at the heart of this conversation.[4]

We begin here, with this explanation of our common humanity, because no doctrine save the doctrine of God is more contested today. In fact, I would go so far as to say that anthropology has become the central question of the

---

2. See my forthcoming *Reenchanting Humanity: Biblical Anthropology for the 21st Century* (Nashville: B&H Academic, forthcoming).

3. On the nature and spread of paganism, see Peter Jones, *The God of Sex: How Spirituality Defines Your Sexuality* (Colorado Springs: Victor, 2006), esp. 19–84. Almost no one today discusses paganism in its newer forms, making Jones's salient critique all the more needed.

4. For more on the gospel, see the classic work by John Stott, *The Cross of Christ* (Downers Grove, IL: InterVarsity, 1986); Leon Morris, *The Atonement: Its Meaning and Significance* (Downers Grove, IL: InterVarsity, 1983); D. A. Carson, *Scandalous: The Cross and Resurrection of Jesus* (Wheaton: Crossway, 2010); and Greg Gilbert, *What Is the Gospel?* (Wheaton: Crossway, 2010).

age.[5] The liberal theologians of the prewar years affirmed the existence of God, albeit in terms more theistic—even deistic—than Christian; the philosophers of the postwar years seemed convinced that God was dead, or at least so shrouded in the mists of twentieth-century warfare and apocalyptic human suffering as to be inapproachable and past engaging.[6] We know what the postmodern world thinks of God and the study of God by virtue of the academy's long shuffling of spiritual things from "divinity" to "religion" to "religious studies" to "social change."[7]

God is invisible. But man and woman are not. The invisibility of God seems, in the postmodern mind, to allow for the marginalization of God. But man and woman are before us, physical, tangible, concrete. We see one another; therefore we exist. But what *is* man, precisely? What is woman? What is humanity? The problem with this central question is that one may only answer it satisfactorily with reference to the aforementioned matter—namely, the existence of God. Centuries ago, Calvin knew where the conversation would go: "The knowledge of ourselves not only arouses us to seek God, but also, as it were, leads us by the hand to find him."[8]

This last point matters greatly for the pages to come. In what follows, we will sketch a biblical understanding of man and woman with reference to delineated differences and gender dysphoria. We will see that the Scriptures speak with conviction and compassion on the contested matters before us. My view, the historic view of the millennia-old Christian church, is that the sexes are binary—man and woman.[9] Further, while we all undergo suffering as a result of Adam's fall, men and women who experience gender dysphoria should not undergo bodily changes but instead, with vivified awareness of the

---

5. One sees the interplay of the metaphysical and the anthropological in the pilgrimage of Roger Scruton, the justly famed (now knighted) British philosopher and critic. See Scruton, *Gentle Regrets: Thoughts from a Life* (New York: Continuum, 2005).

6. See Lily Rothman, "Is God Dead? At 50," *Time*, 2016, http://time.com/isgoddead/.

7. For more on the American academy's shift away from its roots, see George Marsden, *The Soul of the American University: From Protestant Establishment to Established Nonbelief* (Oxford: Oxford University Press, 1994); James Tunstead Burtchaell, *The Dying of the Light: The Disengagement of Colleges and Universities from Their Christian Churches* (Grand Rapids: Eerdmans, 1998); and Kevin J. Vanhoozer and Owen Strachan, *The Pastor as Public Theologian: Reclaiming a Lost Vision* (Grand Rapids: Baker Academic, 2015).

8. John Calvin, *Institutes of the Christian Religion: 1536 Edition*, trans. Ford Lewis Battles (Grand Rapids: Eerdmans, 1985), 1.1.1.

9. It seems worth stating up front that the binary view I am advocating in this chapter is without doubt and without question the historic view of the Christian church. This is true in all its branches, denominations, and iterations. For more on this ethic, see William Weinrich, "Women in the History of the Church: Learned and Holy, but Not Pastors," in *Recovering Biblical Manhood and Womanhood: A Response to Evangelical Feminism*, ed. John Piper and Wayne Grudem (1991; repr., Wheaton: Crossway, 2006), 263–79.

witness of Scripture and a moral imagination ignited for God, should pursue something greater and more effectual than any transition: *transformation*.

To these possibilities, accessible through the plan of the Father, the atoning accomplishments of the Son, and the restoring agency of the Spirit, we now turn.

God Made Two Sexes: A Biblical Exploration of Binary Gender

The discussion among the four views in this book is, at its core, a conversation over the Bible. For any true Christian, the Bible is our authority—it is inspired, inerrant, and authoritative. The Bible is not one guide among many; the Bible, according to the Protestant Reformers, is *norma normans*—the "norm of norms," the standard that rules all others.[10] As with other ethical matters, this discussion of transgender identity among professing believers is at base a referendum on biblical authority and biblical sufficiency. Much, in other words, is at stake in this conversation.

Genesis 1–3 and the Created Order

The Scripture begins with the creative activity of Yahweh, who dynamically makes all that is. Yahweh does not use existing material, but rather speaks and causes life in various forms to take shape from chaos. When God makes the stars by his Word, he makes actual stars. When he makes birds and beasts and fish, he makes actual birds and beasts and fish. There is a one-to-one correspondence between what God intends and says and what comes to pass.

So it is on the sixth day, when the Lord's aesthetic ingenuity reaches its peak. The creation of the man and the woman, the bearers of God's image, is the height of all God's initial activity (Gen. 1:26–27). The man and the woman each bear the image of God, even as the man is given responsibility to lead and guide the woman. There is thus an order to creation: the image-bearers have dominion over the animal kingdom.[11] Within the one-flesh covenant, the man has God-given spiritual authority. In Genesis 2, he is formed first, made from the dust of the ground; the woman's body proceeds from his own, as a rib is taken from him; he names the woman, even as he has named the animals; at the chapter's close, he is tasked in the plan of the ages with leaving father

10. See Matthew Barrett, *God's Word Alone: The Authority of Scripture* (Grand Rapids: Zondervan Academic, 2016), 44–45.

11. Victor Hamilton notes that this is "royal language" and that "man is created to rule." *The Book of Genesis, Chapters 1–17*, New International Commentary on the Old Testament (Grand Rapids: Eerdmans, 1990), 138.

and mother, and he is called—not the woman—to hold fast to his wife. All this speaks to the man's God-given and God-focused spiritual authority.[12]

The woman possesses a distinct, God-ordained identity as well. She is a "helpmate," one fashioned by God to complement her husband. Dorothy Patterson's reflections are helpful here: "There is nothing demeaning about being a helper. It is a challenging and rewarding responsibility. God Himself assumed that role on many occasions (Ps. 40:17, 'You are my help and my deliverer; O my God, do not delay'; Heb. 13:6, 'So we say with confidence, "The Lord is my helper"'). . . . The fact is that there is no suggestion in Scripture that women are inferior or incapable in any sense—neither in personhood, which is the same as man's, nor in function, which is different from man's."[13]

This does not suggest that she is lesser than the man but rather that she bears distinct capabilities and gifts that the man does not have. The woman looks to the man for leadership and sees herself as the one given to him by the Lord to aid and bless him. She is not in competition with him; she sees no inherent threat in his God-rendered authority, for she sees that he is indeed the one who will answer to God for his oversight. His strength is not his own; she knows that the man's body was given for her, and thus his physical ability is her blessing, not her cursing. Finally, he is called and bound by God to hold fast to her, to care for and provide for her, and to never let her go.[14]

Sadly, in Genesis 3 we see the undoing of this holy plan (see vv. 1–13). The serpent subverts the created order, seeking dominion over the woman, who leads her husband. Adam does not rise up and crush the serpent's head as he should, using his force and honor to destroy the one who has targeted his wife. Instead, he meekly, passively submits to satanic subversion. But though the devil has destabilized divine design, he has not overturned it. After the eating of the forbidden fruit, the Lord goes to Adam and addresses him, not the woman.[15] He holds the man responsible. It is his leadership that has failed. The man blames the woman and, ultimately, God himself for his sin.[16]

12. Raymond C. Ortlund Jr. does a masterful job unpacking these implications in "Male-Female Equality and Male Headship: Genesis 1–3," in Piper and Grudem, *Recovering Biblical Manhood and Womanhood*, 95–123.

13. Dorothy Patterson, "The High Calling of Wife and Mother in Biblical Perspective," in Piper and Grudem, *Recovering Biblical Manhood and Womanhood*, 373. See also the careful treatment of *ezer* by Andreas Köstenberger and Margaret Köstenberger, *God's Design for Man and Woman: A Biblical-Theological Survey* (Wheaton: Crossway, 2014), 35–40.

14. For exposition of these duties, see John Piper, *This Momentary Marriage: A Parable of Permanence* (Wheaton: Crossway, 2012), 73–94.

15. See Köstenberger and Köstenberger, *God's Design for Man and Woman*, 44–45.

16. Denny Burk points out that "the apostle Paul indicates that it was indeed the undoing of this order that was the basis for the fall of humanity into sin (1 Tim. 2:13–14)." *What Is*

So the Lord curses the order he has made. The sentence he pronounces is stern and strong as iron: for disobeying God, the man will now abuse his authority over the woman and discharge his duty of provision in pain and toil. The woman, by contrast, will know great pain in bearing children and will seek her husband's place, battling him in the home; she has usurped his authority already, which he received passively instead of rebuking his wife and rejecting the serpent's word-twisting, and now she will do so throughout the ages (see Gen. 3:16–19). Thankfully, although the serpent will bruise the heel of the woman's offspring, this same figure will crush the serpent's head. The work of the Messiah, in other words, is the restoration of creation order. The atonement will put all things to rights in the end.

There is no more important passage of biblical text for our present conversation than this. Genesis 1–3 gives us reality, not a theological fairy tale. God makes the man, and God makes the woman. For this reason we believe in "binary gender." Said better: we believe in the sexes. The sexes are not arbitrary or colorless in Genesis 2 but are clearly and evocatively presented for our instruction. In contradistinction to our gender-neutral society, and even a fuzzy-headed evangelicalism that plays down differences, the Bible begins by sketching a clear portrait of divine design, with the man and the woman front and center in this elegant creation.

All biblical anthropology, as we will see, rests on this foundation. The next sixty-five books of the Bible will do nothing to confuse the doctrine of the sexes; instead, in numerous places, various authors of the old and new covenants will build on it, fleshing it out, offering further exposition of it, unfolding just how beautiful God's vision of humanity truly is.

Prohibition of Cross-Dressing in the Mosaic Law

In our tour of biblical wisdom, our second stop lands us in the old covenant law—the Deuteronomic law. The old covenant law no longer binds, as the law of love—the law of Christ—does (John 13:34). But it does give us priceless guidance into the moral will of almighty God. In the course of several prohibitions of ungodly behavior, Deuteronomy 22 says this: "A woman shall not wear a man's garment, nor shall a man put on a woman's cloak, for whoever does these things is an abomination to the LORD your God" (v. 5 ESV). Jason DeRouchie points out the iron-clad nature of this prohibition: "God chose to frame these prohibitions as durative, so that we should read the 'not' as a 'never': 'A woman shall *never* wear a man's garment, nor shall a man *ever* put

---

the Meaning of Sex? (Wheaton: Crossway, 2013), 166. See also Eugene Merrill, *Everlasting Dominion: A Theology of the Old Testament* (Nashville: B&H, 2006), 207–9.

on a woman's cloak.'" The takeaway here is clear for DeRouchie: "From God's perspective, there is never a permissible time for the type of cross-dressing that this passage addresses."[17]

The use of "abomination" language marks out this principle. There are not many behaviors and practices that merit such condemnation, but we take note of those that do. Spiritual idolatry is called "abomination" in the Deuteronomic code (Deut. 7:25; 13:14; Isa. 44:19); child sacrifice is as well (Jer. 32:35); aberrant sexuality is also regularly classed in such terms. Adultery, incest, homosexuality, temple prostitution, and unlawful marriage draw the dread sentence, showing us just how seriously the Lord takes sexual sin (Lev. 18:22, 27–30; 20:13; Deut. 24:2–4; Ezek. 16:22, 58; 22:11; 33:26).[18] What displeases God most draws this term.

The various behaviors identified as "abomination" allow us to draw a line between ungodly sexuality and cross-dressing. The command to wear the clothes that befit one's sex is not isolated or random.[19] It is part of an anthropological superstructure, a personal order set in stone by the Lord for Israel. Under the law, men must present themselves as men per the standards of the day, just as women must present themselves as women.[20] Failure to do so offended the Lord personally: "Whoever does these things is an abomination to the LORD your God," quoth the code.[21] The cross-dresser did not dishonor abstract reality; not only did such persons broach what some call "natural law," but the cross-dresser dishonored God in a direct and very personal way.[22]

17. Jason S. DeRouchie, *How to Understand and Apply the Old Testament: Twelve Steps from Exegesis to Theology* (Phillipsburg, NJ: P&R, 2017), 445.

18. See DeRouchie, *How to Understand and Apply the Old Testament*, 446.

19. According to Robert Bratcher and Howard Hatton, this prohibition could include "anything that pertains to a man: this seems to include other things besides clothes, such as adornments and weapons." Robert G. Bratcher and Howard A. Hatton, *A Handbook on Deuteronomy*, UBS Handbook Series (New York: United Bible Societies, 2000), 366.

20. DeRouchie shows that the Hebrew term in question refers not merely to a husband but to a man more generally. This passage thus applies not only to married couples, who must not confuse their "gender expression," but to all Israel. *How to Understand and Apply the Old Testament*, 445.

21. The issue here, according to Eugene Merrill, is that of ungodly "mixtures." God wants creation to function as he intends it to function, not in any other way: "Another linkage between the verse and its context is the chiasm connecting [Deut. 22] vv. 5–8 with 9–12: dress (v. 5), animals (vv. 6–7), house (v. 8), field (v. 9), animals (v. 10), dress (vv. 11–12). There is thus a strong tie-in between death and mixtures, that is, between the expositions of the sixth and seventh commandments. The sin in improper mixtures is brought out in the laws of purity that follow (22:9–23:18)." *Deuteronomy*, New American Commentary 4 (Nashville: Broadman & Holman, 1994), 297–98.

22. One scholar argues that the Deuteronomic code may be prohibiting Amorite sexual practices here: "Pertinent to the suggestion that it was a pagan practice is a Babylonian adage, according to which a person who is apparently an Amorite says to his wife, 'You be the man

God, after all, had invested great significance in clothing—after the fall he provided Adam and Eve with animal skins, a little glimmer of his forgiving grace and alien righteousness. Clothing mattered, in more ways than one; clothing could save your soul, or it could undo it.

The abomination motif points us to the conflict of visions that unfolds throughout Scripture. Sexuality is a major battleground in the war between God and Satan. There are not merely certain practices that are ideal for a Christian, a follower of the true God, and certain practices that are less than ideal. There are in truth two visions of sexuality that vie for human adoption. One is divine, given us by the very mind of God. The other is pagan, given us by the serpent.[23] The first vision shows us the ordered beauty of the world; the second dissolves order into chaos, divinizing the natural order and effecting a kind of un-creation. In the first, we have duties before the Lord; in the second, our sexuality has no holy bonds, and we have no higher authority.

Embracing the serpent's vision—whether willfully or without knowing of it—means that we do as we wish, surfing the wild waves of our sinful nature. Sex has no design; our bodies have no script. We are individually a blank slate, free to chase our passions where they lead us. The body is a canvas, not a gift to receive, the masterpiece of God to treasure. We see how this conception of the body fits with a postmodern conception of the self. Our lives are governed not by submissive worship and holy obedience but by "expressive individualism."[24]

In this common cultural view—rarely stated but widely practiced—we are human when we "express ourselves," treating life as a performance. Expressing yourself does not involve placing yourself under standards but rather—at least in the pop-culture form—rebelling against all standards (except those of the cultural elite). It involves relentlessly asserting your individuality (insofar as it accords with the counterculture), your uniqueness (while conforming scrupulously to peer attitudes), your inner superstar (contingent on external affirmation), and your inability because of your authenticity to possibly submit to any external expectation, whether divine or otherwise (while submitting yourself wholly and wordlessly to a nameless, faceless cultural reign).

---

and I'll be the woman.'" Jeffrey H. Tigay, *Deuteronomy*, JPS Torah Commentary (Philadelphia: Jewish Publication Society, 1996), 200.

23. See Peter Jones, *Pagans in the Pews: Protecting Your Family and Community from the Pervasive Influence of the New Spirituality* (Ventura, CA: Regal, 2004).

24. This phrase has now passed into everyday usage in Western discussion. Robert Bellah popularized it. See Bellah, *Habits of the Heart: Individualism and Commitment in American Life* (Berkeley: University of California Press, 1996), 333–35. Bellah contrasts "expressive individualism" with "utilitarian individualism," consistent with a self-interested ethic, and "republican individualism," in which a citizen seeks not only personal flourishing but the civic good.

Our consideration of identity in this volume is not merely a matter, then, of whether it's okay to take certain pills or comb your hair a certain way. The matters before us on the subject of transgender identity are bound up within a much bigger, broader worldview conflict. We do not merely disagree over the particulars of handling gender dysphoria. We disagree, sadly, over the self. We disagree over the nature of submission, the burning heart of God-honoring faith (James 4:7).

My point in this discussion lands here: being pulled by ungodly, sinful, God-dishonoring desires to cross-dress is not new. It is ancient. It is as old as the fall. The old covenant understood the wildness that courses through human blood and did not respond to this wildness in psychological or emotional or medical terms. Moses's law addressed cross-dressing in the stoutest moral-theological language possible, showing us that the creation of the man and woman is not incidental to human identity but foundational. As we said above: everything builds off of Genesis 1–3. The prohibition in Deuteronomy 22 simply reinforces the original blueprint of God.[25]

Evidence in Israel's Life of Differing Expectations for the Sexes

The case I am building is no new concept. For millennia, the people of God understood that men and women are different and called to different roles. One of the key ways the men of Israel imaged the glory of Yahweh was by putting their lives on the line for women and children. Their willingness to enter battle and even die was an extension of the very handiwork of God: he made the woman from the man, and thus the man's body was for the woman, given to strengthen and protect her. This conviction was not merely private, to be treasured up in the confines of the home; this conviction had to go public. Men went to war; men fought Israel's enemies; men won nobility for their courageous sacrifice.

Don't take my word for it, though. It is a woman in Scripture who articulates this truth:

> She sent and summoned Barak the son of Abinoam from Kedesh-naphtali and said to him, "Has not the LORD, the God of Israel, commanded you, 'Go, gather your men at Mount Tabor, taking 10,000 from the people of Naphtali and the people of Zebulun. And I will draw out Sisera, the general of Jabin's army, to meet you by the river Kishon with his chariots and his troops, and I will give

---

25. DeRouchie sums it up well: "From God's perspective, the fact of maleness and femaleness bears implications beyond the home or gathered worshiping community. It also impacts daily life in society." *How to Understand and Apply the Old Testament*, 445.

him into your hand'?" Barak said to her, "If you will go with me, I will go, but if you will not go with me, I will not go." And she said, "I will surely go with you. Nevertheless, the road on which you are going will not lead to your glory, for the LORD will sell Sisera into the hand of a woman." Then Deborah arose and went with Barak to Kedesh. (Judg. 4:6–9 ESV)

Barak apparently had a summons from the Lord to enter into battle with the forces of evil Sisera. He had not only a summons but, according to Deborah, a guarantee of victory (v. 7). Nonetheless, Barak balks at this divine commission. To put it in technical language, he quakes in his boots. Unless Deborah travels with him, he will stay home, guarding his own skin. To her eternal credit, Deborah assures him of her coming but does so with a humdinger of a rebuke: Barak's course of action "will not lead to your glory" because the deathblow will come from "the hand of a woman" (v. 9).[26]

The people of God held, you might say, to "binary gender." They understood what the Bible makes plain in its earliest chapters: not only has the Lord made men and women for his glory, but he has called them to certain duties and roles. In Deborah's mind, the sexes were not interchangeable. Barak dishonored divine design by playing the coward instead of the man. The man was not to tuck himself away in the biblical mold; he was to be a God-oriented glory seeker. His strong physical form signaled that he was made for adventure and initiative. But he was not (relatively) stronger, taller, and faster than the woman so that he could win footraces in his village; he was fashioned in this way so that he would lead his family, protect his wife and children, and answer the call to fight and, if necessary, die for the safety of the nation and his loved ones.[27]

Deborah saw this and knew this. She knew that a God-fearing man should leap at the chance to show himself a warrior, to steel his face like a flint and brave death in order to obey God and bless women and children. She knew that this was a rare chance, that Barak had an opportunity most men

26. Daniel Block points out the unusual nature of this conversation: "The narrative should have moved directly from v. 7 to v. 10, but Barak's response provides one of the keys to the rest of the chapter. Despite Yahweh's assurance of victory, Barak resists the call." Barak's "cowardly" demeanor hijacks the stated desire of the Lord. So it is with all cowardly men. See Block, *Judges, Ruth*, New American Commentary 6 (Nashville: Broadman & Holman, 1999), 199.

27. A useful book on this theme is J. C. Ryle, *Thoughts for Young Men* (1865; repr., Carlisle, PA: Banner of Truth, 2015). For a solid example of masculine courage in action, see Iain Murray, *J. C. Ryle: Prepared to Stand Alone* (Carlisle, PA: Banner of Truth, 2016). For a stirring portrait of a civic leader along these lines, see the matchless volume by William Manchester, *The Last Lion: Winston Spencer Churchill*, vol. 2, *Alone: 1932–1940* (1988; repr., New York: Little, Brown, 2012).

only dream about. With God's favor behind him, Barak could slay a wicked ruler and put his name in the mouths of future generations, becoming the kind of man that the bards write songs about, weaving stories of heroism around nighttime campfires. Deborah is saying to Barak, "God made you for this. He has vouchsafed his favor to you. You are the one he would have slay the tyrant." The warriors of Israel, including Barak, were intended by the Lord to be images of the coming warrior-king. But if they chose weakness as Barak did, the Lord would still accomplish his aim, albeit through a woman, the sex not called by God to protect, intervene, and die for the other.

This is a remarkable passage for those who honestly and earnestly search out biblical gender roles. Though Deborah is often portrayed as a proto-feminist hero, she pointedly urges the man before her to step into his rightful place. She is not called a "judge" in the text but a "prophetess," and she expects Barak to lead the people, not her.[28] Deborah is godly and worthy of praise, but she understands with crystal clarity that men are different from women and must prove their manhood or wither. The irony is thick: the woman given a chance by a feckless man to step into his shoes did not wish to do so, but only went with him in order to aid the people of God.

The Old Testament is filled with more such instances and teachings. Throughout, we see that God's old covenant people understood that there were two sexes and that God was glorified by faithful living as a man or woman. Men, we learn from Isaiah, were expected to guide the people of God:

> My people—infants are their oppressors,
>   and women rule over them.
> O my people, your guides mislead you
>   and they have swallowed up the course of your paths.
>
> (Isa. 3:12 ESV)

The plan of God did not include, ideally, oppression from infants. Neither did it include womanly rulership. Men were called to lead in ancient Israel, and so deviation from this blueprint meant that God was dishonored and the people adversely affected. Women were not inferior to men, we note; the call to authority on the part of men hinged not on ability or intellect but on God's own wisdom and intent.[29] The one who made an ordered universe structured it for the glory of his name and the good of his followers.

28. See Köstenberger and Köstenberger, *God's Design for Man and Woman*, 67–68.
29. Alec Motyer concludes that the form of Isa. 3:12 is that of "outraged exclamation," a judgment that if correct serves to heighten the sense of displeasure that pervades this verse.

Christ's Words on Divine Design

It is stunning to think that anyone could read the Bible and conclude anything but that it affirms the sexes—so-called binary gender. With a host of other voices, Jesus Christ, the Lord of the church, the Messiah, the Alpha and the Omega, the one who not only spoke truth but ontologically *is* truth, weighed in directly on the creational design of the Lord. His affirmation of the sexes, we note, crops up in a discussion of sexual ethics and marriage. These subjects are inescapably intertwined, we see: "And Pharisees came up to him and tested him by asking, 'Is it lawful to divorce one's wife for any cause?' He answered, 'Have you not read that he who created them from the beginning made them male and female, and said, "Therefore a man shall leave his father and his mother and hold fast to his wife, and the two shall become one flesh"? So they are no longer two but one flesh. What therefore God has joined together, let not man separate'" (Matt. 19:3–6 ESV). No stronger word on the sexes can be found in the cosmos than this. Jesus Christ, the Word, the Logos, the Son of God, straightforwardly interprets Genesis 1 and 2. The Lord made humanity either "male" or "female." Christ reinforces his interpretation by quoting Genesis 2:24, which offers not one but two reinforcements of this design: there is "father" and "mother" in view, and "man" and "his wife." In other words, in two short but striking verses, the Lord of the church gives three separate—but connected—arguments for the reality of two sexes, manhood and womanhood.

We can scarcely understate the import of these words. If there were not another comment on the sexes save this (and Gen. 2), we would still have everything we need to understand the nature of manhood and womanhood. We do have much more testimony on this now-controverted subject than just Matthew 19; but this passage alone has normative authority for our conception of human identity.[30] Without this framework, the one-flesh union that Christ commends makes no sense. It is apparent that Jesus does not mean that two people become one physical, cojoined entity; he does mean that a man and woman can come together and procreate, and the exclusive God-honoring expression of this reality is marital union.

Sex is not given to humanity as a utilitarian pleasure, to be accessed however and wherever one sees fit. Sex belongs to marriage. Take sex away from

---

See Motyer, *The Prophecy of Isaiah: An Introduction and Commentary* (Downers Grove, IL: InterVarsity, 1993), 62. Whether a "sarcastic remark" or not (and it may well be), it hearkens back to the calling of men to lead the nation. See Gary E. Smith, *Isaiah 1–39*, New American Commentary 15A (Nashville: B&H, 2007), 149.

30. Leon Morris puts it straightforwardly: "Our sexuality is of divine ordinance; it is intended to be exercised in monogamous relationships." *The Gospel according to Matthew*, Pillar New Testament Commentary (Grand Rapids: Eerdmans, 1992), 481.

marriage, and we are robbed of the fullness of one-flesh union; take marriage away from sex, and the spiritual dimension of one-flesh union is diminished. Sex becomes a merely physical act, whereas God intends it to have numerous dimensions, each of them pleasing to him, each of them a blessing to his creation.

Sex in the biblical mind is not the act of amorous romantic contractors joining together for a spasm of fun. Sex is deeply unitive and is in fact designed to concretize the spiritual bond of a couple. Jesus is at pains to make sure his audience understands this point and grasps the cohesive nature of biblical marriage. He quotes the Genesis passage on one-flesh union, then repeats this phrase in his authoritative exposition of the passage, and finally underlines the idea a third time: that which God "has joined together" should not be dissolved.[31] The point could not be clearer: sex of the complementary kind brings a couple together, and it is God's will that they remain in this state until death.

We should not miss the significance of the connection made by Christ here. Marriage is grounded in sexual complementarity. In other words, God did not create marriage as an institution for anyone to enter—of whatever type or bent or number—and then bid Adam and Eve enter it. This man and woman were not merely the first humans to experience holy wedlock, an experience that most anyone of any bond can feel free to enter. God first made the man and the woman. He then joined them together. Marriage depends on sexual complementarity. We do not have the authority to remake manhood and womanhood; neither do we have the freedom to remake matrimony. Just as God formed the man and woman for his glory, so his Word sets the terms for what marriage is: a man leaving father and mother and holding fast to one wife. The Word of God is not editable; it is not subject to change; it stands forever.

We take away from Christ's testimony in Matthew 19 that both the sexes and marriage are carved in stone. The idea of gender bending is not new; it is ancient. Jesus knew the old covenant law; further, he knew the wildness, the brokenness that is in the heart of every sinner of every type. He would not have boggled at the modern concepts of gender dysphoria and sexual orientation. His words are not normed, then, by modern psychology; it is modern psychology, as with all anthropology, that is shaped by Christ. This is a lordship issue before it is a physical or medical issue.

---

31. Morris calls attention to the rebuke Christ offered both the Hillel and Shammai schools: "The typical attitude of the people of his day had reduced a God-given unity to a casual union, dissolvable at the whim of the male. This was not what Scripture meant when it spoke of what God did at the creation." *Gospel according to Matthew*, 482.

Paul Calls for Faithful Bodily Presentation in First Corinthians

The biblical depiction of the sexes is not laid out in an A-B-C format as in an IKEA instruction booklet. To the saints in ancient Corinth, a city rife with sexual confusion and idolatry, the apostle gives new covenant teaching that is built squarely on the foundation of old covenant law.[32] There is an order to marriage, and to manhood and womanhood, that we cannot miss:

> But I want you to understand that the head of every man is Christ, the head of a wife is her husband, and the head of Christ is God. . . . For a man ought not to cover his head, since he is the image and glory of God, but woman is the glory of man. For man was not made from woman, but woman from man. Neither was man created for woman, but woman for man. That is why a wife ought to have a symbol of authority on her head, because of the angels. Nevertheless, in the Lord woman is not independent of man nor man of woman; for as woman was made from man, so man is now born of woman. And all things are from God. Judge for yourselves: is it proper for a wife to pray to God with her head uncovered? Does not nature itself teach you that if a man wears long hair it is a disgrace for him, but if a woman has long hair, it is her glory? For her hair is given to her for a covering. (1 Cor. 11:3, 7–15 ESV)

There are two essential matters for us to cover here. The first is the order of creation, introduced in Genesis 2 but spelled out in much greater detail here. Every man is under Christ as his head, his authority; every wife is under the headship of her husband, her earthly authority; Christ himself honors the Father as his head, his authority.[33] This passage fills out our understanding of the workings of the holy Trinity as few others do. Jesus, the Son of God, honors his Father by gladly yielding to the Father's oversight and initiative. If the second person of the Godhead embraces submission, how much more should we human creatures, in our respective roles?

Paul's comments on the rightful response to God-constituted authority speak to the nature of the sexes.[34] We do not have the freedom to switch our

---

32. Dan Cole sets the stage well: "Corinth's reputation was as notorious in Paul's day as it had been in the Classical Age five centuries before. The account by the Roman geographer Strabo that a thousand cult prostitutes once served the temple to Aphrodite on the Acrocorinth, overlooking the city, may have been exaggerated. But the steady stream of sailors, traveling salesmen, and the ancient equivalent of soccer fans doubtless kept a good number of the cult prostitutes' secular counterparts busy." "Into the Heart of Paganism," *Christian History* 47 (1995), http://www.christianitytoday.com/history/issues/issue-47/into-heart-of-paganism.html.

33. For more on trinitarian relations and their import for faithful Christian living, see Bruce A. Ware and John Starke, *One God in Three Persons: Unity of Essence, Distinction of Persons, Implications for Life* (Wheaton: Crossway, 2015).

34. I concur on this matter with Anthony Thiselton, who writes that "gender differentiation relates to that which God wills, decrees, and expresses in creation or in the creation order." *The*

positions, so to speak. Women cannot grow tired of their wifely calling and decide to take on the identity and institution of the man; neither can a man shirk his God-given call. Men do not *earn* their role as head of the home; in terms now familiar to us, they are given it, and thus receive it in a posture of worship and obedience. In the same way, women do not decide whether they wish, in marriage, to embrace their husband's headship; their husband is their head, whether or not they honor him as such. Paul's teaching takes us back to the organizing concept of biblical anthropology: we are in an ordered world, a God-ordered world, and nothing we do can change that.

The second principle handed down by 1 Corinthians 11 is that which the old covenant introduced: based on our bodies—and thus our identities—we must present ourselves as a man or woman. To be sure, this swatch of Scripture contains some of Paul's more complex phrases, but the central idea is evident: the sexes need to honor God's design of their bodies by presenting themselves as a man or woman. "Does not nature itself teach you that if a man wears long hair it is a disgrace for him," Paul says, "but if a woman has long hair, it is her glory?" (1 Cor. 11:14–15 ESV). Corinth, we remember, included people—temple prostitutes among them, it seems—who took on a different "gender expression." But the church of the Lord Jesus Christ had no such option. Men and women were to honor the Lord by looking different from one another. It was disgraceful, according to the apostle, for men to look womanly; it was righteous and God-glorifying for a woman to have long hair (whenever possible, we assume).

I suspect that this passage is one of the primary reasons some modern readers dislike Paul. Paul taught in the clearest terms in all Scripture the distinct beauty of manhood and womanhood, and the distinct roles that flow from manhood and womanhood. An autonomous, design-denying, authority-rejecting, order-refusing culture is not disposed to look kindly on such teaching. If we buy the lie of expressive individualism and personal lordship, we will surely look askance at these ancient words or will, if we are more careful, write them off as "culturally conditioned."[35] But Christians—born-again believers in the Lord Jesus Christ, the atoning sacrifice of his people—cannot buy a doctrine of personal lordship. It is too expensive; it costs eternity. We are not

---

First Epistle to the Corinthians: A Commentary on the Greek Text, New International Greek Testament Commentary (Grand Rapids: Eerdmans, 2000), 836–37.

35. Mark Taylor differs with the argument that the passage in question deals only with first-century dynamics. He argues, "Paul's use of the intensive construction ('nature itself') and his prior appeal to the created order in 11:7–10 suggests that mere human convention is not Paul's meaning here." *1 Corinthians*, ed. E. Ray Clendenen, New American Commentary 28 (Nashville: B&H, 2014), 265–66.

our own lord, our own master. We were bought with a price. Once slaves to our sin, ensnared in the lusts of the flesh, we gladly and without reservation have become a slave to Christ.

In commenting on this passage, I do not deny that there are cultural differences in terms of dress and appearance. What I do deny is that we have a right, whatever culture we hail from, to effectively outmode Paul's apostolic instruction on this controversial matter. Our androgynous culture, bereft of belief in theistic creation, feels free to blur boundaries and embrace sameness.[36] There is no reason, after all, to dress as a man or a woman; manhood and womanhood are mere constructs. There is nothing *behind* these terms, nothing save cultural stereotypes. But the Bible has a different take. It opens our eyes to the wonder of twoness.[37] We are not in a drab, formulaic laboratory for oneness, a collection of misfits who end up sounding the same notes and all rebelling against the same reign. Our God is one in three, unity in diversity, and the world this God has made is bursting with aesthetic feasts, delights made possible by difference, God-made and God-revealing.

This is not to deny the existence of the medical condition called "intersex," in which a child possesses genitalia of both sexes. This condition, it is crucial to note, is not a voluntary choice, but is experienced involuntarily and from birth. If a Y chromosome is present, the child should be treated as a man. The counsel of Denny Burk is sound on this matter, and worth quoting at some length:

> First, parents should be extremely reluctant about—if not altogether against— corrective surgery when the child is an infant. This is especially the case when the surgery would involve the modification of the child's genitals or reproductive organs. Perhaps surgical procedures would be in order at some point during the child's life, but do not rush a child into surgery simply out of a desire to make the child "normal." Second, try to determine as soon as possible the chromosomal make-up of the child. If there is a Y chromosome present, that would strongly militate against raising the child as a female, regardless of the appearance of the genitals and other secondary sex characteristics. It would also suggest that medical treatments designed to make the child into a female are out of line. Third, understand that not all doctors and medical professionals share your biblical convictions. Worldviews affect the treatment of intersex conditions.

36. Burk, *What Is the Meaning of Sex?*, 180–82.

37. See Craig Blomberg's helpful commentary on verses 7–10: "For a Christian man to appear gay or pagan dishonors God; for a woman to appear lesbian or unfaithful dishonors her husband. Obviously husbands also dishonor their wives and wives dishonor God when they act in these inappropriate ways, but if an authority structure is implicit in this passage, Paul's less inclusive wording becomes understandable." *1 Corinthians*, NIV Application Commentary (Grand Rapids: Zondervan, 1994), 211–12.

Some doctors may view gender as a social construct and therefore would not let biological markers (such as a Y chromosome) determine the child's gender. Fourth, parents need to take an active role in understanding the condition and pursuing treatment options in keeping with their biblical convictions.[38]

I concur with Burk's careful pastoral approach to the intersex condition. Sadly, this involuntary state has been politicized in our time. Let us do all we can, whatever our precise position on transgender identity, to treat children who have this condition—and have done nothing to ask for it—with great sensitivity, discretion, and love. They are suffering the effects of the fall in a bodily sense. This point, in fact, reminds us once more of the disordered nature of a post-fall world. Our bodies, sadly, do not always work as they should, and when this is the case, we will benefit not from ideological crusading, but from the very opposite: from pastoral care, from compassionate and discrete and slow-moving wisdom, from love for the person in question as a being made in God's image who needs theological, spiritual, and even medical attention.

Marriage as the Metanarrative of the Bible

The final biblical prong to cover we have already introduced. Marriage is not merely a neat part of God's plan for humanity. Marriage is in truth the endpoint of all things. In Ephesians 5:22–33, the apostle Paul expands on previous biblical material on marriage and drops the bombshell that every marriage images, in an imperfect but real way, the relationship between Jesus Christ and his blood-bought church. The passage is worth quoting in full:

> Wives, submit to your own husbands, as to the Lord. For the husband is the head of the wife even as Christ is the head of the church, his body, and is himself its Savior. Now as the church submits to Christ, so also wives should submit in everything to their husbands.
>
> Husbands, love your wives, as Christ loved the church and gave himself up for her, that he might sanctify her, having cleansed her by the washing of water with the word, so that he might present the church to himself in splendor, without spot or wrinkle or any such thing, that she might be holy and without blemish. In the same way husbands should love their wives as their own bodies. He who loves his wife loves himself. For no one ever hated his own flesh, but nourishes and cherishes it, just as Christ does the church, because we are members of his body. "Therefore a man shall leave his father and mother and hold fast to his wife, and the two shall become one flesh." This mystery is

38. Burk, *What Is the Meaning of Sex?*, 181–82.

profound, and I am saying that it refers to Christ and the church. However, let each one of you love his wife as himself, and let the wife see that she respects her husband. (Eph. 5:22–33 ESV)

This section in Paul's writing completes the sad story of Genesis 3, where the first union was cursed, and brings it to a brilliant resolution. The gospel of Jesus Christ overcomes the effects of the fall in all respects, including the curse on husbands and wives. In Christ, the husband may be a self-sacrificial head of his wife; in Christ, the wife may be a churchlike blessing to her husband, submitting to him. In Adam, marriage is damaged and left perilously fragile; in Jesus, marriage is restored and shored up.

This vision of gospel-imaging union depends indissolubly on complementary humanity. A man and a man cannot marry in the sight of God; this means there are two "heads." A woman and a woman cannot marry in the sight of God; this means there is no "head."[39] No other form of union images the Christ-church relationship. Marriage in the teaching of the new covenant is dependent on the old covenant vision of the sexes, but it also works in the promise of the *protoevangelion*, and expands on it.[40] The seed of the woman crushes the serpent's head, but not only this—he marries the one the serpent sought to destroy, his bride, the church. He gives his body for his beloved, showing us in high-resolution detail the essence of manhood. Christ, the head of heads, does not consider his life precious but gives it for the church. As in the beginning, so in the end of Scripture: men and women have distinct but bound-together callings.

The book of Revelation completes this picture. In Revelation 21:9–14, one of the seven angels shows John the end of all things. He tells him, "Come, I will show you the Bride, the wife of the Lamb" (v. 9). We then meet the bride: "the holy city Jerusalem coming down out of heaven from God," the city that is the people of God (v. 10).[41] This is a living city, a city representing the saints. The people of God dwell forever with Christ in the city where he

39. For more on the term "head"—*kephale* in the Greek—see Wayne Grudem, "Does *Kephale* ('Head') Mean 'Source' or 'Authority Over' in Greek Literature? A Survey of 2,336 Examples," *Trinity Journal* 6, no. 1 (Spring 1985): 38–59. See also Grudem, "The Meaning of *Kephale* ('Head'): An Evaluation of New Evidence, Real and Alleged," *Journal of the Evangelical Theological Society* 44, no. 1 (2001): 25–65.

40. The short book by Ray Ortlund elegantly fills out this assertion: *Marriage and the Mystery of the Gospel: Short Studies in Biblical Theology* (Wheaton: Crossway, 2016).

41. A chapter by James M. Hamilton Jr. is bursting with insight and appropriate biblical imagination on this matter: "How to Condone What the Bible Condemns: Matthew Vines Takes on the Old Testament," in *God and the Gay Christian? A Response to Matthew Vines*, ed. R. Albert Mohler Jr. (Louisville: SBTS Press, 2014), 25–42.

is the light, and there is no need of sun (Rev. 21:21–27). The Bible thus begins with marriage and ends with it.[42]

So we see that the metanarrative of the Scripture depends on what modern people call "binary gender," though as we have seen, the end result involves so much more than merely recognizing manly and womanly bodily identities. Bodies are important—very much so. But bodies speak to spiritual realities; they shape personal self-understanding; read in the light of Scripture, they show us who God has made us to be and a significant portion of how we are to live. Our bodies point us upward, to Christ the head of his church, and to the church who is his bride. More than we can comprehend, our manhood and womanhood bear the utmost significance. Scrambling or embracing any distortion of this picture, whether intentionally or unintentionally, compromises not only our own identity but God's protological and eschatological vision.

Engaging Social Science from a Christian Worldview

We have lingered over the biblical text up to this point for a very good reason: the Bible is the authority of the Christian. We are freed as believers to appreciate truth wherever we may find it in this world, for the very existence of truth is a signpost to God and a gift of his kindness, but we take care in our study of our surroundings that we rightly prioritize the witness of the Scripture. Put more simply: if we don't know the biblical perspective on an issue, we're in trouble. If we do know it, we have all the intellectual fortification we could possibly need to wade into the brokenness of our fallen realm.

Social science plays in the key of tragedy on transgender matters. We know that individuals who underwent sex reassignment surgery suffered rates of mental disturbance and suicide that were over twenty times higher than the general population.[43] No Christian can read such a statistic and come away

42. Commenting on the theme of marriage in Revelation 19–21, G. K. Beale sums up the point well: "Saints are to glorify God at the end of time because of the consummation of the marriage of the Lamb with his bride, who will be finally and perfectly adorned for the occasion. Focus on the adorned bride is intended to lead the saints to glorify God." *The Book of Revelation*, New International Greek Testament Commentary (Grand Rapids: Eerdmans, 1999), 1120.

43. See Cecilia Dhejne, Paul Lichtenstein, Marcus Boman, Anna L. V. Johansson, Niklas Långström, and Mikael Landén, "Long-Term Follow-Up of Transsexual Persons Undergoing Sex Reassignment Surgery: Cohort Study in Sweden," February 22, 2011, e16885, http://journals.plos.org/plosone/article?id=10.1371/journal.pone.0016885. For professional commentary on this study, see Paul McHugh, "Transgender Surgery Isn't the Solution," *Wall Street Journal*, June 12, 2014, http://www.wsj.com/articles/paul-mchugh-transgender-surgery-isnt-the-solution-1402615120. Before retiring, McHugh served as psychiatrist-in-chief at Johns Hopkins Hospital and was a nationally renowned specialist.

unmoved. Though different groups read this data in opposing ways, it is my view that this horrific suicide rate speaks to the trauma that accompanies and in some cases provokes gender dysphoria, as well as the baleful effects of embracing gender dysphoria at any level. Whether an individual has made transgender identity a public cause or has experienced the quiet angst of internal confusion, the church cannot fail to make clear that an unbiblical approach to gender dysphoria is not in any way going to help suffering people. This is true in the cases when familial breakdown, failure to connect with one's same-sex parent, and abuse occur. At least some individuals who experience gender dysphoria have undergone devastating harm in their past. We must take care to counsel them well when they come to the church for help. Though they may not in any way have asked for their dilemma, their personal confusion, they need to know that embracing unbiblical identity and behavior will never aid them. They need what every sinner and sufferer of evil needs: the hope of glory, the grace of Jesus Christ, the clarity of complementarity, and the Spirit who dwells in us in all our earthly travail.

This surely bears on our training of children. We know from doctors like Paul McHugh, longtime Johns Hopkins psychiatrist, that close to 80 percent of children who experience gender confusion at a young age "abandon their confusion and grow naturally into adult life if untreated."[44] McHugh is not arguing here from a theological vantage point. He is speaking from simple common sense. His words remind us not to make a disorder, a condition meriting serious treatment and care, an identity. Gender dysphoria is a real problem, one with roots in the fall of Adam. We take it seriously as the church, but we do not make it an identity. We do not encourage or allow children to take on the attitudes, clothes, or identity of the opposite sex, and we certainly do not lead them to think it is a positive expression of self. It is not.

The data on youths who return to their God-given identity tells us much about the malleable nature of the human heart; whether a child or an adult, we are not a fixed entity. Though fully human—and inescapably so—we are

44. McHugh, "Transgender Surgery Isn't the Solution." For correlation of this claim, see the following studies: Thomas D. Steensma, Roeline Biemond, Fijgjie de Boer, and Peggy T. Cohen-Kettenis, "Desisting and Persisting Gender Dysphoria after Childhood: A Qualitative Follow-Up Study," *Clinical Child Psychology and Psychiatry* 16 (2010): 499–516; Annelou L. C. de Vries and Peggy T. Cohen-Kettenis, "Clinical Management of Gender Dysphoria in Children and Adolescents: The Dutch Approach," in *Treating Transgender Children and Adolescents: An Interdisciplinary Discussion*, ed. Jack Drescher and William Byne (New York: Routledge, 2014), 10. Taking these studies together, it appears that anywhere from 2 to 27 percent of dysphoric teens persist in a cross-gender identity in their adolescent years. See Glenn Stanton, "'BOYS GIRLS OTHER': Making Sense of the Confusing New World of Gender Identity," Family First New Zealand, June 30, 2015, https://www.familyfirst.org.nz/research/gender-2015/.

filled with potential because of the design of God. Though we drift from God and his good design, we can change. We can grow. The story of Scripture is this, from one angle: God taking people who are trapped in their sin, hostage to their past, concretized in their habits, unable to see a hopeful future, and ruining all our self-made ruin. God loves nothing more than to take a creature—a person—destroyed by the fall and to remake them. This is the very lifeblood of the Christian faith: Copernican change. Marvelous undoings. Spiritual upending. Damned sinners destined to taste the just effects of wrath for eternity instead becoming trophies of divine grace. The Christian faith, after all, is a cruciform faith. On Golgotha's mount, the Father took the worst possible thing—the death of his spotless Son—and made it the best possible thing. Through the vicarious death and resurrection of Christ, we are saved, and healed, and made new.

Gender dysphoria requires a careful, thoughtful, unhurried response. The church is equipped for just this kind of work, for it is a spiritual hospital. Pastors are not medical professionals and should feel free to interface with doctors as they help parents and family members care for individuals who experience gender dysphoria. But pastors must not shirk their duties to their people. The Bible possesses and hands down all we need for "life and godliness" (2 Pet. 1:3 ESV). The pastor's spiritual purview thus includes maladies and sins and awful events of the past. The pastor is the theologian-shepherd of souls. He is able to listen carefully to stories involving gender dysphoria; he is able to offer moral-theological guidance on the sinfulness of gender bending and cross-dressing, whether at the impulse level—the level of desire—or at the level of physical practices; he preeminently offers the atoning blood of Jesus Christ, which cleanses every wrong, and which makes filthy sinners brand new.[45]

In no instance should a pastor or Christian leader commend surgical transition. The Bible leaves no room for such an undertaking. Neither should a pastor or Christian leader encourage individuals to wear the clothing of the

---

45. It is essential on this and other related questions that we understand that we act sinfully in terms of not merely our behavior but also our desires (Matt. 5:21–30). The New Testament is not voluntarist; that is, it does not locate sin only in spoken words and acted-out behaviors. The central problem with lost humanity is that we do not desire God and the things of God. Therefore, conversion and a faithful walk with Christ must necessarily involve killing sin (Col. 3:1–11) in all stages, including the all-important stage of our desires. This is no new doctrine of sin; this is simple Reformation anthropology derived from biblical testimony. For more on a (closely) related question, see Denny Burk and Heath Lambert, *Transforming Homosexuality: What the Bible Says about Sexual Orientation and Change* (Phillipsburg, NJ: P&R, 2015); and Owen Strachan, "A Referendum on Depravity: Same-Sex Attraction as Sinful Desire," *Journal for Biblical Manhood and Womanhood* 20, no. 1 (Spring 2015): 24–34.

opposite sex or take on the persona of the opposite sex. Nowhere does the Scripture encourage or allow for such responses to gender dysphoria. Instead, pastors should help men and women take steps to own once more the body, and bodily identity, that God has given them.

This first means repentance for the sin of dishonoring God, whether consciously or unconsciously, through rejecting the body given by the Lord. It also entails pastor-led biblical study of manhood and womanhood so that the man or woman in question can glorify their maker according to divine wisdom. It further involves leaving behind all former identification with a cross-gender expression—leaving behind an opposite-gender name, clothing, personal traits, drugs that have repressed or interfered with the body's natural state, and undoing surgeries as much as is possible. Again, pastors and elders should closely consult with virtuous doctors on these matters, particularly if the person in question has attempted physiological transformation.

The pastor should make clear that sanctification is a long process (or, for the unrepentant, that rejecting a transgender identity is right but not necessarily easy). This is why the church exists: to take those ruined and disfigured by their own sin and, by the matchless grace of God, to present them holy in Christ. The man or woman may face gender dysphoria all their days; it may weaken significantly, it may disappear, but no matter what, every Christian must fight for faith every day they live. We do not expect, in other words, that all such persons will trust Christ and then be spiritually zapped into wholeness. God did not give us a checkpoint for the Christian life; he gave us a church. He made us members of a body, one to which we will be attached throughout this life and all of eternity. We need the church. The church is equipped to walk faithfully with men and women who must fight this battle, as it is equipped to help all who persevere in godliness.

The pastor leads the congregation in offering this biblical soul care to all people. But he does so with an eye attuned to the apparent patterns before him. He knows from limited research that gender dysphoria seems to affect men at a disproportionate rate. According to one study, boys and men apparently transition at a considerably higher rate than women—roughly three out of four are man-to-woman.[46] To a gender-neutral, even gender-blind society, this last point does not matter much. But to those of us who have a worldview shaped by the Bible, this makes us sit up in our seat.

46. See Femke Olyslager and Lynn Conway, "On the Calculation of the Prevalence of Transsexualism" (paper, World Professional Association for Transgender Health 20th International Symposium, Chicago, September 2007), http://ai.eecs.umich.edu/people/conway/TS/Prevalence/Reports/Prevalence%20of%20Transsexualism.pdf.

To address men well, we first must accept their innate manliness. This will prove challenging in a society straining to close its eyes to differences between the sexes. Despite its efforts, the data yields straightforward takeaways. Though one can find exceptions to the rule, men on average have 1,000 percent more testosterone than women.[47] As Anne and Bill Moir write, "Men's competitive drive comes from testosterone, and, because in real life not everyone can be a winner, it will come as no surprise that testosterone levels vary between individuals. They also vary enormously between men and women: the adult male's T levels (5,140–6,460 units) are about 11 times higher than a woman's (285–440 units). Give a man the challenge of competition and his already high T level will rise, increasing still further his competitive edge."[48]

It's strange that this is a social-science nugget you will almost never hear, because it matters greatly for understanding the differences between boys and girls and men and women. The God-etched differences between the sexes may seem purely biological, but they are—as I have been at pains to say— constitutive. As one further example, writer Michael Sokolove took serious heat several years ago when he called attention to the huge disparity in injuries between boys and girls who play contact sports: "If girls and young women ruptured their ACL's at just twice the rate of boys and young men, it would be notable. Three times the rate would be astounding." But the picture was worse yet: "Female athletes rupture their ACL's at rates as high as five times that of males."[49] Sokolove is not a conservative voice, but merely discussing such differences proved quite controversial.[50]

47. Gavin Peacock and I have explored what such findings mean in Strachan and Peacock, *The Grand Design: Male and Female He Made Them* (Fearn, Ross-Shire, UK: Christian Focus, 2016).

48. Anne Moir and Bill Moir, *Why Men Don't Iron: The Fascinating and Unalterable Differences between Men and Women* (New York: Citadel, 1999), 56. Anne Moir is an Oxford-trained geneticist with a PhD in the field. This data compares favorably to scientific research from, for example, the Mayo Clinic. See "Testosterone, Total, Bioavailable, and Free, Serum," Mayo Clinic, Mayo Medical Laboratories, https://www.mayomedicallaboratories.com/test-catalog/Clinical +and+Interpretive/83686. One resource, reading the data from the Mayo Clinic, lists the average testosterone ratios as follows: average level for an adult male, 270–1070 ng/dL; average level for an adult female, 15–70 ng/dL. See "Testosterone Levels by Age," *Healthline*, https:// www.healthline.com/health/low-testosterone/testosterone-levels-by-age. Various behaviors are affected by these differing levels: sex drive, aggression, interest in physical violence, and more.

49. Michael Sokolove, "The Uneven Playing Field," *New York Times Magazine*, May 11, 2008, http://www.nytimes.com/2008/05/11/magazine/11Girls-t.html. See also Sokolove, *Warrior Girls: Protecting Our Daughters against the Injury Epidemic in Women's Sports* (New York: Simon & Schuster, 2008).

50. See, for example, Steven D. Stovitz and Elizabeth A. Arendt, "Anatomy Isn't Destiny: A Multidisciplinary Response to Michael Sokolove's *Warrior Girls* (A Sports Medicine Perspective)," *Tucker Center for Research on Girls and Women in Sport* (newsletter), Fall 2008, http:// www.cehd.umn.edu/tuckercenter/library/docs/newsletter/TCN-2008-Fall.pdf. One professor, responding to Sokolove, blamed sexism for the prevalence of female sports injuries. See Jennifer

Even as the church honestly addresses the distinctions between men and women and shows that the biblical teaching on the sexes is not only true but good for us, it also clears its throat and speaks up. Out of love for neighbor (in fulfillment of the second greatest commandment), the church of Christ resists the public lobby of the LGBT movement. Here we note a key distinction between the private and the public. Private individuals are often not politicizing their pain; they may be sinning against the Lord in their handling of gender dysphoria, but they are not attempting to mainstream their behavior. At the public level, however, there is strong and revolutionary pressure being brought to bear on the West to affirm and normalize transgender identity. Provided the distinction holds on the ground, the church must never confuse the private individual with the public cause.

Even as the church offers spiritual soul care for every sinner, it cannot be silent about the public advocacy of depravity. The church stands against the mainstreaming of LGBT identity for several reasons. First, the glory of God is at stake. The existence of evil does not sit lightly on us. We oppose unrighteousness in principle and in practice because God is holy, God is great, and we are his chosen people. Second, the church has the express duty of being "salt and light" in a fallen place (Matt. 5:11–14). Like John the Baptist, we speak up against immorality, opposing evil wherever it is found (Matt. 14:1–12). The Christian conscience is aflame, and none can douse it. The gospel creates ethics. In other words, it awakens our moral instincts and fans them into a flame.[51]

Third, we know that any encroachment of the darkness will first affect not the strong but the weak. It is children who are being indoctrinated to think that there are no essential differences between men and women. It is children who are hearing that homosexuality is a totally viable choice. It is children who stand to suffer in a society that normalizes sin, for children are vulnerable and weak and cannot protect themselves from physical and intellectual and spiritual conflict. The church must speak about sexual depravity, not because it has a partisan bone to pick, but because it cares for children.

Doyle, "Sexism Hurts: ACL Injuries and Women's Athletics," *From a Left Wing* (blog), May 12, 2008, http://fromaleftwing.blogspot.com/2008/05/sexism-hurts-acl-injuries-women.html.

51. On this point, I am thankful that the Council on Biblical Manhood and Womanhood, under the leadership of President Denny Burk, partnered with the Ethics and Religious Liberty Commission of the Southern Baptist Convention to produce the Nashville Statement (https://cbmw.org/nashville-statement). It is a sound and compassionate reference for churches and Christian groups and, in conjunction with the Danvers Statement (https://cbmw.org/about/danvers-statement), will function well as a guide to congregations and Christian institutions on modern sexual ethics and the biblical worldview. Many churches and institutions have adopted these statements already.

This means that our engagement with the transgender community is going to be difficult. We love those who oppose the truth; we love those who disagree with us, perhaps vehemently; we must never demonize the other side. But on the matter of norming transgender identity, as with the mainstreaming of homosexuality, we have no option but to oppose this cultural trend. We do not hate those who disagree with us; in fact, we do all we can to show those who disagree with us that we love them *more* than any unbeliever loves them, for we know their true, God-signaled worth.[52] They are image-bearers—no more enchanted conception of human identity exists in the universe. But they are image-bearers who have fallen, as we all have, in Adam. Their hearts, like everyone's before conversion, are "desperately wicked" (Jer. 17:9 NLT). We have all gone astray (Rom. 3:10–18). Our—and their—only hope is Christ.[53]

But whether they trust Christ as Savior or not, we will not bow to the public normalizing of sin. Doing so is not compassionate. Standing for the truth is compassionate. Telling hell-bound men and women the whole counsel of God, with special attention to the transforming grace of Christ, is loving. This is our commission; this is our call from God. It is why we exist on the earth. The church is embattled and, frankly, may not win the struggle for public virtue. But whether we succeed or we fail in public terms, whether our accreditation is secure or revoked, whether we lose our jobs for not affirming LGBT views, whether the community applauds us or ostracizes us for acting in their eyes as a "hate group," we will not cease to believe God, to speak the truth, and to love fellow sinners.

Brief Synthesis of a Moral-Theological Approach to Transgender Identity

We should note several points quickly, in sum.

First, God created two sexes. There is no question about it; if we trust the Word and take Genesis as truth inspired by the Spirit, then we have no possibility of denying the reality of the sexes. The divine mind accounts for the

---

52. For clarity on the church's pastoral response to individuals who hold a "transgender identity," see Andrew Walker, *God and the Transgender Debate: What Does the Bible Actually Say about Gender Identity?* (Purcellville, VA: Good Book, 2017).

53. Thankfully, we have a growing chorus of voices who have wrestled through fallen sexual and bodily desires and trusted Christ. See the testimonies of Rosaria Champagne Butterfield, *Secret Thoughts of an Unlikely Convert* (Pittsburgh: Crown & Covenant, 2013); Jackie Hill-Perry, "From Lesbianism to Complementarianism," *9Marks*, March 11, 2015, https://www.9 marks.org/article/from-lesbianism-to-complementarianism; and Sam Allberry, *Is God Anti-Gay? And Other Questions about Homosexuality, the Bible and Same-Sex Attraction* (Purcellville, VA: Good Book, 2015).

man and the woman. God desired unity in diversity. He accomplished this by making two image-bearers, full of dignity and worth, who nonetheless differed from one another. We cannot compromise on this point. The Scripture is not an impressionistic painting but an introduction and summons to ordered reality.[54]

Second, the Bible never wavers from its two-sex vision. As we have seen, there is no disharmony between the old and new covenants on this point. From the first to the last, we receive a complementarian vision of humanity from God.[55] This intention for humanity is not problematic, unkind, or opposed to human flourishing. Instead, human flourishing depends on obeying God, a part of which is honoring God with our God-given body.

Third, not only does the Bible affirm two sexes as biological fact, but it builds out differing roles, practices, and even mind-sets in the sexes. We have only begun to sketch these differences in this chapter. The biblical authors writing under the Spirit's inspiration—thus producing an inerrant, authoritative, and sufficient text—do not shy away from exhorting the people of God to behave in manners appropriate to their God-given sex. The dying David instructs Solomon, his son, to "be strong, and show yourself a man" (1 Kings 2:2 ESV). The apostle Paul tells the whole Corinthian church to be brave: "Act like men" (1 Cor. 16:13 ESV). The apostle Peter calls Christian women to exude a "gentle and quiet spirit," distinct from an unruly, unsubmissive demeanor (1 Pet. 3:4). Men are summoned by the Scripture to function as elders of the church, providing comprehensive spiritual leadership for it (1 Tim. 2:8–15; 3:1–7; Titus 1:5–9). In all dimensions of life, manhood and womanhood matter.[56]

54. The church has long understood the ordered nature of creation. See J. I. Packer, "Marriage and the Family in Puritan Thought," chap. 16 in *A Quest for Godliness: The Puritan Vision of the Christian Life* (Wheaton: Crossway, 1990), esp. 272.

55. By "complementarian" I mean that the sexes are equal before God but given different roles to play in the home, church, and daily vocation (to an extent). This is different from the "egalitarian" view that the sexes are equal before God without clear differentiation of roles in the home and church. For more, see Strachan and Peacock, *Grand Design*, 19–43; and Jonathan Parnell and Owen Strachan, eds., *Designed for Joy: How the Gospel Impacts Men and Women, Identity and Practice* (Wheaton: Crossway, 2015). For the egalitarian perspective, see Ronald W. Pierce and Rebecca Merrill Groothuis, eds., *Discovering Biblical Equality: Complementarity without Hierarchy* (1991; repr., Downers Grove, IL: InterVarsity, 2005). I hasten to add that, thankfully, although complementarians and egalitarians disagree on various matters, to date very few evangelical egalitarians have embraced and advocated for acceptance of "transgender identity." In personal communication with egalitarian brothers and sisters, including several whose friendship I treasure, I have been heartened to hear affirmation of basic bodily complementarity.

56. To better understand these truths, I commend the work of R. Albert Mohler Jr., *We Cannot Be Silent: Speaking Truth to a Culture Redefining Sex, Marriage, and the Very Meaning of Right and Wrong* (Nashville: Nelson, 2015).

Fourth, the Bible's presentation of the sexes is given to us as an ideal, not a museum piece. The Lord does not want us merely to gaze at certain verses in Scripture, stunned by how countercultural they are. The Lord wants us to own the body and the bodily identity he has given us. None of us lives perfectly as a man or a woman. We are each a work in progress. We are each called to grow as a man or a woman.[57] This is no unique encumbrance on the shoulders of the gender-confused. On a daily basis, every Christian man or woman faces his or her weakness and sin. On a daily basis, every believer must die to his or her own plans and obey the Lord's plan in the power of the Spirit.

Fifth, we must get the identity-nature relationship right—and only the Bible does so. In our natural state, we quest after an identity. We are all destabilized and destitute from the fall, and so we seek to craft for ourselves a stable sense of being. But the reality is this: though we can affect a posture, the leopard cannot change his spots. In other words, we have a fallen, sinful nature. Try as we might, we cannot undo our depravity. No matter what identity we select for ourselves, the self-identification project is bound to fail. We cannot look inside ourselves, in some vast psychological well, to discover who we are. For as long as we are lost and far from Christ, we will wander, not knowing who we are or who we were made to be.

The Bible solves this quandary. In conversion, we gain a new nature (Rom. 6:6). We die to sin and live to Christ. This means that we are no longer slaves to unrighteousness, no longer bearers of a fallen identity. Now, because of God's grace, we are a new creation, and we have a new name: Christian. We are not one type of Christian: we are not an alcoholic Christian or a social-climbing Christian or a Pinterest-obsessed Christian or a gay Christian or a sexist Christian or a politically idolatrous Christian or a transgender Christian.[58] We have broken with our old nature and thus our old identity. We no longer define ourselves by our sin. Now, by the Spirit's power, we have a new nature—regenerate—and a new identity: Christian, beloved of God. There is no moniker or modifier that we add to our God-granted status. We used to be unfaithful and unrighteous, committing all manner of wickedness and

---

57. Accordingly, as fathers and mothers we want to raise our boys and girls to treasure and embody their God-given sex. We want to raise boys to be boys and girls to be girls. Of course, this will take wisdom, and there is some room for cultural difference on such matters. But if we are faithfully living out the biblical vision of humanity, we will not blur gender or baptize androgyny. Instead, seeking wisdom from the Spirit (see nearly every chapter of the book of Proverbs), we will do all we can to raise boys in distinctly masculine ways and to raise girls in distinctly feminine ways. This is a major way the church will stand out and shine amid a fuzzy, gray, foggy culture.

58. See Owen Strachan, "Should the Church Speak of 'Gay Christians'?," *Journal for Biblical Manhood and Womanhood* 19, no. 1 (Spring 2014): 4–7.

glorying in evil; now, we have been transformed by God, who has shone in our hearts and showed us the miracle of Christ's atoning death and life-giving resurrection.

The flesh wants us to cling to our old nature and make our own identity. The gospel enables us to lose our old nature and embrace our God-given identity. We are not making up who we are; we discover who we are and how valued and loved we are when we, ironically, confess how wicked we are, and when we repent of all our sins in the name of Jesus Christ.

Sixth, because of God's transformative work, we should embrace the messiness of spiritual and personal restoration. This means that we should seek as much as is humanly possible to help people experiencing gender dysphoria to disengage from an opposite-sex identity. We want them to see that their body is not lying to them. Their body is a gift from God. It may be that they must face down a storm of emotions and events in their past. They may have to fight at a visceral, intensive level to leave their fallen practices behind. But this they must do. At the level of desire, when we feel pulled to bend our gender, we should confess this sin to God and repent. This is no new calling unique to a certain category of Christian; this is the mark of the Christian life.

It is essential that, in counseling, Christian pastors, elders, and leaders help struggling individuals see that they are not victims. They may once have been victimized, to be sure; the biblical doctrine of depravity accounts in full for the terrible misdeeds happening all around us. But even if they have gone through deep waters, they will find hope and healing in rejecting victimhood. They must come out of the waters. They must see that they are not held hostage to evil. We must help them recover a sense of agency, profound agency—and the Spirit is ready to bestow it.

The Bible does not lift up our heads in quite the same way as our sin-denying therapeutic culture does. The culture says that we are fine just the way we are and that acknowledging this fact will make us whole. The Bible says that we must turn from brokenness and that doing so in view of divine grace will make all things brand new. One view leaves us a victim, trapped in a self-affirmation loop that never truly addresses our sin and our suffering. The other view rejects victimhood, squares honestly with the darkness of our hearts and our world, and calls us all to walk in newness of life.

Conclusion

The church cannot go soft on the issue of gender dysphoria. We have a divine call that we cannot shirk: to stand for what is good and hold fast to what is holy. We will do so, not because we despise fellow sinners, but because we love them. As the cross abundantly shows, Christian love is not cheap. It is not light as a feather. It does not accord with pop-song theology and never asks us to change, only telling us how awesome and great we are, avoiding any mention of our blemishes, our wrongs, our depravity. Christian love is, at its core, catalytic. It ruins us, redeems us, and renews us. Christian love is *costly*.

This is true for us all. The call for those who experience gender dysphoria is not one hair different than the call for any other kind of sinner born into Adam's disgrace. The call for those who experience gender dysphoria is this: to trust Christ, exercising faith in his cross, and to be born anew into Christ's own family. The call for those who do not face this particular struggle: to walk alongside these brothers and sisters, holding up flagging arms, journeying together to the New Jerusalem, where the Lamb is the light of the city of God.

Response to Owen Strachan

Mark A. Yarhouse and Julia Sadusky

What we appreciate first and foremost about Dr. Owen Strachan's chapter is how he opens by noting that those who are transgender are made in the image of God. He emphasizes the personhood of transgender individuals, and many Christians do not do that well. His words bear repeating: transgender people are "fully, substantially, immovably *human*" (p. 55). Their dignity does not hinge on their depicting it but on others seeing the image and likeness of God that is there. There is freedom and joy in this declaration in that it places the burden not on the transgender person to prove their humanity but on others to see and honor this humanity.

It is also helpful to remind the reader that we are all fallen, that we are all sinners in need of the grace of Jesus and a conversion of heart to receive this grace. The primacy of Scripture as our source of authority is also at the heart of Dr. Strachan's chapter, and we share with Dr. Strachan a high view of Scripture as our primary source of authority. Dr. Strachan also looks to Genesis to help us understand God's creational intent for sexuality. He later writes that "the creation of the man and woman is not incidental to human identity but foundational" (p. 63). This foundation is an important starting point for all of us as we take seriously what Scripture offers the present conversation.

We also appreciate Dr. Strachan's emphasis on forming an adequate anthropology, which includes our sexuality. He highlights that our sexuality comes with a duty. It is a gift from God, certainly, but we look to God for instruction on how to live it out. Strachan is right to contrast that with the individualism that is such a part of our contemporary landscape and that certainly infiltrates Christian circles as much as it does every other milieu. The movement toward absolute autonomy over our sexuality is not rooted in Scripture, but it is certainly increasingly popular. We also appreciate how Strachan points to sexuality as "a major battleground in the war between God and Satan" (p. 62). This explains why so much attention has been given in the church to the discussion of sexuality and how our relationship with God ought to inform the integration of sexuality into personhood.

We were glad to read that Strachan recognizes the cultural context in which Scripture was recorded, as when Paul describes in 1 Corinthians 11 standards for hair and clothing. He acknowledges that cultural differences in dress and presentation ought to be considered as we attempt to glean from these passages practical applications for pastoral care in contemporary settings. Yet he later discusses that "the command to wear the clothes that befit one's sex is not isolated or random" (p. 61). We wonder what "clothes that befit one's sex" would be today. What are the cultural considerations here that inform how strongly Christians would assert particular standards of male or female dress and imbue them with moral significance across the board? Is it possible to consider that dress and clothing matter, as is the case with modesty, without hinging one's salvation on one's particular dress?

Dr. Strachan distinguishes between the private individual and the public sphere, writing, "The church must never confuse the private individual with the public cause" (p. 78). We have written elsewhere on the importance of distinguishing between those who are personally struggling with gender identity concerns, those who have taken on a public identity (e.g., coworkers, neighbors), and those political advocates who would offer different opportunities to engage around pastoral care and Christian witness.

Dr. Strachan also directs the reader to larger points of disagreement. For Strachan, this has to do with anthropology, one's sense of self, and submission. He may be on to some important considerations. We agree that Scripture provides an adequate anthropology, and we appreciate the way he looks to Scripture as a reliable guide to be taken seriously. Toward the end of his chapter, he writes, "The Scripture is not an impressionistic painting but an introduction and summons to ordered reality" (p. 80). Even with this common adherence to Scripture as the primary authority, we think there is nonetheless disagreement about how we approach science and human experience and how these are understood in relation to the primacy of Scripture. We also find that there are differences as to what practical pastoral care looks like and the degree to which it is informed by each of these.

In the opening paragraphs, Dr. Strachan frames the topic in terms that resonate for him. He talks about conversion and repentance, as well as the need for transformation, which places the discussion of gender dysphoria in moral categories: "In repentance and faith, you will find all the happiness and Godward fullness you can imagine, and more" (p. 56). We wonder what is realistic to anticipate in this life when it comes to transformation in the realm of gender identity. What is the tangible measure of transformation? We also wonder whether there is any distinction here with regard to what is placed in moral categories as it relates to gender identity.

Dr. Strachan discusses that transgender people "need what every sinner and sufferer of evil needs: the hope of glory, the grace of Jesus Christ, the clarity of complementarity, and the Spirit who dwells in us in all our earthly travail" (p. 74). What is unclear is what this looks like practically. The reader who comes to this chapter may wonder, as we did, what pastoral care actually looks like here. How does one offer the clarity of complementarity in an operationalized way? This chapter is strong on saying, in essence, that one ought not to identify as transgender or dress in ways that would help one manage one's gender dysphoria, regardless of whether one pursues hormonal treatment or surgical interventions. It fails to cast a positive vision for how the person will live today, in the "not yet" transformed process that he points to. Strachan is strong on the "no" but leaves us with little sense for the "yes" of a life in which a person can flourish, insofar as their gender identity is not "healed" and they suffer in enduring ways with gender dysphoria.

"We take [gender dysphoria] seriously as the church, but we do not make it an identity. We do not encourage or allow children to take on the attitudes, clothes, or identity of the opposite sex, and we certainly do not lead them to think it is a positive expression of self. It is not" (p. 74). Again, such a declaration begs the question: What is a positive expression of self?

Dr. Strachan identifies renewal, or remaking, as the way God encounters humanity. "God loves nothing more than to take a creature—a person—destroyed by the fall and to remake them. . . . Through the vicarious death and resurrection of Christ we are saved, and healed, and made new" (p. 75). What are realistic expectations for the person with gender dysphoria? What does it mean for them to be saved? We know many Christians who suffer from gender dysphoria. Does their being saved take the form of healing in this life? We know that most do not experience an alignment with their biological sex. Does their being saved take the form of being made new? What does that mean or look like this side of eternity?

We would agree with the assertion that "the sexes are not arbitrary or colorless in Genesis 2 but are clearly and evocatively presented for our instruction" (p. 60). The question emerges as to how intersex conditions are instructive. Apparently, after the fall, not every human body offers clear instruction for the sex of the person. This need not render the sexes as arbitrary in Genesis 2, but it does force us to wrestle with the application of this text to those whose experience of sexuality is outside the norm.

Dr. Strachan seems sympathetic to gender experiences that are known to be tied to medical conditions, even as he attaches moral significance to the experience of gender incongruence. For Dr. Strachan, intersex conditions are those he recognizes as involuntary, but the contrast seems to suggest that gender dysphoria is a voluntary choice. That intersex conditions are experienced from birth seems important to Strachan but also appears to preclude the development of other conditions that may have an unclear origin but are perhaps equally involuntary, as is gender dysphoria. Other sections of the chapter seem to suggest that Strachan recognizes that gender dysphoria is not volitional, as when he writes, "They may not in any way have asked for their dilemma, their personal confusion" (p. 74). Later he writes about gender dysphoria as a disorder and as a condition that has ties to the fall and so seems to speak from more of a disability perspective, often indicating a lack of autonomy in the experience.

We then turn to how Dr. Strachan moralizes "gender bending and cross-dressing, whether at the impulse level—the level of desire—or at the level of physical practices" (p. 75). Is there any distinction between desire and behavior? Is the gender incongruence itself thought of in moral categories? It appears to us to be treated as such. To what degree can there be moral significance attached to a desire, if the desire is not chosen or willed by the person?

Additionally, could motivation matter when it comes to cross-dressing? Dr. Strachan points to Deuteronomy 22 in his condemnation of this behavior, highlighting that the type of cross-dressing addressed in the passage is never permissible. This seems to leave room for different types of cross-dressing, which may be worth considering when it comes to applying these passages to every person who engages in cross-dressing as a means of managing gender-related distress. Is it possible that when a biological male with gender dysphoria wears female undergarments, there is more to the story than "rebelling against all standards" and a refusal to "submit to any external expectation, whether divine or otherwise" (p. 62)? Is it fair to label all desires to cross-dress as "ungodly, sinful, God-dishonoring" desires (p. 63)? In conversations with those with gender dysphoria, it seems unclear that the desire flows from a place of rebellion, refusal to submit to God, or volitional sin.

For the purposes of this analysis, we are going to mostly set aside Dr. Strachan's reflections on pastoral care for intersex conditions, which we found inadequate. Here, he offers chromosomes as being instructive, but we would assert that even chromosomes could be, and in some cases are, touched by the fall. Strachan states that we ought to approach those with this condition with love, as those in need of "theological, spiritual, and even medical attention" (p. 71). But it is unclear what this medical attention would look like, or even, for that matter, what form the theological and spiritual attention might take.

But let's look at pastoral care for gender dysphoria, which appears to be a two-step model of care. As we read it, the pastoral care steps Dr. Strachan recommends for reclaiming one's gender identity (so that it aligns with one's biological sex) are (1) to repent "for the sin of dishonoring God, whether consciously or unconsciously, through rejecting the body given by the Lord" (p. 76) and (2) to be taught that "sanctification is a long process" that may not abate (p. 76). Sanctification appears tied to accepting one's "innate manliness" (p. 77).

Dr. Strachan's notions of maleness and femaleness also leave room for disagreement. The exposition of maleness is given in reference to Barak and Deborah. Barak is said to have "dishonored divine design by playing the coward. . . . His strong physical form signaled that he was made for adventure and initiative" (p. 64). Dr. Strachan goes on to say that the man was made "stronger, taller, and faster . . . so that he would lead his family, protect his wife and children, and answer the call to fight" (p. 64). While it seems clear that this could be true for Barak, what is less clear is how this applies to the man who feels afraid, or the one who is not stronger, taller, and faster than his female counterparts, or the one who has no family, no wife or children. Is each man who does not exhibit these qualities merely dishonoring divine design in the feelings he has or the physical form he has been given? And for the Christian women who lived and died as radical protectors of Christianity, what does it mean that the woman would not be "called by God to protect, intervene, and die for the other" (p. 65)? Do Christian martyrs who are women dishonor God?

Taking from Scripture a literal interpretation of what is said about male and female roles leaves some room for concern, especially when passages like 1 Corinthians 11:3 and 7–15 are cited. It does not seem that Dr. Strachan is encouraging all women to wear head coverings, which leads us to wonder how we can distinguish between what is to be taken literally and what is not. When he says we ought to "present ourselves as a man or woman" (p. 69), we wonder what this looks like, in light of the cultural considerations that he himself points out are worth thinking through. Does the choice of having short hair or long hair have moral significance attached to it in every case? Or solely in the case of the person with gender dysphoria? Again, does motivation matter? If so, it is unclear from this exposition.

With every prohibition of something, whether cross-dressing, gender bending, hormonal treatments, or surgeries, comes the burden to offer a tangible alternative. Dr. Strachan boldly states that "nowhere does the Scripture encourage or allow for such responses to gender dysphoria" (p. 76). This is the area that needs more attention in his chapter. It is not clear that Scripture explicitly speaks of gender dysphoria or of the particular responses to be allowed. That perhaps is the dilemma we face. It seems insufficient, though, to encourage someone to take steps to "own once more the body, and bodily identity, that God has given them" (p. 76) if we have not developed tried-and-true strategies for this to be done.

Many of the people we have worked with have tried the very things Dr. Strachan suggests: prayer, repentance, conformity to gender stereotypes and cultural standards for dress, and yet they continued to endure the gender dysphoria they hoped to see resolved. How would they know they were "converted" in the way Dr. Strachan means? Is there mercy, in the face of enduring conditions like gender dysphoria, that applies to each person, allowing them to accept "a new nature—regenerate—and a new identity: Christian, beloved of God" (p. 81), regardless of whether they have adopted a transgender identity? Can they walk in "newness of life" (p. 82) even while experiencing enduring gender dysphoria, even if they never acquire the standards of dress posed as an adequate measure of their holiness?

Response to Owen Strachan

Megan K. DeFranza

n his award-winning book *Exclusion and Embrace*, evangelical theologian Miroslav Volf draws from his experience of ethnic warfare to provide wisdom for approaching other conflicts as followers of Jesus. Volf notes how, in times of peace, diverse groups can and do live together: tolerating, helping, occasionally even mixing and marrying. But in times of conflict, identities become hardened, and loyalties are demanded.[1]

> I have Czech, German, and Croatian "blood" in my veins. . . . But the new Croatia, like some jealous goddess, wanted all my love and loyalty. I must be Croat through and through, or I was not a good Croat.
>
> It was easy to explain this excessive demand of loyalty. After forced assimilation under communist rule, the sense of ethnic belonging and cultural distinctness was bound to reassert itself.[2]

Volf got the message that, even if his mixed ethnic heritage was true, it shouldn't be talked about. In times of war, better to keep the lines between "us" and "the enemy" crystal clear.

Dr. Strachan sees the contemporary church in a battle for true Christianity, for the gospel, for manhood and womanhood; thus, any Christian of mixed "blood"—a different theological tradition or a different interpretation of the Bible—is presented as untrustworthy, disloyal. Strachan's desire for us to think Christianly about gender and gender identity is praiseworthy, but he appears to believe that only those Christians who think exactly like him, who have a pure (complementarian) bloodline, are trustworthy. It seems as if he believes any diversity of opinion among Christians will cost him the culture war.

---

1. Miroslav Volf, *Exclusion and Embrace: A Theological Exploration of Identity, Otherness, and Reconciliation* (Nashville: Abingdon, 1996), 14–16.
2. Volf, *Exclusion and Embrace*, 16–17, emphasis added.

90

When one is at war, differing opinions about tactics can undermine an operation. Thus, military cadets are taught not to think, but rather to simply take orders. Better they don't know Augustine's arguments for just war. Better they simply follow the black-and-white commands of their superior officers. Like a drill sergeant, Dr. Strachan doesn't present evidence of complexity or ask his readers to weigh evidence. Maybe he believes this information is better kept for higher-ranking officers (e.g., pastors and seminary professors) rather than lay readers of this volume.

In this way, Dr. Strachan's approach differs significantly from that of Dr. Yarhouse and Dr. Sadusky, who highlight nuance and diversity on many levels—complexity at the level of biblical interpretation (three interpretive lenses), diversity of transgender experiences (including the reality of transgender Christians seeking God's guidance in how to manage their dysphoria), and nuances in how to best support transgender Christians in their quests for wholeness and health (examples of policies put forth by three different Christian colleges). Where Yarhouse and Sadusky invite their readers to weigh the evidence and arguments for differing Christian perspectives, Strachan insists there is only one Christian approach to the question of gender identity.

This military approach seems to fit with his vision of biblical masculinity (pp. 63–65). In a culture war, it is not the military hero but the theologian or the pastor who gives orders and asserts his authority. Unfortunately, Dr. Strachan presents his authority (i.e., his interpretation) as biblical authority and as the authority of the church through the ages, which no believer would dare to question. "This discussion of transgender identity among professing believers," he writes, "is at base a referendum on biblical authority and biblical sufficiency. Much . . . is at stake in this conversation" (p. 58). He continues: "The binary view I am advocating in this chapter is without doubt and without question the historic view of the Christian church. This is true in all its branches, denominations, and iterations" (p. 57n9).[3]

This authoritarian approach can be effective, especially for Christians used to being told by their pastors what they should think and how they should interpret the Bible. The problem with this model is that it is not the whole truth. The truth is more complex. The Bible is more complex. Christian history is more complex. Transgender experiences are more complex. Pastoral

---

3. See the following for evidence that both Eastern and Western church traditions show knowledge of and theological reflection on sex and gender diversity: Megan K. DeFranza, *Sex Difference in Christian Theology: Male, Female, and Intersex in the Image of God* (Grand Rapids: Eerdmans, 2015), chaps. 2–3; and René Grémaux, "Woman Becomes Man in the Balkans," in *Third Sex, Third Gender: Beyond Sexual Dimorphism in Culture and History*, ed. Gilbert H. Herdt (New York: Zone Books, 1996), 241–83.

care is more complex. And mature Christian adults should be trusted with the whole truth, even if they are not pastors or professional theologians.

Conversely, I would argue that the gospel, as evangelicals have understood it, is simple. To the gospel of salvation by grace through faith Dr. Strachan wants to add a gospel of faith and works. Faith in the saving work of Jesus must be accompanied by works of gender performance, or all is lost. "As we will see, understanding the gospel—and specifically the significance of conversion—is at the heart of this conversation" (p. 56).

As I explain in my chapter, it is not "biblical authority" that is at stake but whether we are reading the *whole* Bible, and reading it carefully—allowing Scripture to interpret Scripture, reading to understand the unfolding of God's redemptive story, a complex story that doesn't end where it begins. My reading of Genesis differs from Strachan's because it integrates truths revealed in other parts of the Bible—passages that affirm what science is confirming today. Ancient Jews and Christians knew that *most* people are born clearly sexed as male or female, but they also knew that a significant minority are born with bodies that do not fall on one side of the binary or the other, people who are also God's beloved children.

In Matthew 19, Jesus affirms the majority male/female story, but he goes on to add that there are those who don't fit into this majority model, people who are born different, eunuchs from their mother's womb. Augustine speaks of those born in between male and female using the language of his day, "**hermaphrodite**" and "**androgyne**," in his famous text *The City of God.*[4] Neither Jesus nor Augustine attempts to deny the existence of these humans; Jesus doesn't heal a eunuch, and Augustine doesn't pray for the healing of hermaphrodites. Why? Maybe because they remembered Isaiah 56, in which God promises eunuchs not a restoration to the binary but something "better than sons and daughters" (better than the way typical men would be blessed in the passing on of their name). God blesses them *as they are* with "an everlasting name" (Isa. 56:5).

These biblical passages about those who do not fall into the majority binary sex pattern are essential to our conversation about transgender people. Rather than attending to ancient and modern people who do not fit the binary, Dr. Strachan speaks only of the majority, of men and women, whom he calls back to patriarchal roles in home, church, and world.[5]

---

4. See my chapter, p. 61.

5. Because innumerable books have been written debating how best to interpret the Bible on gender roles (i.e., complementarianism vs. egalitarianism), I need not address these arguments but will instead focus on the topic assigned to us in this volume. Resources defending

I find it difficult to explain why Dr. Strachan takes many paragraphs to unpack the significance of Jesus's words about divorce and remarriage in Matthew 19:1–9 but does not complete his exegesis of the passage, which ends at verse 12. Why stop, when Jesus is about to speak more directly to our current topic than he does in the previous nine verses? Why stop before our Lord talks about eunuchs, those he is *differentiating* from men and women (pp. 66–67)? Dr. Strachan is a signatory of the Nashville Statement and former president of the organization that created and published the document. The Nashville Statement acknowledges both the reality of people born intersex and their presence in the Scriptures—connecting them directly to the words of Jesus in Matthew 19:12—but Dr. Strachan fails to mention this in his chapter.[6]

To his credit, Dr. Strachan does eventually acknowledge the reality of intersex people, but not in connection with Matthew 19. Unfortunately, not only is his explanation incomplete, but it is also incorrect on several points. First, intersex is not "*the* medical condition" (p. 70, emphasis added). It is not one kind of thing; rather, intersex is an umbrella term for many variations in human sex development that create bodies different from the majority male/female pattern. Second, only a minority of intersex variations produce "genitalia of both sexes," or, as it is more accurately described, "ambiguous genitalia."[7] Third, Strachan's quoting of Burk on the presence of the Y chromosome as determinative of male sex reveals that neither has done sufficient research on the subject. The Y chromosome does not always determine male identity; production and receptivity to androgens is more influential, as I explain in my chapter (pp. 154–55n13).

It looks to me like Dr. Strachan's inadequate treatment of intersex reveals either that he has not done sufficient research to serve the readers of this volume or that he is choosing to present only *some* of the evidence. Does he not trust that his readers can handle the whole complex truth? Is it possible that he is "simplifying" complexity and misrepresenting scientific facts for the sake of mustering his culture warriors?

When Dr. Strachan presents scientific research on the differences between non-intersex men and non-intersex women, he is similarly selective. At some

---

complementarianism can be found at www.cbmw.org, while www.cbeinternational.org is a good place to find resources defending egalitarianism.

6. Nashville Statement, Council on Biblical Manhood and Womanhood, August 29, 2017, art. 6, https://cbmw.org/nashville-statement/.

7. Nashville Statement, art. 6. It is humanly impossible to have the genitalia of both sexes as the phallus develops either as a penis or a clitoris, labia fuse to create the scrotum, etc. When the phallus is smaller than expected for a penis or larger than a typical clitoris, or when labia are partially fused, or a child has a vaginal opening and a phallus large enough to pass for a penis, these are considered "ambiguous genitalia."

points, he looks to scientists to defend his arguments, but at others, he seems to be warning his readers not to trust doctors or scientists who study sex and gender differences.[8] By contrast, Dr. Yarhouse and Dr. Sadusky carefully review scientific studies that support their arguments and those that challenge their assumptions, modeling how to evaluate complex phenomena and scientific debate.

Where Dr. Yarhouse and Dr. Sadusky differentiate varieties of transgender experiences, Dr. Strachan's refusal to acknowledge these distinctions once again leaves him open to the question of whether he is willfully misleading his readers, unfamiliar with the facts, or unwilling to listen to the testimonies of Christians who struggle with gender dysphoria.[9] Certainly, children raised in loving Christian homes who experience gender dysphoria long before they are exposed to the "expressive individualism" of the world undermine his argument that "transgenderism" is merely a new secular philosophy (p. 62).

As Christians, we need not fear the whole truth, even when it is complicated, because we have been given the Spirit who has promised to "guide [us] into all the truth" (John 16:13 ESV). Thanks be to God!

---

8. Contrast his presentation of Dr. Paul McHugh (p. 74) with his warning, quoting Burk, about doctors who may not "share your biblical convictions. Worldviews affect the treatment of intersex conditions. Some doctors may view gender as a social construct and therefore would not let biological markers (such as a Y chromosome) determine the child's gender" (pp. 70–71). In this example, it is Strachan's worldview that has influenced him to reject the consensus of the medical community in viewing the Y chromosome as determinative.

9. He uses the term "cross-dresser" as if it were interchangeable with "transgender" (p. 61).

Response to Owen Strachan

Justin Sabia-Tanis

et us begin with Christ's witness. Jesus was asked by an expert in the law, in Luke 10:25, what was necessary for eternal life.

> "What is written in the Law?" [Jesus] replied. "How do you read it?"
>
> He answered, "'Love the Lord your God with all your heart and with all your soul and with all your strength and with all your mind'; and, 'Love your neighbor as yourself.'"
>
> "You have answered correctly," Jesus replied. "Do this and you will live."
>
> But he wanted to justify himself, so he asked Jesus, "And who is my neighbor?"
>
> In reply Jesus said: "A man was going down from Jerusalem to Jericho, when he was attacked by robbers. They stripped him of his clothes, beat him and went away, leaving him half dead. A priest happened to be going down the same road, and when he saw the man, he passed by on the other side. So too, a Levite, when he came to the place and saw him, passed by on the other side. But a Samaritan, as he traveled, came where the man was; and when he saw him, he took pity on him. He went to him and bandaged his wounds, pouring on oil and wine. Then he put the man on his own donkey, brought him to an inn and took care of him. The next day he took out two denarii and gave them to the innkeeper. 'Look after him,' he said, 'and when I return, I will reimburse you for any extra expense you may have.'
>
> "Which of these three do you think was a neighbor to the man who fell into the hands of robbers?"
>
> The expert in the law replied, "The one who had mercy on him."
>
> Jesus told him, "Go and do likewise." (Luke 10:26–37 NIV)

Jesus is clear here about the conditions for eternal life: love God and love our neighbors. Jesus does not mention gender, sexuality, marriage, conformity, respectability, or any other social condition in connection with eternal life. Jesus, in fact, lifts up a despised outsider—the Samaritan—as the true neighbor, because he was the one who showed mercy. Will not, then, transgender people who love God with all their heart and with all their soul and with all their strength and with all their mind, and who love their neighbor as themselves, be saved, regardless of their physical status? If we carefully read Jesus's words here and in John 3:16, I think the answer is undoubtedly yes.

Love and mercy lie at the core of Jesus's statements about eternal life. We need to be clear that Christ does not mention gender and sexuality at any time *in relation to salvation*. We are not "hell-bound" because of gender or **gender transition**. I think it is important to be honest and direct about that. What we are debating here is how best to live out a Christian life, and we have differences of opinion about that.

I want to raise three substantive issues: first, the perception of gender dysphoria in this chapter; second, the role of women; and third, why many people have come to see the Christian church as a hate-filled institution.

This chapter does not reflect current knowledge about transgender people. Nowhere do I see any reflection of engagement with transgender people; this only speaks about transgender people abstractly as the sinful other. Characterizing transgender people as confused (p. 81) is heard by most transgender people as very condescending; I would argue that it is not confusion but our *certainty* that our identity does not match aspects of our physical bodies that is challenging. Just because our condition may be puzzling to those who do not share it does not mean that we ourselves are confused.

Fortunately, Dr. Strachan does acknowledge God will not simply "zap" away gender dysphoria; it is not a realistic expectation to simply pray this issue away. Yet at the same time, he holds out the idea of "transformation" as an alternative to physical transition. He does not offer a realistic or even clear view of this transformation, other than barring medical transition and consigning a transgender person to live with gender dysphoria. What specifically and realistically would this spiritual transformation look like? Transgender people can attest that Bible study, prayer, and attempts to follow the norms of their birth gender have not, in fact, relieved their gender dysphoria; these may even increase anxiety and depression.

Dr. Strachan lists several unsubstantiated ideas about the causes of gender dysphoria (p. 74), including a very misleading conclusion: "We know that individuals who underwent sex reassignment surgery suffered rates of mental disturbance and suicide that were over twenty times higher than the general population" (p. 73).[1] Dr. Strachan goes on to state, "Though different groups

1. See Cecilia Dhejne, Paul Lichtenstein, Marcus Boman, Anna L. V. Johansson, Niklas Långström, and Mikael Landén, "Long-Term Follow-Up of Transsexual Persons Undergoing

read this data in opposing ways, it is my view that this horrific suicide rate speaks to the trauma that accompanies and in some cases provokes gender dysphoria, as well as the baleful effects of embracing gender dysphoria at any level" (p. 74). This implies that "embracing gender dysphoria at any level" leads to elevated levels of suicidality. The quoted article comes to a different conclusion than implied here and compares post-transition individuals with the general population, not with transgender people who had not undergone reassignment. The original article concludes, "Even though surgery and hormonal therapy alleviates gender dysphoria, it is apparently not sufficient to remedy the high rates of morbidity and mortality found among transsexual persons. Improved care for the transsexual group after the sex reassignment should therefore be considered."[2] I urge readers to track down the original article and also familiarize themselves with other literature, which shows no higher rates of underlying psychological problems among transgender people (something I discuss in my chapter).

In addition, this chapter skips a number of biblical passages to arrive at its conclusions about women and transgender people. The description of the role of women ignores or distorts the roles of female leaders in the Bible, such as Lydia, Deborah, and Martha's sister Mary, who is praised by Jesus for turning away from household service. Moreover, the presentation of rigid gender roles with men as protectors of vulnerable women ignores the tremendously violent treatment of women in the Bible. Women in the Bible are not simply the helpmate Eve or the blessed Mary, mother of Jesus; they are often the chattel and property of men, who have all the authority. In the Bible, this results in the banishment of the unwilling Hagar into the wilderness (Gen. 21); the horrifying, undeserved execution of the daughter of Jephthah (Judg. 11–12); the rape of Tamar (2 Sam. 13); the rape and dismemberment of the Levite's concubine (Judg. 19–21); and more. Claiming a God-given authority of men over women has had disastrous, immoral consequences for women in the Bible.

Biblical scholar Phyllis Trible, in *Texts of Terror*, which explores some of these violent stories, states that we should see the Bible as a mirror. "If art imitates life, scripture likewise reflects it in both holiness and horror. Reflections themselves neither mandate nor manufacture change; yet by enabling

---

Sex Reassignment Surgery: Cohort Study in Sweden," *PLoS One* 6, no. 2 (February 22, 2011): e16885, http://journals.plos.org/plosone/article?id=10.1371/journal.pone.0016885.

2. Dhejne, Lichtenstein, Boman, Johansson, Långström, and Landén, "Long-Term Follow-Up."

insight, they may inspire repentance. In other words, sad stories may yield new beginnings."[3]

Seeing the Bible as a mirror helps us understand that we are called to discern which parts of the Bible are mandates and which are cautionary tales. Consider, for example, the dangerous ease with which one can justify slavery based on the Bible (e.g., Eph. 6:5, or the pro-slavery argument that Jesus interacted with enslaved people yet never condemned slavery). As people of faith, we have come to recognize that, while slavery is frequently described and condoned in the Bible, it is a moral evil. In the same way, we should recognize that the treatment of women as subject to male domination does not reflect the morality under which we should live. The stories of male domination may tell us what to avoid, not what to practice. The dominant-male/submissive-female paradigm has not only been used to justify acts of violence against women but has led to women being unable to follow their callings in ministry and other aspects of life. For women and men who feel called to live in this kind of authoritarianism, I support your right to choose this for yourselves but not your attempts to subject others to it.

Finally, I sense that the amount of attention given in this chapter to the charges of hate and intolerance reflects the pain of being called those terms. I understand that name-calling does not move the conversation forward and that to be called such things is a difficult experience. Early in the chapter, Dr. Strachan writes, "The Christian preacher, known today as 'intolerant' and a charter member of a 'hate group,' is in point of fact the figure most poised to affirm the full humanity of every person, including those who hate him" (p. 56). While this is theoretically true—the Christian preacher *is* poised to affirm the full humanity of every person—we know it is not realized truth at this time, as the author himself recognizes when he delineates at the outset of his discussion some of the pejorative terms that are leveled at transgender people. The full affirmation of humanity is nonetheless a standard that I think we can agree is both Christlike and a worthy goal. We should be about the business of affirming the full humanity of every person.

Why is it, though, that Christian preachers are often called "intolerant" or a member of a "hate group"? Consider for a moment the fruits of some of these sermons and teachings. To the underage child who has been thrown out of their Christian home because of same-sex desires or gender nonconforming behavior, too young to get a real job, who must turn to survival sex work to obtain a meal, it certainly feels hateful. To the young people contemplating

3. Phyllis Trible, *Texts of Terror: Literary-Feminist Readings of Biblical Narratives* (Philadelphia: Fortress, 1984), 2.

suicide after being denied access to gender-affirming therapy or treatment, it is not life giving. These attitudes are not saving souls but stealing lives.

Not only has the conservative church driven people away, but it has failed to even take a stance against the violence inflicted on transgender people. While some Christians have spoken in favor of laws aimed at preventing violence and discrimination based on gender identity, often the only opposition to these measures comes from conservative Christians. Thus, progress toward ending violence and discrimination is both supported and blocked by Christians. How is the church's mission furthered by tolerating people being evicted from their homes, fired from their jobs, assaulted, or murdered because of their gender identity? Surely we could agree to take steps against violence and discrimination.

In the not-too-distant future, people will read accounts like this and think of them the way we now think of Christian treatises in favor of slavery or against interracial marriage. Those future readers will wonder then what we ask now: Why do people, in the name of Christ, try to limit the human potential and flourishing of others—in this case, particularly women and transgender people?

In fact, I would argue that much of the Christian church's attitude toward sexuality and gender has created a swath of destruction through some people's lives, while justifying the exclusionary behavior of others. When people characterize the church as hateful, they are stating their belief that the church has been deeply sinful through its actions that harm individuals, families, and communities. This is a call to account for condemning and alienating people from their families and their churches for the crime of loving or identifying differently.

2

The Complexities
of Gender Identity

*Toward a More Nuanced Response
to the Transgender Experience*

Mark A. Yarhouse and Julia Sadusky

The title of this book, *Understanding Transgender Identities*, raises these questions: What does it mean to be transgender? and Who is transgender? Although these appear to be straightforward questions, their answers are far from clear, at least if measured by consensus among professionals or among those who identify as transgender today.

To describe oneself as transgender is sometimes done in contrast with people who are cisgender. Trans-, "the other side of," indicates an alternative gender identity from what is expected to correspond with biological sex, and cis-, "on this side of," indicates congruence with one's biological sex. But "transgender" is considered an umbrella term for the many ways people experience, express, or live out a gender identity that is different than what is experienced by people whose gender identity corresponds with their biological sex.

The broader answer to the question of who is transgender might include transsexual persons (persons who adopt a cross-gender identity through the use of cross-sex hormones and/or sex reassignment surgeries or desire to pursue such medical interventions); drag kings and queens (who may engage in cross-dressing behavior primarily for entertainment purposes); people who have a transvestic fetish (in which cross-dressing has come to reflect an emotional attachment to specific attire); people with intersex conditions (various experiences—chromosomal, gonadal, or genital—in which a person is born with sex characteristics or anatomy that does not allow clear identification as male or female); people who push against norms through gender-bending behaviors, nonbinary gender identities, or what we might refer to as emerging gender identities (e.g., genderqueer, genderfluid, agender, **gender expansive**, and so on); and people who suffer from gender dysphoria (the experience of distress associated with incongruence where one's psychological and emotional gender identity does not match one's biological sex). Gender dysphoria can be thought of as residing along a continuum of intensity. At the far end of the continuum, there is clinically significant intensity or impairment in functioning, by which a person could meet the formal mental health diagnostic criteria for gender dysphoria.

Is Gender a Binary Phenomenon, or Is It a Continuum?

"Sex" and "gender" are frequently distinguished with reference to biology and societal role or expression. In other words, "sex" often refers to biological sex and so reflects chromosomal, gonadal, or anatomical differences between males and females, whereas "gender" is often thought of as a reflection of societal role or expression of one's biological sex. Gender identity conveys one's psychological and emotional experience of oneself as male or female or another gender identity other than male/female and may at times be related to how masculine or feminine a person feels.

Three Interpretive Lenses

In our previous work, we describe three frameworks for understanding the topic of gender identity and the people who are navigating gender identity concerns.[1] These frameworks—integrity, disability, and diversity—function as "lenses" through which people "see" research findings, theological matters, and pastoral care.

The integrity framework reflects one evangelical theologian's observation that gender identity conflicts are best understood with reference to "the sacred integrity of maleness or femaleness stamped on one's body."[2] Many

1. Mark Yarhouse, *Understanding Gender Dysphoria: Navigating Transgender Issues in a Changing Culture* (Downers Grove, IL: InterVarsity, 2015), 46.
2. Robert Gagnon, "Transsexuality and Ordination," August 2007, www.robgagnon.net /articles/TranssexualityOrdination.pdf.

conservative Christians resonate with the integrity framework and the emphasis placed therein on the creation story in Genesis 1 and 2, which reflects a God-ordained, male/female sex differentiation. For example, in Genesis 1:26–27, we read,

> Then God said, "Let us make humankind in our image, according to our likeness; and let them have dominion over the fish of the sea, and over the birds of the air, and over the cattle, and over all the wild animals of the earth, and over every creeping thing that creeps upon the earth."
>
> So God created humankind in his image,
>   in the image of God he created them;
>   male and female he created them.

Likewise, in Genesis 2 we read,

> Then the LORD God said, "It is not good that the man should be alone; I will make him a helper as his partner." So out of the ground the LORD God formed every animal of the field and every bird of the air, and brought them to the man to see what he would call them; and whatever the man called every living creature, that was its name. The man gave names to all cattle, and to the birds of the air, and to every animal of the field; but for the man there was not found a helper as his partner. So the LORD God caused a deep sleep to fall upon the man, and he slept; then he took one of his ribs and closed up its place with flesh. And the rib that the LORD God had taken from the man he made into a woman and brought her to the man. Then the man said,
>
>   This at last is bone of my bones
>   and flesh of my flesh;
>   this one shall be called Woman,
>   for out of Man this one was taken.
>
> Therefore a man leaves his father and his mother and clings to his wife, and they become one flesh. And the man and his wife were both naked, and were not ashamed. (vv. 18–25)

Scripture, viewed through the integrity lens, likewise raises concerns when people have pushed back against the male/female binary through cross-dressing behavior associated with sexual practices or when other conditions or experiences are noted. For example, Deuteronomy 22:5 reads, "A woman must not wear men's clothing, nor a man wear women's clothing, for the LORD your God detests anyone who does this" (NIV). Other passages, such as Deuteronomy 23:1—"No one who has been emasculated by crushing or cutting may enter the assembly of the LORD" (NIV)—are often cited as prohibitions for the use of medical interventions to facilitate a cross-gender identity.

Yet Christians have also voiced concern that there is not much treatment in Scripture of all that resides under the transgender umbrella. The question has been asked whether simply citing these passages risks treating the Bible as "a sort of ethical cookbook,"[3] whereas some might conclude that acknowledging gender dysphoria as a real mental health concern, identifying as transgender, or taking steps to manage gender dysphoria are all things that are prohibited in the cited passages. We also see in Scripture "a clear progression . . . which culminates in the implied acceptance of the genitally-mutilated by Jesus in Matthew 19:12, and the conversion, baptism and acceptance into the Kingdom of God of the Ethiopian eunuch in Acts 8:26–39."[4] Deuteronomy 22:5 appears to reflect a caution that the ancient Israelites not participate in religious rituals that were practiced by the Canaanites, which included changing sex roles and cross-dressing behaviors. We have to grapple with how that applies to contemporary discussions about gender dysphoria and the broader transgender umbrella.

This brings us to the second framework: disability. If the strength of the integrity lens is Genesis 1 and 2, the strength of the disability lens is in acknowledging the reality of Genesis 3. When people experience a lack of fit between gender identity and biological sex, those who use this lens may be inclined to think of it as an unfortunate departure from what typically happens. In other words, not everything is lining up properly in rare cases. This lens sees an incongruence between one's gender identity and one's biological sex and doesn't consider it to be a moral issue as such, which is contrasted somewhat with the integrity lens. It leans toward compassion, as the person is not seen as choosing this experience.

In thinking through biblical support for this lens, Christians might be drawn to the emphasis on the reality of the fall (Gen. 3), which has resulted

3. We agree with the Evangelical Alliance Policy Commission, however, when they note that the Hebrew word translated "detests" or "abomination" does convey a response such that "in the sight of God such practices were fundamentally incompatible with the identity of God's people." Evangelical Alliance Policy Commission, *Transsexuality* (Carlisle, UK: Paternoster, 2000), 45.

4. Evangelical Alliance Policy Commission, *Transsexuality*, 46. The story of Philip and the Ethiopian eunuch is sometimes referenced by those who believe there is warrant here for a "third sex" or that perhaps points to what we today describe as gender dysphoria. However, we do not see evidence that eunuchs were either a different gender or gender dysphoric. The reference to eunuchs being "born that way" may refer to people born with ambiguous genitalia; that is the suggestion by Adrian Thatcher. One could also consider a condition comparable to a diminished sexual capacity, although it may be hard to speculate beyond that. The eunuchs in these contexts were most frequently either court officials or slaves. See Adrian Thatcher, *God, Sex and Gender: An Introduction* (West Sussex, UK: Wiley-Blackwell, 2011), 147.

in all sorts of consequences that a person is not directly culpable for. This may shed light on how gender could be experienced along a continuum: in a fallen world, a small percentage of individuals may experience their gender differently than, in between, or outside of the male/female binary. A biblical Christian open to the disability lens would likely see some experiences of transgender identification as an understandable but potentially misguided search for identity. The recent and dramatic increase in referrals to gender specialty clinics has been documented,[5] as has an increase in the number of younger persons identifying as transgender, which may represent this search for identity to some extent. But they would still want to respond with empathy to the distress faced by people with gender identity concerns, especially those struggling with life-threatening dysphoria.

The third lens is the diversity lens. This is the lens that is captivating the culture today. Those who see through the diversity lens see differences in gender identity as signaling an identity and a sense of personhood (a transgender person) to be embraced and celebrated.

Adherents of the diversity lens tend to view people who adopt a cross-gender identity (e.g., a biological male who experiences himself as a woman) or other-gender identity (e.g., an adolescent who identifies as gender expansive) as part of a people group and part of the larger lesbian, gay, bisexual, and transgender community. Diversity advocates may also see the transgender movement as an ideological and political movement indicating progress in deconstructing views of sexuality that they believe are hurtful to transgender persons. They would often reject the existence of a binary for male/female sex difference and would not see it as intended by God from creation. Although we see these claims as lacking biblical support, we can appreciate how they address concerns for identity and community in a way that is quite compelling to many people navigating gender identity concerns.

Biology and Physiology

We think of sex as a binary, meaning that, generally speaking, people are born either male or female. As we indicated above, this is typically with reference to biological sex or chromosomal, gonadal, and anatomical differences.

---

5. In a recent report from The Amsterdam Cohort of Gender Dysphoria Study, Wiepjes and colleagues reported a twenty-fold increase in referrals per year between 1980 and 2015. C. M. Wiepjes, Nienke M. Nota, Christel J. M. de Blok, et al., "The Amsterdam Cohort of Gender Dysphoria Study (1972–2015): Trends in Prevalence, Treatment, and Regrets," *Journal of Sex Medicine* 15 (2018): 582–90. This is a study looking at referrals associated with gender dysphoria. For news coverage on the increase in transgender identification, see https://www.nytimes.com/2016/07/01/health/transgender-population.html.

There are relatively rare exceptions to this binary, of course, including biological intersex conditions. These exceptions could be thought of as proving the rule. Very rarely have we known people with intersex conditions who have celebrated their intersexuality (although this does occur); more often these conditions are a source of significant distress. Examples include a person diagnosed with Klinefelter Syndrome, a genetic disorder of gonadal differentiation in which there is an extra X chromosome (XXY); a person born with incomplete or mixed ovarian and testicular tissues; or a person with Androgen Insensitivity Syndrome as a result of malfunctioning gonads and other prenatal concerns. Christians we have met with have typically understood these experiences to be a reflection of the fall and not God's original, creational intent. If anything, the distress they feel confirms the contrast between their experience and God's plan for their sexuality.

The question that arises with transgender experiences is how best to conceptualize them. How experiences of being transgender are understood is often related to recommended responses. Some assert that this phenomenon is very clearly a problem in the mind rather than in the body. They derive that the solution is mental health counseling rather than medical interventions.

Others view experiences of gender dysphoria as representing what Milton Diamond refers to as "a form of brain intersex."[6] Diamond's conclusion is based on research of the "brain-sex" theory. Briefly, there are areas of the brain that are considered sexually dimorphic structures, meaning they are different between males and females. The brain scripts male and female ways of organizing the world. Male/female differentiation occurs in utero, although the differentiation is solidified later, particularly in puberty. There are two distinct processes in utero that, through exposure to testosterone, lead to the development of male genitalia and a male-differentiated brain. One theory of gender dysphoria is that in rare instances we are witness to the genitalia mapping one direction and the brain mapping the other direction: "a discrepancy may exist between prenatal genital differentiation and brain differentiation such that the external genitals develop, for example, as male while the brain develops as female."[7]

Some of the older research in this area involved studying the brains of male-to-female transsexual persons postmortem and comparing their brain structures to those of cisgender male and female brains. The findings here

6. Milton Diamond, "Transsexuality among Twins: Identity Concordance, Transition, Rearing, and Orientation," *International Journal of Transgenderism* 14, no. 1 (May 2013): 24–38.
7. Cindy Meston and Penny Frohlich, "Gender Identity Disorder," The Sexual Psychophysiology Laboratory, University of Texas at Austin, https://labs.la.utexas.edu/mestonlab/?page_id=582.

were suggestive, but the problem with the design was that the regions of the brain being studied would also be affected by the use of cross-sex hormones, which all participants had been exposed to.

A review by Antonio Guillimon and his colleagues of more recent studies suggests improved methods, where brains of still-living transgender persons who had not yet been exposed to cross-sex hormones could be looked at with the use of MRIs and compared to the brains of cisgender persons.[8] Limitations of these studies include small sample sizes and the presence of some mixed studies that include both homosexual and nonhomosexual individuals with gender dysphoria, where scientists might expect to see differences in specific brain structure.

In light of the findings of these improved studies,[9] the intersex hypothesis seems more plausible. Even without the impact of cross-sex hormones, people with early-onset gender dysphoria (referred to as the "homosexual type" because the person is attracted to persons of the same sex) "have much in common with" people with intersex conditions.[10] These individuals, often referred to as male-to-female (MtF), appear to have a unique "expression of sex differences in their brains." For example, main structures of MtF brains (intracranial volume, gray matter, white matter, and cerebrospinal fluid) are similar to those of cisgender males. However, some cortical regions show feminine volume and thickness and brain cortical thickness, which differed from both cisgender males and cisgender females. Some white matter fascicles (bundled fibers) in MtFs are demasculinized, mainly in the right hemisphere, while others are still masculine.

For biological females who identify as male (female-to-male or FtM), the areas of the cortex that mainly affect body perception are different from those of cisgender males and cisgender females and MtFs. In other words, FtMs appear to have their own phenotype.

These studies appear to support Diamond's observation and raise an interesting question: Is it possible that people who suffer from gender dysphoria may actually be reflecting a "neurodevelopmental condition of the brain" that is analogous to an intersex condition?[11] Put differently, if a person with an intersex condition has shared male/female tissue that makes it difficult

8. Yarhouse, *Understanding Gender Dysphoria*, 68–74.

9. Antonio Guillamon, Carme Junque, and Esther Gomez-Gil, "A Review of the Status of Brain Structure Research in Transsexualism," *Archives of Sexual Behavior* 45, no. 7 (October 2016): 1615–48.

10. Guillamon, Junque, and Gomez-Gil, "Review of the Status of Brain Structure Research," 1627.

11. See Milton Diamond, "Transsexualism as an Intersex Condition," last updated May 20, 2017, https://www.hawaii.edu/PCSS/biblio/articles/2015to2019/2016-transsexualism.html.

to identify the child's sex at birth, is it possible that gender dysphoria is a manifestation of shared "feminine, defeminized, and masculinized morphological traits" (if FtM) or shared "masculine, feminine, and demasculinized traits" (if MtF)?[12] Are we witness to what is analogous to an intersex condition of the brain?

In our previous research, we noted that a biology-based theory is not the only type of theory explaining the etiology, or causes and origins, of gender dysphoria. Other theories highlight environmental factors such as parental preferences for a specific sex in a child, parental indifference to behavior that is **gender atypical**, and insufficient role models (of one's gender identity).[13] The available studies are correlational, which means some of these variables could be either the cause or the result of gender dysphoria.

The question remains: Is gender a binary? Again, we understand Genesis 1 and 2 as indicating that God's creational intent was a male/female binary for sex and alignment between one's gender identity and one's biological sex. The reality today is that, for a small percentage of persons, gender identity does not align with biological sex. In other words, some people don't live at either side of the binary (they live in between or outside the binary) when it comes to gender identity or gender expression. Some of these persons meet diagnostic criteria for gender dysphoria. Of these, some will have a traditional onset and course (childhood or early onset), while we are now seeing an increase in late-onset cases (or rapid onset), potentially reflecting a different developmental trajectory or, in some cases, another phenomenon entirely.[14] We see this as evidence that the fall touches every aspect of human experience, including sex differentiation and gender identity.

Political, Public, and Private Identities

Genderqueer and gender expansive are examples of emerging gender identities, to which we could also add genderfluid, bigender, agender, gender creative, and others. These would be considered nonbinary gender identities because they do not reflect a cross-gender identity (a shift in identity from male to female that relies on the binary itself).

12. R. Fernandez, A. Guillamon, J. Cortes-Cortes, et al., "Molecular Basis of Gender Dysphoria: Androgen and Estrogen Receptor Interaction," *Psychoneuroendocrinology* 98 (2018): 165.

13. Yarhouse, *Understanding Gender Dysphoria*, 76–79.

14. Riittakerttu Kaltiala-Heino, Maria Sumia, Marja Työläjärvi, and Nina Lindberg, "Two Years of Gender Identity Services for Minors: Overrepresentation of Natal Girls with Severe Problems in Adolescent Development," *Child and Adolescent Psychiatry and Mental Health* 9 (2015): 1–9.

It may be helpful to distinguish gender dysphoria from at least some of these emerging gender identities. Gender dysphoria, as noted above, is a diagnosable disorder in which a person is distressed by a lack of congruence between their gender identity and biological sex. Emerging gender identities do not always include dysphoria or personal distress.

How have emerging gender identities come about? Some of what accounts for emerging gender identities is related to the history of the development of a public and political transgender identity. Although we are unable to do justice to all of the relevant history, we would like to review the more salient points, restating an argument we first made in a monograph on the topic.[15]

What we have witnessed in the last century is a shift away from a medical and psychiatric frame of reference to a public and political framework.[16] The designations of "transsexual" (those whose cross-gender identity is facilitated by medical intervention) and "transvestite" (those who engage in cross-dressing behavior) were at one time the salient categories for gender variance. These were medical and psychiatric terms that depended on a relationship between biological sex (related to chromosomes, gonads, etc.) and gender identity.[17]

In his account, Zein Murib notes how in the early twentieth century the medical and psychiatric community separated "inherited traits" (such as chromosomes, hormones, etc.) from "gender identity" (one's awareness and expression of oneself as masculine or feminine) and from "sexuality" (desires and attractions/behaviors).[18] Parsing out biological sex, sexuality, and gender identity was important to the emergence of transgender identity as public and political. A public transgender identity is predicated on the notion that "the sex of the body does not bear any *necessary* or *deterministic* relationship to the social category in which the body lives."[19] In other words, if there is no necessary relationship between one's biological sex and one's gender identity, then gender identities can and ought to be experienced and expressed as a reflection of one's psychological and emotional internal experience.[20]

The language of being "transgender" (as opposed to previous psychiatric categories of "transsexual" or "transvestite") was reportedly the result of an

---

15. Mark A. Yarhouse and Julia Sadusky, *Approaching Gender Dysphoria*, Grove Ethics (Cambridge: Grove Books, 2018), 10–11.

16. Zein Murib, "Transgender: Examining an Emerging Political Identity Using Three Political Processes," *Politics, Groups, and Identities* 3, no. 3 (2015): 381–97.

17. Yarhouse and Sadusky, *Approaching Gender Dysphoria*, 10.

18. Murib, "Transgender," 384.

19. Murib, "Transgender," 384, quoting Susan Stryker, *Transgender History* (Berkeley: Seal Press, 2008), 11.

20. Yarhouse and Sadusky, *Approaching Gender Dysphoria*, 11.

attempt to find a political identity through identifying norms regarding sex and gender as a source of oppression. According to Murib, having a shared source of oppression would allow diverse experiences of gender identity to connect to a broader identity (transgender) and to subsequent "political action." "Transgender," then, became the broad and encompassing term for gender-diverse persons that "marked an important shift away from the identity categories derived by doctors and psychiatrists and imagined a future for transgender as an explicitly public and political identity."[21]

The establishment of a unifying term for diverse gender identities created a more coherent, public, and political gender identity. It also made it possible to set one's gender identity apart from the norm of cisgender experiences and opened up space for an increasing number of what we refer to as emerging gender identities.[22]

A Looping Effect and Emerging Gender Identities

This concise account sets the stage for a discussion of emerging gender identities. Here it may be helpful to draw on what Ian Hacking refers to as a "looping effect" in mental health categorization.[23] The looping effect refers to what happens over time when people respond to their own categorization, how professionals interact with various stakeholders, and whether these labels and categories and interactions may at times bring into existence new ways people experience themselves and the corresponding identity labels that capture that experience.

The looping effect begins by differentiating between human beings and natural phenomena. Hacking offers an example by articulating the difference between labeling a substance and labeling a human being.[24] When a scientist categorizes a substance, such as a chemical compound, that compound does not react to the categorization it has been given. However, when mental health professionals categorize people, this categorization inadvertently expands ways people think about themselves and their history of being categorized in this way.

With gender dysphoria, we have witnessed a shift over time in both the diagnosis (in the shift from "gender identity disorder" to "gender dysphoria" as a diagnostic label) and the criteria (away from an identity concern and today

21. Murib, "Transgender," 387.
22. Yarhouse and Sadusky, *Approaching Gender Dysphoria*, 11.
23. Ian Hacking, *The Social Construction of What?* (Cambridge, MA: Harvard University Press, 1999), 34.
24. Hacking, *Social Construction,* 2–22.

reflecting gender incongruence, which can be distressing) and the interactions with the broader transgender community. Categorizing gender incongruence as a mental health concern is a shift away from seeing it as an *identity* problem to seeing it as an issue of *distress* associated with one's gender incongruence. This was, in part, a result of interactions with members of the broader transgender community who reacted to the stigma associated with mental health labels and viewing their gender identity as a sign of pathology. The larger question is whether shifts in conceptualizations and various interactions, as well as the emergence of specialists who determine categories that inform ways of understanding diverse gender identities, contribute to emerging gender identities (e.g., gender expansive) as "ways of being" gendered in our present culture.

In other words, by making a diagnosis dependent on distress rather than identity, it is possible for people to have or express gender identities without distress. These individuals would not be thought of as having a mental health concern in and of itself; rather, they can now be understood with reference to alternative or emerging gender identities associated with the broader LGBTQ+ community.[25] By moving away from discussions of cross-gender identities toward alternative identities, it is also possible to account for emerging, nonbinary gender identities, which we see as more prevalent today.

Gender Transitioning

How should a Christian who experiences gender dysphoria respond to their experience? Is gender transitioning a solution? The answer to this question for us has been "It depends" or "Only with great caution." We do not see it as the first or best option, and this is reflected in how we integrate the three lenses of integrity, disability, and diversity.

Interpretive Lenses

Earlier in the chapter we discussed common passages in Scripture that support the integrity framework insofar as they establish a biblical account of God's creational intent to distinguish male/female as a binary. Additional passages present strongly worded prohibitions around cross-dressing behavior that raise flags about how best to respond to conditions such as gender dysphoria.

25. Yarhouse and Sadusky, *Approaching Gender Dysphoria*, 12.

In our view, the integrity lens says that there are real, God-given differences between males and females that were intended by God from creation. These differences lay the foundation for morally permissible sexual behavior. As we noted above, this lens is concerned that the integrity of male/female distinctions is forfeited if a person were to adopt a cross-gender identity or pursue medical interventions, such as hormonal treatment or sex reassignment surgery. In contrast with the diversity lens, we find that the exceptional cases of gender incongruence, characterized by a desperate need to cope, support the verity of original male/female distinctions. The experience of these individuals may actually reinforce the importance of the integrity lens. We discover a great deal about God's creational intent by our own experiential knowledge of the consequences when the world is not as it was meant to be.

The theological underpinnings found in the integrity lens certainly give us pause when we consider medical interventions to facilitate gender transitioning. There is also room for reflection about cross-gender identification because of the strength of condemnation of cross-dressing activities associated with pagan religious practices. However, as much as we focus on creational intent in Genesis 1 and 2, we provide care and counsel to people in the reality of Genesis 3; we live in a world touched by the fall, so we thoughtfully consider the implications of that as well.

We can expect that gender identity and the potential for incongruence and distress associated with that incongruence demonstrate the fallen reality in which we live. It seems likely that the sense of maleness or femaleness, in varying degrees with different people, would be fallen like every other aspect of human experience. There is also much we do not understand about causation, which has to at least be a consideration when we think of whether gender identity or anatomy (or both), in the case of those with gender dysphoria, has been touched by the fall. This highlights the importance of being honest about what we currently do and do not know about causation, realizing how future research may further inform the decision-making process.

If one's gender identity is tainted by the fall, it remains a difficult decision whether to bring one's anatomy into accordance with one's gender identity. After all, a person's chromosomes, gonads, and genitalia are intact and are typically understood as instructive of creational intent. However, a person's gender identity—again, as a result of the fall—may be due to something akin to an intersex condition of the brain, which may present a different decision tree for Christians. Consider the possibility of further research supporting that, in rare instances, one's anatomy may have mapped differently than one's brain. Would we then consider that one's gender identity is, in some cases, instructive? Could cross-gender identity and subsequent interventions then be used to facilitate alignment? Such steps might still be reserved for cases of life-threatening gender dysphoria; consequently, gender dysphoria would be likened to other medical or psychiatric diagnoses that have a variety of treatments available, some of which are much more invasive and have more significant consequences over time yet appear to be the only steps available for those who have tried other treatment approaches and found them to be ineffective. In cases of clinical depression, for instance, we begin with talking therapy, medication, or a combination of the two, but more invasive procedures, such as electroconvulsive therapy (which induces a seizure and has more serious side effects, such as potential memory loss), are available when severe depression does not respond to other protocols.

People who draw exclusively from the integrity framework tend to see pastoral care as returning the person to God's creational intent, by which they mean the congruence of gender identity with biological sex. We prefer this too, if at all possible. But our point at the moment is that this lens often emphasizes returning all levels (physical, emotional, psychological, and spiritual) toward God's original creational intent. In pastoral care, this shifts the focus to healing.

This raises the question, How often are people healed of gender incongruence? Our experience has been that, once a person reaches adulthood, it rarely occurs. We have known of a few cases, mostly testimonials, and we do not mean to detract from those stories. Still, they are remarkably few and far between. We have also known people to **detransition**; they experienced regret or conviction that the transition was not what they thought it would be or was no longer in line with how they felt they should live. While we expect this to rise in the coming years, something we will consider in more detail in the next section, it does not at present appear to be a common experience.

We do see evidence that gender dysphoria in childhood tends to resolve on its own in the vast majority of cases. However, once a person reaches late adolescence or adulthood, if their gender dysphoria has not resolved, it does not tend to. The person is living with more of an enduring condition. What does pastoral care in that context look like? Does it matter if the causal pathway may be more likened to an intersex condition of the brain? While we do not know the causal pathway, does that theory give us pause when we think of counsel that might encourage individuals to think of their anatomy as instructive of God's creational intent?

The question is whether ministry is meant to restore creational intent in the way it is commonly talked about. What is restoration of our original creational intent after the fall? We are called by God to be moving closer to our original creational intent—that is, unity with God and perfect conformity to his will. After the fall, this original unity was marred. Physical, emotional, and psychological distress complicate our own sense of unity with God and bring up questions of God's sovereignty and goodness in the midst of our suffering. A theology of healing could imply that God intends that we would experience total healing of distress in this life. This is a challenge for those with enduring conditions, who may receive the message that God's healing will come if they pray harder or do more.

Perhaps another way to think about a theology of healing, though, is that God is more concerned with our spiritual healing than with the healing of our physical, psychological, and emotional wounds in this life. Spiritual healing does not always hinge on the degree to which other wounds are healed. In this way, it is possible for a person to move toward greater spiritual healing and restoration of God's creational intent for their life, and unity with him, while not experiencing healing in physical or psychological aspects of life. Could we take seriously creational intent without making it our goal to be healed of physical or psychological pain?

This is not to say that God does not heal or that we could do whatever we would like to manipulate our physical selves in our fallen experience. This would run the risk of rejecting the value of the body as a way of reflecting God's plan for humanity and dismissing God's miraculous works in every age. Nevertheless, we have seen the damage that comes from expecting God's will for our lives to be synonymous with our own desire to be free from suffering. An emphasis on healing in the material realm can only leave those who do not experience this healing embittered. It also lends itself to people making judgments about what this means about God, or about their own quality of faith. If and when suffering remains in an enduring way, a robust theodicy becomes more pressing. This is where the disability lens is important. It acknowledges both the painful reality of our human condition and the invitation to glorify God in the midst of the time of redemption, as we await the resurrection, our ultimate healing. Even the resurrected body of Christ, though, still bore the wounds of the cross, which can be an additional point for reflection.

The disability lens offers context for the ways in which God may not intend for us to experience the perfect restoration of our creational intent in this life. In making the goal physical or psychological healing, we could assume that a person's spiritual health is evidenced by the degree to which they experience healing in these other spheres of life. If we were to shift the focus to spiritual health, which certainly is not mutually exclusive of other aspects of health, we may find much to consider there. Even as the body may reflect our original creational intent less and less over the course of our life, and ultimately does not reflect this intent in death, we can experience increasing spiritual healing and restoration that coexists with this decline. In fact, we can think of many people who, despite physical and psychological difficulties, demonstrated heroic virtue through increasing unity with God.[26]

In the same way, it seems plausible that we can journey with those whose physical bodies are not healed of the distress of dysphoria, and even those who use various strategies to manage the pain that comes from this, without neglecting the opportunity to attend to and witness their spiritual restoration. The goal then is fostering a person's relationship with God and accompanying them as they allow their relationship with God to inform the decisions they make while navigating life with an enduring condition. In doing so, we bear witness to the fact that they can glorify God in and through their current state and that God's plan for their life is not derailed by their difficulties.

Is there anything to be gained from the diversity lens? This is by far the most challenging lens for us as Christians, as it has tended to uphold individual autonomy and self-determination rather than discerning God's plan for the human person. While we disagree with the answers typically offered within the diversity lens for those with gender-related concerns, it is the only lens attempting to specifically meet the longing for identity and community among those with gender dysphoria. A Christian ministry that wants to be effective will have to address these concerns. It will have to do this in a way that is emotionally and spiritually compelling in order to compete with the siren call arising from the diversity lens and going out to people with transgender concerns.

Psychological and Scientific Perspectives

In our previous work, we offer a more expanded treatment of the psychological and scientific contributions to our understanding of hormonal therapy (HT) and sex reassignment surgery (SRS).[27] We want to revisit that material here, beginning by outlining the various ways a person might pursue a gender transition.

26. Pope John Paul II was diagnosed with Parkinson's disease in the 1990s and yet continued to maintain a rigorous schedule of prayer, speaking, writing, and traveling. He saw the visibility of his own suffering as important, particularly as Parkinson's continued to challenge him, even to the point where he could no longer speak. It was a witness to many of the ways God can be glorified and our lives can have meaning, purpose, and value, even when psychological and physical problems limit our functional capacities.

27. Yarhouse, *Understanding Gender Dysphoria*, 101–24; and Mark A. Yarhouse and Julia Sadusky, "A Christian View of Sex Reassignment Surgery and Hormone Therapy," https://www.scribd.com/document/371504692/Yarhouse-Mark-A-Christian-Survey-of-Sex-Reassignment-Surgery-and-Hormone-Therapy.

Hormonal blockers may be used as an intervention in order to "buy time" for a young person at the onset of puberty. Blockers keep a person from going through the physical changes that are typical for their peers. Puberty is, in this case, delayed for one or more years. Again, the intention is to allow an adolescent, in light of their own sense of gender identity, to decide the direction moving forward.

HT is the use of cross-sex hormones to facilitate a cross-gender identity or manage the experience of gender dysphoria. In the case of a biological male, the use of cross-sex hormonal therapy would involve injections of progestogens, antiandrogens, and estrogen. Biological females who utilize cross-sex hormones typically would be administered testosterone.

SRS refers to one or more surgeries that are considered by a person seeking to adopt a cross-gender identity or alternative gender identity. For a biological male, some of the more likely surgical procedures would include breast implantation or augmentation. These would enhance the breast development that was already taking place after the use of hormonal therapy. Another common intervention is electrolysis or laser treatment in order to remove facial hair.[28] Surgeries that are typical for biological females would involve removing anatomy that has been experienced as a source of significant distress. This would be the case for a biological female who undergoes chest reconstruction to develop a male chest or who removes the uterus by way of hysterectomy.[29]

Within the psychological community, there is an added emphasis on understanding the benefits and drawbacks of taking more invasive steps to manage gender dysphoria. While the considerations within the mental health community may differ in some ways from those raised in theological discussions, it is still worth exploring the physical and psychological implications of the use of HT or SRS.

The research studies available to date have certain limitations that are worth noting at the outset. We want to be careful to critically evaluate methodology, acknowledging that the limitations impact the generalizability of the findings. Most of the studies are observational and cross-sectional in nature, include small sample sizes collected by convenience sampling, do not have a

28. Additional steps that some individuals might consider would be penectomy, removal of one's penis, or orchiectomy, removal of the testicles. Vaginoplasty is the surgical inversion of the penis so that it can be shaped into a vagina.

29. A biological female pursuing a cross-gender identity might consider other interventions such as metoidioplasty. This involves the partial cutting of the clitoris, which was enlarged by the use of cross-sex hormones, so that it could function similarly to a penis. Alternative procedures that would be more invasive include phalloplasty, which is the use of skin grafting to attach a penis or to construct one; vaginectomy, which is the removal or closure of the vagina; and a Salpingo-oopherectomy, which is the removal of ovaries and fallopian tubes.

comparable control group to evaluate outcomes for those who pursue HT or surgery (or both) versus those who do not, rely primarily on self-reporting, and typically follow individuals for only one year after treatment. This last limitation highlights what makes it difficult to understand the long-term impacts of these interventions. Especially since more individuals have access to these options today than ever before, it is important that we commit to improving the quality of research in this area.

Within the available literature, overall sense of satisfaction, quality of life, psychological distress, and risk of morbidity are the variables of interest when it comes to understanding the efficacy of HT and SRS. These tend to be the very factors that motivate individuals to seek more invasive interventions.[30] Thus, we would expect research to inform decisions about managing gender dysphoria. If, for instance, we were to find that symptoms did not improve with HT or SRS, there would be concern about the incremental value of taking more invasive steps and whether other interventions ought to be developed to manage gender dysphoria. Conversely, if we find that distress is significantly alleviated in multiple areas of functioning, we would expect more people to consider it.

Psychological distress and quality of life among transsexual individuals before and after hormonal intervention have been considered through several longitudinal studies. These studies indicate that there were significant decreases in the report of suicide attempts, anxiety and depressive symptoms, and level of functional impairment one year following HT.[31] Manieri and colleagues found that the male-to-female participants reported improved overall and sexual quality of life and improved body image when they were interviewed one year following the first treatment.[32] In another study, even

---

30. Gunter Heylens, Charlotte Verroken, Sanne De Cock, Guy T'Sjoen, and Griet De Cuypere, "Effects of Different Steps in Gender Reassignment Therapy on Psychopathology: A Prospective Study of Persons with a Gender Identity Disorder," *Journal of Sexual Medicine* 11, no. 1 (2014): 119–26; and Ann Haas, Philip Rogers, and Jody Herman, "Suicide Attempts among Transgender and Gender Non-conforming Adults: Findings of the National Transgender Discrimination Survey," *Williams Institute*, January 2014, https://williamsinstitute.law.ucla.edu/wp-content/uploads/AFSP-Williams-Suicide-Report-Final.pdf.

31. Karine Khatchadourian, Shazhan Amed, and Daniel L. Metzger, "Clinical Management of Youth with Gender Dysphoria in Vancouver," *Journal of Pediatrics* 164, no. 4 (2014): 906–11; Marco Colizzi, Rosalia Costa, and Orlando Todarello, "Transsexual Patients' Psychiatric Comorbidity and Positive Effect of Cross-Sex Hormonal Treatment on Mental Health: Results from a Longitudinal Study," *Psychoneuroendocrinology* 39 (2014): 65–73; and Rikke Kildevaeld Simonsen, Annamaria Giraldi, Ellids Kristensen, and Gert Martin Hald, "Long-Term Follow-Up of Individuals Undergoing Sex Reassignment Surgery: Psychiatric Morbidity and Mortality," *Nordic Journal of Psychiatry* 70, no. 4 (2016): 241–47.

32. Chiara Manieri, Elena Castellano, Chiara Crespi, et al., "Medical Treatment of Subjects with Gender Identity Disorder: Experience in an Italian Public Health Center," *International Journal of Transgenderism* 2 (2014): 53–65.

when negative side effects of medical intervention were reported, these did not seem to lead to premature termination of treatment or decreased quality of life.[33] This bolsters the position of advocates for HT as an effective treatment of gender dysphoria. At the same time, findings caution that those with higher levels of pre-treatment psychopathology are at greater risk for poor post-treatment outcomes and continued psychopathology.[34] This tempers the expectations of some clients that HT will always improve functioning in other areas of life.

As we move into the literature on SRS, we find that most of those who pursue this option report satisfaction with their choice, although the evidence is limited.[35] Earlier studies indicate that candidates for these surgeries do not tend to doubt their decision, and that both level of satisfaction and surgical outcomes are improved with consistent post-surgery use of hormones.[36] Even in the studies where individuals have indicated some level of dissatisfaction with surgery, most participants reported an overall sense of satisfaction and improved quality of life. There are certainly reports of dissatisfaction with surgery, but these are rare in the research thus far and have been attributed to dissatisfactory physical results of surgery, elevated distress, or inadequate information and support throughout care.[37]

33. Khatchadourian, Amed, and Metzger, "Clinical Management," 906–11.

34. Colizzi, Costa, and Todarello, "Transsexual Patients' Psychiatric Comorbidity," 65–73.

35. Lea Karpel, Berenice Gardel, Marc Revol, Catherine Bremont-Weil, Jean-Marc Ayoubi, and Bernard Cordier, "Psychological and Sexual Well Being of 207 Transsexuals after Sex Reassignment in France," *Annales Medico Psychologiques* 173 (2015): 511–19; and Mohammad Hassan Murad, Mohamed B. Elamin, Magaly Zumaeta Garcia, et al., "Hormonal Therapy and Sex Reassignment: A Systematic Review and Meta-Analysis of Quality of Life and Psychosocial Outcomes," *Clinical Endocrinology* 72 (2010): 214–31.

36. Yarhouse, *Understanding Gender Dysphoria*, 101–24; Richard A. Carroll, "Gender Dysphoria and Transgender Experiences," in *Principles and Practice of Sex Therapy*, 4th ed., ed. Sandra R. Leiblum (New York City: Guilford, 2007): 477–508; Annika Johansson, Elisabet Sundbom, Torvald Hojerback, and Owe Bodlund, "A Five-Year Follow-Up Study of Swedish Adults with Gender Identity Disorder," *Archives of Sexual Behavior* 39, no. 6 (2010): 1429–37; Louis J. Gooren, Erik J. Giltay, and Mathijs C. Bunck, "Long-Term Treatment of Transsexuals with Cross-Sex Hormones: Extensive Personal Experience," *Journal of Clinical Endocrinology and Metabolism* 93, no. 1 (2008): 19–25; Bram Kuiper and Peggy Cohen-Kettenis, "Sex Reassignment Surgery: A Study of Dutch Transsexuals," *Archives of Sexual Behavior* 17, no. 5 (1988): 439–57; and Karpel, Gardel, Revol, Bremont-Weil, Ayoubi, and Cordier, "Psychological and Sexual Well Being," 511–19.

37. Kuiper and Cohen-Kettenis, "Sex Reassignment Surgery," 439–57; Marsha C. Botzer and Bryant Vehrs, "Psychosocial and Treatment Factors Contributing to Favorable Outcomes of Gender Reassignment" (paper presented at the 14th International Symposium on Gender Dysphoria, Germany, 1995); Anne A. Lawrence, "Factors Associated with Satisfaction or Regret following Male-to-Female Sex Reassignment Surgery," *Archives of Sexual Behavior* 32, no. 4 (2003): 299–315; Luk Gijs and Anne Brewaeys, "Surgical Treatment of Gender Dysphoria in Adults and Adolescents: Recent Developments, Effectiveness, and Challenges," *Annual Review*

There are mixed findings of morbidity rates and psychological distress following SRS. Karpel and colleagues followed individuals who pursued both HT and surgeries between 1991 and 2009 and found that, for the 207 participants, mortality rates were 1.5 percent.[38] Eighty-six percent indicated positive mental health and physical health following surgery. Another study made significant improvements on previous methodology by being the first to use a nationally representative and population-based sample with both a control group and longer-term post-surgery follow-up. Key findings from this study included indication of "substantially higher rates of overall mortality, death from cardiovascular disease and suicide, suicide attempts, and psychiatric hospitalizations" in those who transitioned when compared to the control group.[39] A subsequent study indicated continued risk for suicide among transsexual persons, even ten or more years following transition.[40] Murad and colleagues conducted a systematic review that indicated lower suicide rates post-surgery, although it also showed that male-to-female transsexuals may be prone to worse outcomes than female-to-male transsexuals.[41]

Better understanding the post-surgery risk for morbidity and mortality will be important in subsequent research. Some researchers are concerned that this data may be difficult to come by and that some groups may be uninterested in investing in it, largely due to the trending sociocultural narrative that cross-gender identification or an alternative identity is the solution for those with gender identity concerns.[42] Increases in atypical presentations (e.g., late-onset or rapid-onset cases) and the trend toward decreasing the role of mental health professionals as gatekeepers to medical interventions have led us to wonder whether we will also see increased rates of regret among those who pursue HT and SRS.

One surgeon with over twenty years of experience in the area of reconstructive surgery has noted a trend of increased regret and subsequent requests from his former clients to provide reversal surgeries, particularly among natal

of Sex Research 1 (2007): 178–224; and Karpel, Gardel, Revol, Bremont-Weil, Ayoubi, and Cordier, "Psychological and Sexual Well Being," 511–19.

38. Karpel, Gardel, Revol, Bremont-Weil, Ayoubi, and Cordier, "Psychological and Sexual Well Being," 511–19.

39. Cecilia Dhejne, Paul Lichtenstein, Marcus Boman, Anna L. V. Johansson, Niklas Langstrom, and Mikael Landen, "Long-Term Follow-Up of Transsexual Persons Undergoing Sex Reassignment Surgery: Cohort Study in Sweden," PLoS One 6, no. 2 (2011): 7.

40. Simonsen, Giraldi, Kristensen, and Hald, "Long-Term Follow-Up of Individuals Undergoing Sex Reassignment Surgery," 241–47.

41. Murad, Elamin, Garcia, et al., "Hormonal Therapy and Sex Reassignment," 229.

42. Joe Shute, "The New Taboo: More People Regret Sex Change and Want to 'Detransition,'" Surgeon Says," National Post, October 2017, http://nationalpost.com/news/world/the-new-taboo -more-people-regret-sex-change-and-want-to-detransition-surgeon-says.

females.[43] This cautions us from assuming that all individuals with gender dysphoria ought to pursue a cross-gender identity by way of medical and surgical interventions. We advocate for more research in order to better understand the presentations that are increasingly common, such as late-onset cases of gender dysphoria, nonbinary presentations, and increased rates of natal females experiencing gender dysphoria.

Until more research is available, the broader consensus is that medical and surgical interventions may be helpful in reducing gender dysphoria, at least in the short term, while not necessarily abating psychological distress for some individuals. We do not fully understand the long-term implications of HT and SRS, although financial strain from the need to maintain HT permanently, and other concerns such as infertility, medical complications, and social consequences due to stigma, are noteworthy.

Scientific research does not mitigate the spiritual significance or moral concern regarding such steps for many Christians. Rather, this highlights the challenges for Christians as they wrestle with the broader cultural trends toward pursuing such interventions and the lived experiences of transgender Christians who have already done so. In the cases where gender dysphoria does not abate with less invasive methods, it is clear that individuals and families are faced with weighty decisions, especially when the majority of research to date shows that gender dysphoria is effectively managed through these more irreversible steps. Similarly, since there is little evidence of promising alternative treatments for gender dysphoria, the options for families are limited.

The question for Christians remains how to move beyond discussing issues on which we may not find scientific consensus to considering postures toward real persons within the transgender community.

Responding to the Transgender Community

Perhaps the most important consideration in developing a distinctively Christian response to the transgender community is that we must avoid a one-size-fits-all approach. We see the need to distinguish among (1) those who wish to advance a political identity (advocates), (2) those who are living a public identity (neighbors, acquaintances, etc.), and (3) those who are sorting out a personal identity and may be facing difficult decisions today in light of their gender dysphoria. And we see the value of integrating the three lenses in our response to each. Even this third group, those who have been diagnosed with

43. Shute, "New Taboo."

gender dysphoria or are otherwise navigating gender identity concerns, are not a monolithic group. No single response will be sufficient to capture the nuances we are seeing today. If we continue to see the transgender community as a homogenous group, we will continue to miss the very people we are invited by Christ to respond to. In doing so, we will either choose not to respond, as we would be more comfortable avoiding that which we misunderstand, or we will respond inadequately. This would confirm cultural messages asserting that Christians are unequipped to walk with the marginalized. In order to speak into the lives of others, it is better to get to know them by investing more energy into entering their lives than into talking about them.

People within the transgender community are navigating life with significant challenges, even as cultural norms move to embrace transgender identities. As we noted above, those who identify as transgender are historically at greater risk for significant psychological distress, including anxiety and depression, which, in some cases, result in suicide.[44] There is a fragility to this group that must be kept in mind, but also a resiliency. Conversations about the difficulties faced by transgender people can evoke compassion, but also a sense of fear of saying the wrong thing. This can be enhanced if we only focus on the negatives associated with being part of this community. We may benefit from noting the strength it takes to navigate life when something as integral as sexuality is experienced in a radically different way than it is experienced by most others.

When thinking broadly about forming relationships with members of the transgender community, another consideration is the possibility that many transgender people are wary of Christians. At times, hurtful responses to transgender Christians have been justified by those advocating for "tough love." In some cases, this takes the form of mockery and ridicule by those who claim Christ. It is not surprising, then, that there would be a level of hesitancy on the part of transgender people to invest vulnerably in relationships with other Christians. This may be most evident in those who assert a political identity and are advocates for sociocultural shifts and gender ideology that many Christians would disagree with. As an act of resilience, some advocates, who at one point may have been rejected or deeply hurt by Christians, might be hostile toward Christian faith. Their shared Christian roots may be hard to see. It can be difficult for Christians to know how to engage, especially when culture wars incline us to argue first rather than begin by seeking to understand one another better.

When we think of those who have suffered abuse at the hand of a religious leader, we can understand how difficult it would be to approach God. We can

---

44. Simonsen, Giraldi, Kristensen, and Hald, "Long-Term Follow-Up of Individuals Undergoing Sex Reassignment Surgery," 241–47.

also understand how the victim may generalize all religious representatives as a threat in order to avoid continued painful interactions. The person might subsequently boldly profess their rejection of Christian faith. While we are increasingly able to acknowledge the far-reaching effects on the spiritual lives of victims of abuse and their families, we may be less ready to acknowledge the alienation suffered by transgender Christians in the Christian communities they are part of, and the consequences over time. To acknowledge the hurt and the way that culture wars have exacerbated division can be a helpful first step in building relationships among those we might disagree with when it comes to norms around sex and gender.

Turning now to relationships with those sorting out a personal identity, we are mindful that common Christian language, such as the encouragement to "pick up your cross and follow Jesus" or to "rejoice in suffering," can be less helpful at the outset, particularly when such comments are not made in the context of a relationship and lived out by others in the faith community, including leadership. Anyone who has suffered and heard these phrases can likely attest to this. More often than not, such comments are made by those who have little interest in helping "carry the cross." These phrases more frequently distance the painful experience of the transgender person, as if to say, "Pick up your cross and follow Jesus, but I am not able to help you do it." This is not an uncommon experience, unfortunately, of many in Christian communities. In moments of grief and pain, it can be easier to apply trite one-liners than to acknowledge the angst of the moment and the many questions without answers. When individuals are considering how to cope with something like gender dysphoria, the gravity of the decisions they wrestle with is significant. Remaining in the tension is a challenge for all. This is not to say that Jesus does not call each of us to carry our crosses. Rather, it is a matter of how this is modeled by leadership and communicated in ways that do not negate just how challenging picking up the cross actually is. We fear that if we cannot learn to do it, those experiencing gender dysphoria will assume that their cross is to be carried in isolation. Or they may exchange the cross for the crown that is offered by the diversity lens, potentially rejecting Christian faith as a result.

We turn now to what it would look like to accompany individual transgender people as church bodies and to willingly help them as they navigate the challenges of daily life with gender identity questions.

In our experience, there is no single way that churches engage in ministry to transgender people. This is evident in what we have seen through institutional consultations, particularly with Christian colleges that have begun to develop policies around sex and gender. There is great variety in the policies implemented, and we have found it helpful to organize these policies based on the degree to which they integrate the three lenses while still weighing one more heavily than the others. We hope that this can help us better understand how different Christian churches may draw from the best of the three lenses in their ministry approach. This may also shed light on how individual Christians might develop ministry postures that integrate theological convictions and pastoral care.

Integrated with Elements of the Integrity Lens in the Foreground

One Christian college that is grounded in the "teachings of the Bible as understood in the Protestant Evangelical theological tradition" has a document stating that "God's original and ongoing intent and action is the creation of humanity as two distinct sexes, male and female."[45] While there is recognition of our fallen state (e.g., "due to sin and human brokenness, our experience of our sex and gender is not always that which God the Creator originally designed"), the emphasis is on God's ability "to heal and transform" human "brokenness." Toward this end, the institution does "not affirm attempts to change one's given biological birth sex via medical intervention in favor of the opposite sex or of an indeterminate identity." This understanding informs practical decisions about housing, admission, hiring, student and employee retention, and so on. It sets a tone, letting potential students and staff know how the environment might be for those who experience human brokenness in the area of sex and gender. It also gives clarity about the posture taken toward specific management strategies, such as adopting a cross-gender identity, and sets an expectation that identity, meaning, and purpose are to be found in living a gender identity that is in keeping with one's biological sex.

Integrated with Elements of the Disability Lens in the Foreground

A second Christian college has a policy affirming that people are created with "gifts designed to bring glory to God and edification to the world" and that one of these gifts is our body.[46] It asserts that "all aspects of our bodies and identities should seek first to exalt Christ, recognizing God's deep love for each person." The policy affirms that "God created humans in the Divine image: male and female." However, the reality of the fall means that "complete physical and emotional wholeness for humanity will never fully occur on earth." Specifically, experiences "of sex and gender . . . may not always

---

45. Wheaton College Student Handbook, 2017–18, last updated January 2018, https://www.wheaton.edu/media/student-development-related/student-handbook.pdf, 26–28.

46. George Fox University Position Statement, 2018, https://www.georgefox.edu/transgender/index.html.

be as the Creator originally designed." Whereas the first college emphasized healing and transformation, this policy underscores that "God cares deeply about every person, including their pain and suffering. Hope and contentment in life rely on the knowledge of God's love, compassion and redemption." Turning explicitly to gender identity, this policy states, "Understanding that one's gender identity might not conform to his or her birth sex, we want all students to feel embraced within our faith-imbued community of learning." The policy goes on to say, "Given the varying circumstances of students identifying as transgender, addressing their particular needs will be evaluated on a case-by-case basis, prioritizing the well-being of the individual and community alike." The focus on applying Christian principles of compassion to all, including transgender students, is intentional. This translates into the inclusion of things on campus like gender-neutral bathrooms, in an effort to balance the support for transgender persons with the considerations of the broader community they belong to. Meaning and purpose here could be found in experiencing God's care, love, compassion, and redemption within pain and suffering, even though this may not be realized now.

Integrated with Elements of the Diversity Lens in the Foreground

A third institution offers a "Guide for Students Who Identify as Transgender or Genderqueer."[47] The guide identifies a point of contact at the institution and provides information on relevant services, such as gender-inclusive bathrooms, name change on identification card and some databases, housing options, and communication with professors about gender identity and preferred name and pronouns. This institution also provides information on a group for LGBTQ+ persons, a counseling center support group for LGBTQ+ persons, counselors and chaplain information, opportunities to educate others about gender identity and related experiences, and mentoring options for transgender students. The college offers information on health care and a provider who has years of experience working with transgender persons. It provides insurance benefits for cross-sex hormones (although not for surgery). This institution is intentional in providing resources and visible support on campus as an extension of compassion and a sense of both identity and community to individuals navigating gender identity.

This is what we have seen in terms of the diverse approaches to gender identity and transgender experiences at Christian colleges and universities. We are simply citing these as examples of different approaches among Christian

---

47. Calvin College, "Go-To Guide for Students Who Identify as Transgender or Genderqueer," May 4, 2016, https://calvin.edu/dotAsset/3a87b0de-2a36-44f9-ae1b-5878fdcc9c65.pdf.

institutions. The question remains: How could we translate this for an eccle-
siastical setting that is trying to be faithful to biblical norms regarding sex
and gender?

Integrated Ministry with Elements of the Integrity Lens in the Foreground

We imagine that some church settings whose integration is weighted toward
the integrity lens will focus more on Genesis 1 and 2 and place greater emphasis both on creation and on what redemption is to look like in terms
of restoring original creational intent for congruence between one's gender
identity and one's biological sex. This might be referred to as "healing" from
gender-related distress. Such healing could be held out as an expectation, with
the hope that it would be achieved through corporate worship ministries or
counseling models.

Such an approach may also function as a filter to those interested in visiting
or joining the church by communicating expectations for participation or what
it may look like to sit under the spiritual oversight of leadership. Within this
paradigm, the leadership could be more likely to equate certain resolutions
of gender identity with morality. Expectations around dress and presentation
could be reinforced by the community, encouraging individuals to live in accordance with their biological sex. If a person were to experience continued
distress, the pursuit of other avenues to address gender-related concerns, such
as medical interventions, could be deemed unacceptable by leadership.

In adopting any formal approach, there are benefits and risks attached.
For those who are integrity leaning, the benefits include clarity regarding
doctrinal understandings of sex and gender, which would be reinforced by
formal statements and dialogue with pastoral staff. Another strength could
be the ability to communicate norms around sex and gender that provide a
sense of stability to a majority of children and adolescents. Also, individuals
who share such doctrinal beliefs and believe that the best way to communicate these is through an emphasis on healing will likely feel supported and
protected by policies. At the same time, those who experience gender-related
distress may experience increased distress in such environments and may find
it difficult to remain in such churches. Teenagers in particular may not see a
path for themselves, especially if they have prayed for healing for several years
without experiencing it. Relationships could be severed if a person were to
pursue steps other than healing. The integrity lens, which represents a historically Christian view of sexuality, may not foster an environment of missional
engagement with those who have personally relevant questions about such

teachings. While the integrity-leaning approach may be suitable to those who make up the majority of such churches, those navigating the difficult experience of gender dysphoria may feel forgotten if it does not continue to engage with questions of identity and community in a spirit of compassion. Another risk is that the very questions members are asking can be oversimplified, leaving them without a sense of safety to express hurt and frustration with their challenges or with the current church climate.

Integrated Ministry with Elements of the Disability Lens in the Foreground

We can also imagine other churches would integrate the three lenses and give greater weight to the disability lens. They could teach the creational intent of God for congruence between sex and gender but also acknowledge and underscore the effects of the fall. Such churches will approach transgender persons or persons navigating gender identity concerns with empathy and compassion, perhaps comparing challenges people face in these realms not with other sins of volition but with other conditions that do not reflect the original intent of God at creation. This could be modeled after the treatment of those who struggle with depression or anxiety concerns, moving the discussion from a question of morality and healing to a question of living with an enduring condition. Perhaps strategies to cope with gender dysphoria would be understood as supportive care. This also leaves room for discussions of theodicy and how to make meaning out of the sufferings of this life without blaming the person for the difficulties they face.

A church that is reflecting such an approach would create policies and procedures that are broad enough to give the senior leadership the latitude to walk with each person on a case-by-case basis in terms of various resolutions. This could mean that the church is hesitant to take any pathways off the table, as it were, to be able to journey with individuals, so that pastoral care is not contingent on the direction they choose to go for resolution of gender-related concerns.

Within this approach, there is room for flexibility; one standard is not set for all. It allows those who are part of the church the opportunity to learn from and alongside the individuals with gender-related concerns. It allows individuals navigating these concerns to be mindful that God does not reject them in their difficulties, and they may resonate with the framework of disability in light of their significant pain. It also serves as a model for members to respond compassionately to one another. Removing the moral category from one's experience of gender dysphoria can give freedom for families who are wrestling with decisions in this sphere to ask hard questions. It may even give all who, in varying degrees, experience suffering and the effects of the fall on their human experience greater freedom to be transparent with others in an environment where difficulties and challenges do not result in admonishment but in accompaniment.

Still, the disability-leaning approach could leave room for gossip and scandal, especially when individuals pursue a resolution that is deemed immoral by others. Individuals who are more diversity leaning may shy away from such church bodies because the language of disability may not seem to them a robust pathway for flourishing. They may react to the notion that their experience is pathologized, especially if they identify as transgender but do not report experiences of distress. For those who do experience gender-related distress, as we've already noted, pat answers such as "this is your cross to bear" are often insufficient. This is especially the case if a robust theology of suffering is not offered and modeled by others within the church. Suffering in isolation can translate into being subject to pity, rather than compassion. This only enhances feelings of distress and makes it difficult for the person with gender dysphoria to experience community and purpose in their pain. They may desire to find the redemptive value of their suffering but find it lacking.

Integrated Ministry with Elements of the Diversity Lens in the Foreground

Still other churches may prioritize sending messages, both formally and informally, acknowledging that, for many people, transgender identity and cross-gender presentations will be a reality and a preference. Churches of this sort will likely find ways to incorporate transgender persons into the community through various accommodations as an act of hospitality (e.g., single-stall bathrooms), fewer gender-inflected activities (e.g., reducing the number of boy/girl breakout sessions in youth group), thinking through housing arrangements on retreats for those navigating gender identity, and so forth.

Such a church is intentional about how it wishes to be experienced by people who identify as transgender. It is a contrast to those who lean toward the integrity lens in that it does not see various resolutions as involving moral categories as such (similar in a way to the disability lens). It is perhaps missional in this sense, identifying a way of relating to a broader community, even if all members do not see eye-to-eye on the importance of this. This is quite different than the other two approaches because it seeks to make the church an environment that is an oasis for transgender individuals. It takes seriously moving to the margins of society, and it does so without second thought. Not only that, but it makes marginalized groups a priority, which can be incredibly healing to people who often feel invisible in Christian churches. A church here casts a compelling vision for the person with gender dysphoria, so that they can integrate their gender identity and faith. It would communicate that these persons are "at home" in the faith community.

The drawback associated with this approach is that openness to diverse experiences could leave less room to teach norms regarding sex and gender, which have been upheld by conservative churches consistently over time. Such churches may find it to be more difficult to discuss Genesis 1 and 2 and its implications without offending members of the church community. Seeking out the broader community and inviting those who may come with a range of experiences and perspectives on human sexuality may lead to confusion regarding the theological and biblical foundations of the church's understanding of sex and gender. Further, it may distance individuals from the church body who feel that their concerns and questions regarding church policies are not considered.

A Further Integration?

The tension remains as to whether a church could integrate the three lenses in such a way that they could maintain and teach norms regarding sex and gender, facilitate an environment of understanding and compassion for those whose experiences may be outside of those norms, and provide community, meaning, and purpose to transgender persons. No doubt, this is hard to imagine. In a polarized culture, the only solution to this tension is division, in which churches that resonate with one of the three lenses become a hallmark of that lens and reject the others. What we offer is the possibility for churches to consider what it could look like to draw from each of the three lenses in a way that maintains doctrinal positions and offers the gift of hospitality to all persons. Caring as deeply about scandal and gossip as we do about norms of sex and gender can guide leadership to lead by example in calling on all church members to be gracious and understanding of the difficulties faced by transgender Christians.

When it comes to ministry with transgender persons, it can be helpful to take a long-term view. Relationships are not built overnight, and much of the opportunity to speak into the life of another person hinges on relationship. What, then, is a helpful approach to forming and maintaining such relationships over time? Humility goes a long way, as it captures a recognition of what we know and don't know about the experience of the transgender person, about the moral implications of the various strategies a person would consider, or about the possible consequences, both physical and spiritual, of different decisions made over time. As we have already mentioned, sometimes those in ministry can develop a posture of dispensing one-liners that do not apply to the unique experience of the transgender Christian. In general, we have found it helpful to intentionally ask questions and convey a genuine desire to understand their experience, which can go a long way toward establishing the foundation for a healthy relationship.

Perhaps the most challenging consideration is when a person is thinking about transitioning, whether through hormonal or surgical means. What is the ministry posture in this case? Would a church walk with someone through a time of decision making and discernment, even if the person were to consider not to take any options off the table? Under what circumstances would medical steps be taken off the table by church leadership? If the church shepherds people on a case-by-case basis, is there any set of circumstances that would warrant further reflection and discernment? What if management strategies have been considered in a step-wise fashion but most have now been exhausted and the person is in great distress? What if the church leadership had been working as part of a multidisciplinary team that accurately diagnosed gender dysphoria and any co-occurring concerns, and treated the co-occurring concerns but still supported further steps for the well-being of the person? Would the church support the person through that time and afterward and continue to deepen that person's faith and relationship with God?

It is one thing to show empathy to someone who has transitioned, but to stay in that person's life for the long haul raises questions for ministry. For example, if a person has already transitioned from female to male and asks to attend your men's Bible study, what is the best approach? Is the person welcome to attend in the spirit of deepening their relationship with Christ? Is the person expected to share his story or journey with others in attendance? Would you inform others who are in the study in advance? Would you expect the person to detransition or have other expectations the person would need to meet in advance of attending? Would you distinguish between a missional, outward-reaching Bible study and a study for those who are members of the church?

As we have seen throughout this chapter, there is no single experience of navigating gender identity concerns that captures all the experiences of people who identify as transgender. We don't know who is sitting across from you and whether they suffer from life-threatening gender dysphoria or whether their experience is any one of several other presentations we've discussed. But we know that there are helpful approaches to take in forming a relationship. We would recommend a willingness to be "caught up" on the life of the person in front of you, rather than making blanket statements that enact judgment on behavior before understanding the context of a person's life. This is an invitation to learn a person's history, as ministers often seek to do, to learn the chapters of their story that led them to this point and the ways they have looked for and seen God in and through their life. Receptivity to the story, even without knowing the solutions for practical problems, goes a long way.

This willingness to listen is certainly a challenge for all, but an increasingly necessary one, particularly in the polarized state of our nation. Christians are asking questions about gender identity and looking to their faith communities for support. People we have worked with are desperate for pastoral guidance as they make decisions about identity, community, and managing dysphoria. If they do not find support, at least in the form of a listening ear, we often find that they will leave the church. This is not the same thing as agreement with all of the choices a person is making, and we are not sure it ought to be. Rather, it is an earnest wrestling with these questions, for the sake of all. Unfortunately, it is hard for fellow Christians to respond to questions if they have not taken the time to reflect on them. We too often wait to ask questions until the questions become our own.

Ministry is much more complicated when we reflect on the questions faced by transgender Christians and seek to provide an atmosphere of hospitality for them. Nevertheless, this is an invitation to anticipate the needs of those who wonder whether they are wanted when they walk into a Christian church. To make space for individuals and families navigating questions around gender identity means to embrace the suffering of others, suffering that many have the luxury of themselves avoiding. The moment when Simon of Cyrene was commissioned to carry Jesus's cross comes to mind (see Matt. 27:32; Mark 15:21). It was not Simon's cross to carry, he may have thought. He was not familiar with the terrain, did not know where the cross would lead him, and would have had an easier day if he had not been asked. But Simon was asked. And so, he carried the cross. Little did he know that beneath this cross he would come face-to-face with the person of Jesus Christ.

Too often Christians think of ministry with a one-up posture, where we come to serve and uplift the downtrodden. Unfortunately, to be treated in this way is degrading of the dignity of the person and forgets that God is glorified in and through the people we encounter in ministry. We have something to learn from others, even as they also navigate life imperfectly. As any person who has done mission work can attest, the fundamental lesson is that we receive more than we are given when we engage in authentic ministry. We, like Simon, may find that in ministry to people who suffer from gender dysphoria we come face-to-face with the person of Jesus Christ.

Response to Mark A. Yarhouse
and Julia Sadusky

Owen Strachan

commend Mark Yarhouse and Julia Sadusky for their thoughtful, compassionate, and informative chapter. Their compassion for fallen men and women is evident, and the depth of research on the matters at hand is clear. It is worth noting that, in the broader secular academy, Yarhouse and Sadusky might be read as on the right—even the far right—where in the Christian community, the pair would be seen as more in the middle. As a graduate of one of the first colleges to implement a full-fledged embrace of LGBTQIA+ identity—Bowdoin College—I sense the tension they may well face.

The good news for us all is that we are not left to manage these matters by ourselves. As believers, we have an authoritative revelation that frames the way we see the world and approach its fallenness. In the Bible, furthermore, identity as a subject occupies no background role. On the very first page of Scripture, Moses quotes almighty God himself on the identity of the human race. God has made two who are one. The image-bearers who fill the earth, that is, are one race, but they are "male" and "female" (Gen. 1:26–28). We note this carefully: In the first sentence that the Lord utters, recorded in the Word, about humanity, sex figures prominently—binary sex, male and female, man and woman. The binary is carved into the earth.

Yarhouse and Sadusky pay homage to this reality, as every Christian must. But they introduce a destabilizing element as well, an element on display in this paragraph:

> The theological underpinnings found in the integrity lens certainly give us pause when we consider medical interventions to facilitate gender transitioning. There is also room for reflection about cross-gender identification because of the strength of condemnation of cross-dressing activities associated with

131

pagan religious practices. However, as much as we focus on creational intent in Genesis 1 and 2, we provide care and counsel to people in the reality of Genesis 3; we live in a world touched by the fall, so we thoughtfully consider the implications of that as well. (p. 112)

They expand on this idea in the following section:

The question is whether ministry is meant to restore creational intent in the way it is commonly talked about. What is restoration of our original creational intent after the fall? We are called by God to be moving closer to our original creational intent—that is, unity with God and perfect conformity to his will. After the fall, this original unity was marred. Physical, emotional, and psychological distress complicate our own sense of unity with God and bring up questions of God's sovereignty and goodness in the midst of our suffering. A theology of healing could imply that God intends that we would experience total healing of distress in this life. This is a challenge for those with enduring conditions, who may receive the message that God's healing will come if they pray harder or do more. (pp. 113–14)

Yarhouse and Sadusky are quite right. The question before us in this book and in the broader theological discussion in evangelical circles is this: If we agree that God saves and restores sinners, what does this saving and restoring work look like in the life of the born-again believer? This is the central matter in the intraevangelical conversation. My fellow authors rightly identify God's "creational intent in Genesis 1 and 2." Then, however, they suggest that a postfall world complicates our conception of what we could call "re-creational intent." I agree with them that it takes hard work to answer this question well, and that the working out of our salvation will be challenging and sometimes frustrating. I disagree with their contention that our re-creation has no clearcut *telos*, or—to put it differently—that some Christians can find this *telos* while others cannot.

When God saves us, he is not stamping us as redeemed and then leaving us to wander, hapless, in the forest, until he zaps us away. When God saves us, we cease walking on the broad path to destruction and begin walking on the narrow way toward glory. We who are image-bearers are now oriented toward Christ, not toward Adam. Adam was the original image; Christ, the apostle Paul teaches, is the true image (Col. 1:15). Christ is the *telos*. Our sanctification involves the Spirit beautifying us, making us more like Christ, conforming us to his likeness (Rom. 8:29). Once we were in rebellion against God; now we have a new name, a new identity, and a new nature, and we are a new creation (Rom. 6; 8).

This matters greatly for our bodies and our identity. If we are a man who comes to Christ, we are not a gender-neutral Christian but a Christian man. If we are a woman who comes to Christ, we are not a gender-neutral Christian but a Christian woman. In conversion, God begins the lifelong work of purifying us and enabling us to honor God with body, soul, and mind. We now are freed to become a biblical man, and freed to become a biblical woman. But we do not make up what this looks like; we recognize that Scripture teaches us certain truths about the sexes, truths that only the redeemed can consciously and joyfully magnify. We train our sons to be protectors, providers, and leaders in the image of Christ. We train our girls to be feminine and to embody a gentle and quiet spirit as a demonstration of womanly beauty. When we live in these ways as believers, we may know with assurance that we are living as God intended. The "creational intent" was obscured in us to some degree, but now, re-creation has happened for us all.

Such biblical theology in no way suggests that sanctification means "total healing of distress." Every Christian must battle for holiness, fight the flesh, and put the old man to death (Col. 3:1–11). This is a daily fight. Yes, we are saved in an instant, but we fight sin and temptation all our days. This biblical truth does not and must not draw us away from the *telos* though. Those who feel inclined to cross-dress for whatever reason, and who then come to faith in Christ, may well feel the pull of the flesh to a degree for the rest of their lives. They may have to fight the pagan instincts of the old nature, in other words. But this does not mean that they should see these instincts as a "disability," nor does it mean that they should surgically or pharmacologically alter their bodies. It means that they should do precisely what every believer fighting myriad patterns of sin and temptation must do. They must confess their sinful urges, reject ungodly temptations, and pray for fresh strength to honor God by the power of his Spirit.

I understand why Yarhouse and Sadusky point to the three different approaches to transgender. Further, they are far more careful than many. I am thankful for this. But I must also say this: they should not encourage people who experience gender dysphoria or cross-sex instincts to embrace them in any form or fashion. They frame their multimodel approach as more "compassionate" than the essentialist vision, but it is not. Compassion must never be separated from the truth. The ministry of truth *is* the ministry of compassion. There was no more compassionate person than Jesus Christ, and he called sinners to break with their sin in encounter after encounter. There was no perspectival framework he offered the woman at the well; she was to stop committing adultery at once. The rich young ruler heard nothing about managing his interest in wealth or being a slightly less disobedient sinner; he was to sell everything he had and follow Christ. Pontius Pilate was condemned by the silent Christ, and Christ offered him no murmur of understanding given Pilate's extreme political sensitivities; Pilate is the man who sent Jesus to his death, and history will know him as such until the last page turns.

The Bible, we must reiterate, will not allow us to manage our sin. It summons us to kill it. This, Yarhouse and Sadusky rightly note, is no trifling matter. It is difficult. It is a death to self. This is not clean, antiseptic language. It is visceral, bloody, and wrenching. For many of us—perhaps all—following Christ is going to mean struggling against ourselves for the glory of God. No psychological approach can soften this reality. There are no halfway measures that will take the sting away. By God, we are turning away from Satan to God. By God, we are leaving paganism behind.

We may comment on one further matter. I sense that Yarhouse and Sadusky might consider the foregoing material injurious to missiological engagement. They hint at this when they write the following about the "diversity" framework: "Churches of this sort will likely find ways to incorporate transgender persons into the community through various accommodations as an act of hospitality (e.g., single-stall bathrooms), fewer gender-inflected activities (e.g., reducing the number of boy/girl breakout sessions in youth group), thinking through housing arrangements on retreats for those navigating gender identity, and so forth" (p. 127).

With respect, I believe the exact opposite. The church is not to pitch itself somewhere slightly below what we could call the "Ideal Spiritual Mark." In other words, we do not soften our spirituality to attract lost people. Instead, we are to be rich in good works, and so present a powerful testimony to a watching world (Matt. 5:16). It is not our blend of worldliness and faith that draws the lost but our generosity and our "submission that comes from [our] confession of the gospel of Christ" (2 Cor. 9:13 ESV). Our "honorable" conduct and "good deeds" lead unbelievers to "glorify God on the day of visitation" (1 Pet. 2:12 ESV).

This means for the present conversation that local churches should in no way soften their teaching and practice regarding biblical sexuality. We should not seek an artful mingling of culture and Christ in order to attract those wrestling with their "gender identity." We should instead teach and model the beauty, the doxological joy, of living as a man or a woman in captivity to God. We are not our own; we cannot treat ourselves as blank anthropological slates; we are those who have by divine aid submitted to God. We are under his reign. We obey him comprehensively and gladly.

To make this more granular, we must not blur our understanding of the sexes through neutralized bathrooms. We should hold more, not fewer, "gender-inflected activities." Where our culture encourages us to see sexual difference as a negative, we should push the exact opposite way, and celebrate the glory of manhood and the beauty of womanhood. All around us we find people ravaged by fatherlessness, divorce, and destroyed families. Our solution is not to cease talking about the biblical vision of the sexes, the family, and the body. Our solution is to graciously and directly answer the very questions people are raising all around us.

In sum, Mark Yarhouse and Julia Sadusky are absolutely right to counsel compassion for individuals who feel drawn to a different identity than their birth sex. They are correct to call for careful and faithful presence in the lives of such individuals. The gospel of divine grace is the answer for our sexual confusion. The local church is the common hospital for every born-again believer, the place where we fight sin until our final breath. We benefit in many ways from medical wisdom and psychological testimony, but as Christians we are a uniquely Word-driven people. The Word is not lacking when it comes to addressing transgender as an identity and a struggle. The Word is sufficient.

The church that preaches and loves and counsels the Word stands ready—and must stand ready—to speak truth in love to those ruined, as we all are, by the enemy's lies.

Response to Mark A. Yarhouse
and Julia Sadusky

Megan K. DeFranza

D r. Mark Yarhouse and Dr. Julia Sadusky have offered conservative
Christians a valuable resource in this chapter. I found most helpful their (1) admission of complexity, (2) articulation of theological
lenses, (3) evaluation of the current state of scholarship, (4) recommendations
to cisgender Christians on how to build relationships with transgender people,
and (5) illustrations of the practical implications of each lens by examining
policies adopted by three Christian universities and suggestions as to how
these might serve as a helpful guide for policy development by churches with
similar theological views. Although addressed to theologically conservative,
cisgender Christians (with the unfortunate consequence of "othering" transgender Christians), their chapter provides resources for Christians of various
theological persuasions to think carefully about the ramifications of their
theology, pastoral care, and accompaniment of transgender people, Christian and non-Christian alike. My own theological perspective, outlined in
my chapter in this volume, brings me to different conclusions on a number
of points, but I think it is valuable to note much common ground between
our arguments.

Complexity

Too many Christians have responded to transgender people with simplistic platitudes: "God only made male and female!" "Find your identity in
Christ!" "Carry your cross!" Simplistic responses come not only from conservatives but also from liberal Christians: "God loves everyone!" "Don't
judge, lest you be judged!" The truth of the matter, as Yarhouse and Sadusky

136

helpfully explain, is that transgender experiences are diverse, our understanding of the formation of gender identity is in its infancy, and studies
about the benefits and risks of medical interventions are not unanimous in
their findings. Considering this, their call for Christians to adopt a posture
of humility—a humble willingness to learn the science and listen to the
stories of transgender people, especially trans Christians—is the proper
place to begin.[1]

Integrity

I value the integrity of Dr. Yarhouse and Dr. Sadusky's scholarship. They
honestly report when findings from psychological studies do not line up
with assumptions often made by those with a conservative theological
lens. Christians who believe transgender identity is not what God intended
would prefer research showing that transitioning does not bring greater
psychological well-being to transgender people. Indeed, other publications
by evangelicals have tended to downplay the effectiveness of transitioning,
hormone replacement, and surgeries by emphasizing the few exceptions
to these data.[2] But our authors admit that "detransitioning" is uncommon
and that most transgender people who choose surgical transition "report
satisfaction with their choice" even though "evidence is limited" (p. 118).
Similarly,

> both level of satisfaction and surgical outcomes are improved with consis-
> tent post-surgery use of hormones. Even in the studies where individuals
> have indicated some level of dissatisfaction with surgery, most participants
> reported an overall sense of satisfaction and improved quality of life. There
> are certainly reports of dissatisfaction with surgery, but these are rare in
> the research thus far, and have been attributed to dissatisfactory physical
> results of surgery, elevated distress, or inadequate information and support
> throughout care. (p. 118)

It takes integrity to present the facts as one finds them, rather than as
one might like them to be. It also takes integrity to challenge those within
one's own theological tradition. Yarhouse and Sadusky challenge fellow
conservatives to stop treating gender difference as more troubling than other
actions they would consider violations of Christian teaching. "Caring as

---

1. This is spelled out most clearly at the end of their article (pp. 129–30).
2. Evangelical Alliance Policy Commission, *Transsexuality* (Carlisle, UK: Paternoster, 2000).

deeply about scandal and gossip as we do about norms of sex and gender can guide leadership to lead by example in calling on all church members to be gracious and understanding of the difficulties faced by transgender Christians" (p. 128).

While I appreciate their integrity as illustrated by the evidence presented thus far, I am frustrated that they label the traditionalist view the "integrity lens" because this too easily biases the reader. Who, after all, is *not* in favor of integrity? The strengths and weaknesses of each lens are presented with more balance at the end of the chapter than at the beginning, where they write, "Many conservative Christians resonate with the integrity framework and the emphasis placed therein on the creation story in Genesis 1 and 2, which reflects a God-ordained, male/female sex differentiation" (p. 103). They could have written, "which *they believe* reflects a God-ordained male/female sex differentiation." This rephrasing would have reflected a more nuanced appreciation of biblical interpretation. Each of their three lenses is a theological framework through which one reads a text. By its very nature, a lens influences what we see and do not see. Too often conservative Christians fail to admit that their reading of a biblical passage is just that—a *reading* of the text, an *interpretation*. What looks clear to them may not look clear to other Christians, for reasons that also reflect the integrity of their different theological viewpoints.

In my chapter, I show how Christians can employ the diversity lens with integrity by reading the opening chapters of Genesis in the context of the whole Bible. The Scriptures present us with complex, compelling stories that, when read together, reveal the shocking beauty of God's redemptive work— the folding of "others" into the family of God, those whose inclusion is initially a challenge for those already within the fold. We find this thread woven through Isaiah 56; Matthew 19; Acts 8 and 15; and Revelation 7. When read together, they show how those who do not fit the categories found in the garden of Eden or the purity laws of the ancient Israelites are, nevertheless, welcomed and blessed as they are. Eden is not the end of the story. Those deemed outsiders in the earlier parts of God's story are welcomed in later chapters, revealing what nineteenth-century hymnist Frederick Faber penned so beautifully: "There's a wideness in God's mercy."

Intersex

Another area of commonality between our chapters is Yarhouse and Sadusky's acknowledgment of the "plausibility" of the "intersex hypothesis" (p. 107;

see also pp. 112–13). At the same time, it is important to clear up a few in-accuracies in their presentation of some intersex variations. For example, it is untrue that people with Androgen Insensitivity Syndrome (AIS) have "malfunctioning gonads" (p. 106). People with AIS have the typical male chromosome pattern, which initiates undifferentiated gonads (the first stage of prenatal infant development) to change into testes. These testes function normally, producing the typical levels of hormones for other XY people. The difference is that the cells of people with AIS are "insensitive" to the androgens produced by their functioning gonads. Those with Complete AIS cannot process any androgens (even typical female levels). Those with Partial AIS only respond to some of the androgens. Due to this insensitivity in cellular tissue, the genitals do not masculinize as one would expect for a child with XY chromosomes. In Complete AIS (the more common form), the baby looks like a typical female baby. Differences are not usually discovered until puberty, when menstruation never begins. Noteworthy is the fact that these functioning testes continue to produce typical levels of hormones for XY in-dividuals, which are then converted by the body into usable estrogen so that the girl develops female secondary sex characteristics (breast growth, skeletal structure, etc.). Truly, our bodies are "fearfully and wonderfully made" (Ps. 139:14). Unfortunately, because doctors and parents are troubled by a person who identifies as female, whose body appears female on the outside, yet has XY chromosomes and healthy testes, it is sometimes the case that their testes are removed upon discovery (often without their consent). Tragically, this castration in the name of medical care often leads to patients' ill health, as synthetic hormones are not as healthy as the hormones made by their own bodies. The rigid binary framework, which some believe to be decreed in Genesis 1, actually leads to medical malpractice and ill health in the midst of "caring" for women with Complete AIS.

It is the unnecessary assumption of the binary that leads to the mistreat-ment of intersex children—medical attempts to "correct" their bodies through medically unnecessary castration and plastic surgery. It is also the assumption of the binary that leads to feelings of distress among some intersex people. The authors write, "Very rarely have we known people with intersex condi-tions who have celebrated their intersexuality (although this does occur); more often these conditions are a source of significant distress" (p. 106). Yarhouse and Sadusky argue, "If anything, the distress they feel confirms the contrast between their experience and God's plan for their sexuality" (p. 106). But in my own conversations with intersex people, I have learned that the distress that some experience is often relieved simply by meeting other people with intersex variations. It is not the variation that causes the distress but the feeling of isolation that can come from being told one's body is "not right." Kimberly Zieselman, executive director of InterACT (a nonprofit working to establish legal protections for intersex children), insists that "meeting other people is the most important thing, the most important 'therapy' an intersex person can get."[3] Intersex Christians can experience distress due to having no theological framework to view their biological differences as anything other than a "result of the fall." The intersex people I talk with find great relief (and joy!) upon discovering that Jesus mentions intersex variations in Matthew 19:12 in the language of the "naturally born eunuch." Many do come to accept themselves and celebrate their intersex traits once they have another lens through which to understand themselves.

The Logic of Distress

Dr. Yarhouse and Dr. Sadusky employ a similar argument when interpreting the dysphoria that some transgender people feel. "We find that the exceptional cases of gender incongruence, characterized by a desperate need to cope, support the verity of original male/female distinctions. . . . We discover a great deal about God's creational intent by our own experiential knowledge of the consequences when the world is not as it was meant to be" (p. 112). I will concede that sometimes we humans do feel distress from transgressing "the way things were meant to be," but not always. Sometimes distress is ill founded.

I used to be distressed by the fact that I was one of very few women studying theology at my Bible college. I thought there was something wrong with me because I didn't aspire to children's ministry. My distress was caused by enforced rigid gender roles, and my distress was relieved when I learned to name patriarchy for what it is and to accept the ways God made me, even if I differed from many of my female friends. Similarly, my father-in-law felt distress when he was punished for not writing with the "right" hand in parochial school. While left-handedness is not the majority experience, Christians no longer see this biological variation as something troubling or "sinister" (the Latin for "left" is *sinistra*). The distress of left-handed people has been alleviated by acceptance of natural variation in handedness.

We should note that the logic of distress could also be used to point the other way. Given that transgender people experience significant decrease in distress post-transition, our conclusion could be that transition is God's intent.

---

3. Personal interview in the documentary *Stories of Intersex and Faith*, directed by Megan K. DeFranza, Lianne Simon, and Paul Van Ness (Springfield, TN: Intersex and Faith, 2018).

Conclusion

Transgender Christians are likely to find Yarhouse and Sadusky's chapter "othering," as it is written for cisgender Christians ministering "to" transgender people. Nevertheless, theirs is a valuable contribution for the way it calls cisgender Christians to listen to and learn from God's transgender children, even if through the lens of disability. Their encouragement of a humble learning posture in the face of diversity and complexity surely moves conservatives in the right direction. I hope that, one day, they can move past the disability framework to value God's transgender children for the gifts they *are*.

Response to Mark A. Yarhouse
and Julia Sadusky

Justin Sabia-Tanis

Let me begin my response with the conclusion: Mark Yarhouse and Julia Sadusky describe ways in which a church community might pastorally approach the presence of transgender people, including the clear understanding that there is no single narrative. I appreciate the thoughtful tone of their discussion. The variety of experiences the authors articulate is very similar to the range of attitudes I found among religious groups in the late 1990s when I first started researching gender identity and the church. At that time, I spoke with Christians from conservative churches who considered medical treatment for gender dysphoria as a matter between individuals and their doctors, not a spiritual issue. I talked to liberal Christians who felt that transgender people needed counseling to overcome their desire to transition. And, in both cases, I encountered the opposite: conservatives who felt that transgender people needed mental health care and liberals who readily accepted transgender people. What these different positions had in common was a focus on pastoral care and well-being, not on morality and sinfulness. In each case, pastors and church leaders made their own decisions about how best to support an individual in their midst.

As we moved into the new millennium, these positions hardened and moved away from a pastoral focus to polarizing conversations about sin, morality, and policies. I have long felt that a pastoral approach is much more likely to yield faithful, compassionate responses from people of faith, including transgender people, our families, and our church communities. The pastoral approach modeled in this chapter is vital to restoring conversations across the divides in our faith communities and society. I appreciate that the authors lay out different paths that various Christian groups have taken, particularly in higher education. This reminds us that faithful people have come to different conclusions on this issue.

I found the three-lenses approach helpful in organizing the material. However, I have concerns about the naming of the "integrity" lens. This label is drawn from an article that postulates transsexuality as an extension of homosexuality to argue against the ordination of transgender people (an article that lacks the pastoral sensitivity of Yarhouse and Sadusky's chapter; I was surprised they drew on it for such an integral point). In reading the original article, it seems to argue that one's biological sex solely and completely determines one's gender identity. Perhaps a "sex deterministic" lens might be a better name? This concept, however, is problematic because of the many complexities of what makes up biological sex—is it chromosomes? external appearance? genitals? There are many variations and combinations of these (described elsewhere in this volume) that make this simplistic idea impractical to implement. I am also concerned that some might consider those who hold the other views as lacking integrity. Transgender people are seeking to live with authenticity and honesty about who we are, internally as well as physically.

Dr. Yarhouse and Dr. Sadusky helpfully lay out some of the medical treatments available to those with gender dysphoria and acknowledge the research showing that these can be efficacious. I certainly agree with them that additional research is urgently needed so we have more complete answers. Yet I was left wanting to hear more concretely their reasoning as to why those with gender dysphoria should not access these treatments under most circumstances, and what those circumstances would be. In addition, I am interested in the authors' views, as clinical practitioners, on when medical treatment might be appropriate and what alternatives they feel are both effective and compassionate. What is the appropriate course of action for someone who experiences severe and unrelenting depression and anxiety because of gender dysphoria, which counseling and prayer have not been effective in addressing?

For people with gender dysphoria for whom it is appropriate, medical and psychological professional associations consider hormone therapy and surgeries to be medically necessary. How can we reconcile these clinically accepted standards of care with these theological positions?

I am especially troubled by the idea of pastors or other church leaders taking surgery or hormone therapy "off the table" for a transgender church member (p. 129). Clergy are trained in theology and ministry, not in medicine. It is inappropriate for me to make medical decisions on behalf of parishioners or students; even more than that, I believe it would be professionally unethical to do so. Clergy may feel that medical treatment is not an option because of theological considerations but may not have adequate training or knowledge of the psychological or medical needs of their transgender congregants. The authors' suggestion that churches be up-front about this so that transgender people could seek out an alternative, welcoming congregation is helpful; however, it does not address the needs of transgender people and their families who are already part of a nonaccepting church.

There also seems to be some conflation of sexuality and gender in the chapter. They write, "Diversity advocates may also see the transgender movement as an ideological and political movement indicating progress in deconstructing views of sexuality that they believe are hurtful to transgender persons" (p. 105). Human sexuality—our attractions, desires, and intimate actions toward other individuals—is not the same as sex or gender. Transgender people can be any sexual orientation and hold varying views about sexuality. While there is clear overlap between the transgender community and lesbian/gay/bisexual people, and some common aims, they are not synonymous.

If the authors mean to argue instead that the transgender movement is interested in deconstructing views of sex and gender, then that is a different question. That certainly is the goal of some people, but many transgender people live very much according to gender norms, just not those of their natal-identified gender. I often encounter the idea that the transgender movement was developed for the *purpose* of deconstructing gender. In my experience, most transgender people are not, in fact, engaged in a political effort to alter perceptions of gender or gender norms but are simply seeking to live their lives with integrity and in the gender that affords them a holistic sense of well-being.

Relying heavily on the work of a political scientist, the authors describe the development of transgender identity largely in political terms (pp. 109–10). They write, "The language of being 'transgender' (as opposed to previous psychiatric categories of 'transsexual' or 'transvestite') was reportedly the result of an attempt to find a political identity through identifying norms regarding sex and gender as a source of oppression" (pp. 109–10). This focus tells only one aspect of the story and needs additional nuance. It seems to me that people are clear that the source of oppression is others who discriminate against and denounce transgender people. While an enforced system of gender norms can be oppressive, the problem lies in the dehumanization of those who are perceived to live counter to them.

Rather than being solely political, I would say the movement away from a purely medical understanding of transgenderism stemmed from the desire to not be labeled as patients or victims. Instead, people were motivated to develop a positive self-identity beyond the medical and psychiatric labels. A transgender person is a person, not a diagnosis (which I feel that the authors of this chapter would agree with). This new attitude, then, became the springboard for both personal empowerment and the creation of community. The transgender advocacy movement, in turn, developed not for the purpose of abolishing gender but primarily to address the tremendous and overwhelming levels of discrimination and violence the community faced and continues to face.

I appreciated the authors' comment that "there is a fragility to this group that must be kept in mind, but also a resiliency. Conversations about the difficulties faced by transgender people can evoke compassion, but also a sense of fear of saying the wrong thing. This can be enhanced if we only focus on the negatives associated with being part of this community. We may benefit from noting the strength it takes to navigate life when something as integral as sexuality is experienced in a radically different way than it is experienced by most others" (p. 121). Setting aside what again seems to be a conflation of sexuality and gender (here I believe the authors are referring to gender and not sexuality) and focusing instead on the substance of this statement, I think it is key to keep in mind both the resilience and the vulnerabilities of transgender people.

In writing the findings for the National Transgender Discrimination Survey in 2011, our team identified events that we felt were significantly life-disrupting or traumatic, which we defined as "events that would have a major impact on a person's quality of life and ability to sustain themselves financially or emotionally." These included things like losing a job or home, being physically or sexually assaulted, and losing significant relationships as a result of bias. A majority (63 percent) of the 6,450 transgender and gender nonconforming respondents had experienced at least one of these, while 23 percent had undergone at least three of these. We felt that even a single incident would have a significant impact on a person's life; three or more would be catastrophic. Yet almost a quarter of those responding reported three or more such events. We concluded: "These compounding acts of discrimination—due to the prejudice of others or lack of protective laws—exponentially increase the difficulty of bouncing back and establishing a stable economic and home life."[1] In addition to these acts of discrimination, transgender people also face tremendously high levels of violence, though numbers vary significantly, from 7 percent to 89 percent.[2]

1. Jaime M. Grant, Lisa A. Mottet, and Justin Tanis, with Jack Harrison, Jody L. Herman, and Mara Keisling, *Injustice at Every Turn: A Report of the National Transgender Discrimination Survey* (Washington, DC: National Center for Transgender Equality and National Gay and Lesbian Task Force, 2011), 8.

2. Andrea L. Wirtz, Tonia C. Poteat, Mannat Malik, and Nancy Glass, "Gender-Based Violence against Transgender People in the United States: A Call for Research and Programming,"

Transgender people may appear to some to be fragile, but that can be the result of repeated exposure to bias and subsequent trauma; it is not being transgender per se that makes one fragile but the ways in which transgender people are often treated with disdain and violence. I appreciate the acknowledgment of the resilience that it takes to continue living in ways that are different than those experienced by others. It seems to me that these experiences of bias and discrimination need to be of significant pastoral and social concern. The fear of saying the wrong thing pales in comparison with the failure to act in the face of violence and overt prejudice.

Finally, I wanted to comment on the fall as a cause for variations in gender identity. For example: "There is also much we do not understand about causation, which has to at least be a consideration when we think of whether gender identity or anatomy (or both), in the case of those with gender dysphoria, have been touched by the fall" (p. 112).[3] It seems to me that this question was clearly resolved by Jesus, as recorded in John 9. In this passage, Jesus was asked whether a man had been born blind as a result of his own or his parents' sin. Jesus replies, "Neither this man nor his parents sinned; he was born blind so that God's works might be revealed in him" (John 9:3). That is, the condition of our bodies is not the result of sin—our own, our parents', or by extension, our earliest parents in the Bible, Adam and Eve. Rather, what matters is what comes about as a result.

Transgender people—through our resilience and faithfulness—can be witnesses to the glory of God and reveal God's working among us. Differences do not have to be the result of the fall but can be for the purposes of furthering God's aims. The church, too, can reveal the light of Christ through actions of acceptance, compassion, and healing. This chapter raises questions that can help us on that journey.

Trauma, Violence & Abuse, January 1, 2018, 1, https://doi.org/10.1177/1524838018757749 (epub prior to printing). This article has a helpful table of current data and suggestions for additional research that is urgently needed.

3. Further reflections on this theme continue on this same page.

3

Good News
for Gender Minorities

Megan K. DeFranza

The Ethics of Sex Reassignment Surgery: An Evangelical Perspective." This was the title of the first research paper I submitted in the first semester of my doctoral studies. Long before I had ever met a transgender person, much less a transgender Christian, before I was instructed that I should say "transgend*er*" not "transgender*ed*," before I heard that "gender confirmation surgery" had replaced "sex reassignment surgery" as preferred terminology, before I gathered that there is rarely only one surgery and sometimes none at all.

I knew no transgender people and only a little about transgender experiences from articles and books I had read. But I thought that with two seminary degrees I knew enough about the Bible and theology to weigh in on the matter.

I knew the story started in Genesis, where God created two kinds of people—male and female—and declared their creation good. But human rebellion precipitated a fall from the freedom, goodness, and wisdom in which we had been created, a fall down to folly, slavery to sin, the inability to discern right from wrong. The rest of the story recorded the many ways God was at work to put humanity back on track, climaxing in Christ's sacrifice to purchase forgiveness and in the work of the Holy Spirit to grow us in holiness and healing. At the end of the story, Christ returns to make all things as they were back in Eden. Perfect. Sinless. Beautiful. Right.

Creation. Fall. Redemption. Sanctification. Consummation and new creation. These were the theological lenses I had been given in Bible college and seminary, and while my professors never approached the subject, these lessons led me to view transgender people through the lens of the "fall"—as confused or rebellious or mentally ill or suffering the effects of terrible abuse. I thought transgender people needed mental and spiritual healing, not hormones or surgery. I believed it was the mind and heart that needed alteration, not the body or clothes or name.

I'm glad I never published that paper.

I've heard that the best writers are those who write about what they know, and I knew very little back then. I know more now about biblical interpretation, theology, and the science of sex difference. Even more importantly, I have now *met* transgender people, even *transgender Christians*, and am honored to be able to call some of them my friends. Now, when I hear the word "transgender" I don't think of people on TV or on the covers of magazines or of some secular philosophy (i.e., "transgenderism"); instead, I think of Cameron, Kit, Austen, Paula, Ruben, Justin, Adam, Laura Beth, Nicole, and others I've been privileged to meet along the way.[1]

The Role of Experience and Emotion in Moral Reasoning

Before I knew any transgender people, the word conjured images in my mind of tall masculine-looking people wearing very short skirts, extremely high heels, and plunging blouses that showed more cleavage than I'll ever have. They looked like prostitutes advertising sexual availability, and, frankly, they made me uncomfortable. As a Christian woman who still believes modesty is a virtue, I don't dress that way, and as a Christian mother, I am trying to pass those same values on to my daughters (who would never be let out of the house in clothes like that). In my limited experience, transgender identities seemed more about sexuality (and sexual promiscuity in particular) than gender. These feelings of discomfort and mistrust were also factors in my "theological assessment" that transgender identities "are not what God intended."

1. Some of these friends also reviewed this chapter, and while only I should be held responsible for any complaints about the content, credit for its improvement goes, with my heartfelt thanks, to Heath Adam Ackley, Katherine Apostolocus, Austen Hartke, Ruben Hopwood, and Paula Williams. Thanks also goes to Andrew DeFranza, Roy Ciampa, Joanna Greenlee Kline, Christine and Greg Mutch, Lianne Simon, and Paul Van Ness for their feedback on earlier drafts.

Eventually, I learned the difference between drag queens, transvestites, and transgender people. Drag queens are "typically gay men, who dress like women for the purpose of entertainment" (sexual entertainment, hence sexualized apparel). Transvestites or cross-dressers are heterosexual "men who occasionally wear clothes, makeup, and accessories culturally associated with women. . . . This activity is a form of gender expression and not done for entertainment purposes. [These men] do not wish to permanently change their sex or live full-time as women." By contrast, transgender people have a "gender identity and/or gender expression [that] differs from what is typically associated with the sex they were assigned at birth."[2] Like all humans, they vary in the ways they live in the world—conservative or liberal, chaste or licentious. The transgender Christians I know don't call attention to themselves in the sexualized ways I had imagined. Meeting them doesn't raise the same visceral response in me. (Some have also challenged me to be less quick to judge those who find themselves in sex work; for many transgender people, their inability to "pass" makes it difficult or next to impossible to find work that will provide for their needs.)

While we often dismiss "feelings" as irrelevant to moral reasoning (particularly the emotional appeals of those we disagree with), scientific study is demonstrating that human emotion is one of the most powerful factors in our assessment of right and wrong, including our assessment of right and wrong ways of interpreting the Bible. Research shows that most of us make choices because some things (arguments, people, actions) feel right while others feel wrong. After our feelings point the way, we use our heads to articulate reasons why that way is the right way. This is true for liberals and conservatives, Christians and non-Christians alike.[3]

Before reading any further, it would be helpful to identify the feelings you experience when you hear the term "transgender." Do you envision drag queens (as I did)? Or do you picture a five-year-old crying in distress, suicidal upon entering kindergarten? The emotional responses differ significantly. Do you think of people praying for God's guidance about transitioning or of men sneaking into bathrooms to prey on women? Despite the fact that there is no evidence of an increase in sexual assaults in states that have allowed

2. "Glossary of Terms—Transgender," Gay and Lesbian Alliance Against Defamation (GLAAD), *GLAAD Media Reference Guide*, 10th ed., October 2016, 10–11, http://www.glaad.org /sites/default/files/GLAAD-Media-Reference-Guide-Tenth-Edition.pdf.

3. Jonathan Haidt, *The Righteous Mind: Why Good People Are Divided by Politics and Religion* (New York: Pantheon, 2012); and "The Moral Roots of Liberals and Conservatives," Monterey, CA, February 2008, TED Talks video, 19:13, https://www.youtube.com/watch?v=v s41JrnGaxc&list=PLyJ4YDcVdsrywdtk1rcyHyU2r8shzFIjM.

transgender people to use the bathroom of their choice, the mere suggestion triggers fear and protective instincts.[4] Human distrust of those who "look different" is a natural defensive response developed from our tribal past (something we are still trying to overcome when we recognize its influence on racism, xenophobia, etc.).

The idea of deception—that someone is pretending to be someone or something other than they are—naturally arouses suspicion. It certainly did for me. Which is why I found Krista Tippett's interview with Joy Ladin so convicting.[5] Joy explains that finding the courage to live as a woman is the most honest thing she has ever done. Letting the world know one's true gender identity, despite the real dangers that often incurs, takes profound courage. When I was fearing dishonesty from people whose names or clothing didn't match what I assumed was their bodily sex, some of them were putting their lives at risk to tell me the truth.

Still, if I am going to be honest, I must admit that it wasn't meeting transgender people that got me thinking differently about gender identity. I didn't reconsider transgender experiences until I learned about the complexity of human biology, until I met people who would have been labeled "transgender" were it not for some biological difference of sex development that could be verified by a physician. I needed a scientist to prove to me that bodies come in more varieties than the simple categories of male (XY chromosomes) or female (XX chromosomes) that I learned in eighth-grade health class.

Differences of sex development (DSDs) are also known as "intersex" traits or "natural variations" of sex development. Most intersex people do not identify as transgender, but for those who do, the only difference between being labeled transgender versus intersex is that the latter can point to something in their body that is different from most bodies—chromosome patterns other than the typical XX/XY, gonadal variations such as one ovary and one testis or ovarian and testicular tissue in the same gonad, varying hormone levels or cellular reception of hormones, atypical genitalia, or secondary sex characteristics (facial hair, breast development, fat distribution, etc.) that don't fit the usual pattern.

The United Nations fact sheet on intersex states, "Between 0.05% and 1.7% of the population is born with intersex traits—the upper estimate is

4. Katy Steinmetz, "Why LGBT Advocates Say Bathroom 'Predators' Argument Is a Red Herring," *Time*, May 2, 2016, http://time.com/4314896/transgender-bathroom-bill-male-preda tors-argument/.

5. Joy Ladin, interview by Krista Tippett, "Transgender amid Orthodoxy: I Am Who I Will Be," On Being, March 23, 2017, https://onbeing.org/programs/joy-ladin-transgender-amid-ortho doxy-i-am-who-i-will-be-mar2017/.

similar to the number of red haired people."[6] When it comes to identifiable markers of male or female sex, some people's bodies put them in both categories.

Behavioral Gender Differences

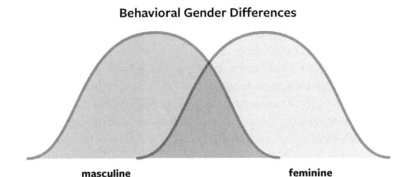

masculine   feminine

Biological Sex Differences

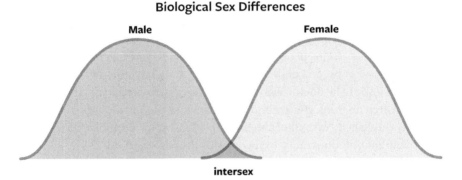

intersex

Differences between males and females fall along patterns, overlapping bell curves. The height of the bell curve indicates a majority, allowing us to speak of what is "typical"—a binary pattern. The baseline reveals (1) diversity between groups, (2) diversity within each group, and (3) the fact that the two groups are not distinct but overlap. Melissa Hines, director of the neuroendocrinology research unit at City University in London, studies biological sex differences and gendered behavior. She summarizes the research: "Few, if any, individuals correspond to the modal male pattern or the modal female pattern. Variation within each sex is great, with males and females near the top and bottom of distributions for every characteristic. . . . In fact, although most of us appear

6. "Fact Sheet: Intersex," United Nations, Human Rights, Office of the High Commissioner, https://unfe.org/system/unfe-65-Intersex_Factsheet_ENGLISH.pdf.

to be either clearly male or clearly female, we are each complex mosaics of male and female characteristics."[7] Scientific studies show that sex difference falls on a continuum, but since it is not an evenly distributed continuum one can also see a binary pattern (i.e., two bell curves).

Human sex is dimorphic, meaning there are two basic bodily patterns, but not strictly so; it also falls on a continuum.[8] There are exceptions to the typical pattern, and it is those exceptions to which we are attending in this volume—asking what God thinks about those who fall in between or outside of the majority. Are those who are not strictly male or female in body or gender identity problematic or benign? Are they beautiful variations or troublesome aberrations? Conservative Christians tend to respond differently to people with verifiable biological variations (intersex) than to people with gender differences (gender nonconforming behavior and/or transgender identities), as we will see.

The Role of Science in Moral Reasoning

Intersex people are sometimes shown compassion for doing the best they can with the biological cards they were dealt. At least when a doctor can prove you have intersex traits, people don't (usually) think you are crazy. Of course, if your intersex traits go "undiagnosed" and your gender identity differs from the best guess of the doctor who filled out your birth certificate, then people can and often do think you are crazy (or rebellious, deceitful, sinful, etc.). The recently published Nashville Statement by the Council on Biblical Manhood and Womanhood illustrates, in theory, this double standard:

> WE AFFIRM that those born with a physical disorder of sex development are created in the image of God and have dignity and worth equal to all other image-bearers. They are acknowledged by our Lord Jesus in his words about "eunuchs who were born that way from their mother's womb." With all others they are welcome as faithful followers of Jesus Christ and should embrace their biological sex insofar as it may be known.

> WE DENY that ambiguities related to a person's biological sex render one incapable of living a fruitful life in joyful obedience to Christ.[9]

7. Melissa Hines, *Brain Gender* (Oxford: Oxford University Press, 2004), 18–19.
8. Wesley J. Wildman provides a helpful discussion of nonstrict dimorphism and its implications for arguments from natural law in *Science and Religious Anthropology* (Burlington, VT: Ashgate, 2009), 143–51.
9. Nashville Statement, Council on Biblical Manhood and Womanhood, August 29, 2017, art. 6, https://cbmw.org/nashville-statement/.

The authors appear to be making a distinction between intersex people, who are viewed more positively, and transgender people, who are not welcomed or affirmed anywhere in the document as "created in the image of God" with "dignity and worth equal to all other image-bearers." There are a number of problems with article 6 as it relates to intersex people, including the fact that too many of my intersex Christian friends tell me they have not felt welcomed in many churches.[10] Despite their acknowledgment of biological complexity, article 6 is preceded by language insisting that "the differences between male and female reproductive structures are integral to God's design for self-conception as male or female" and denying "that physical anomalies or psychological conditions nullify the God-appointed link between biological sex and self-conception as male or female." Article 13 finalizes the distinction the authors are trying to make between intersex and transgender people: "The grace of God in Christ enables sinners to forsake transgender self-conceptions and by divine forbearance to accept the God-ordained link between one's biological sex and one's self-conception as male or female."

The first part of this chapter will explore the assertions above: whether transgender identity is chosen, and thus able to be "forsaken," as well as the "link between biological sex and self-conception as male or female." Afterward, we will look more carefully at the assertions in article 7 of the Nashville Statement: the insistence that "self-conception as male or female should be defined by God's holy purposes in creation and redemption as revealed in Scripture" and denial that a "transgender self-conception is consistent with God's holy purposes in creation and redemption." In other words, we will ask what the Bible says about gender identity.

10. First, the insistence on the language of "disorder" combined with pastoral instruction to "embrace their biological sex insofar as it may be known" encourages traumatic medical and psychological interventions to establish kids' bodies as "clearly" male or female and privileges intersex people who fit into the binary system while discriminating against those who identify as "gender nonbinary" or "inter-gender." Additionally, viewing intersex people as eunuchs is sometimes used to prohibit them from marriage. In other words, intersex people can be tolerated so long as they aren't having sex with anyone. See Cary Gabriel Costello, "Conservative Evangelicals Embrace Intersex Genital Mutilation," *The Intersex Roadshow* (blog), September 2, 2017, http://intersexroadshow.blogspot.com/2017/09/conservative-evangelicals -embrace.html; and Lianne Simon, "Barren Women and the Nashville Statement," Intersex and Faith, October 5, 2017, https://www.intersexandfaith.org/news/2017/10/5/barren-women -and-the-nashville-statement. For a more detailed exegesis and interpretation of eunuchs, see Megan K. DeFranza, *Sex Difference in Christian Theology: Male, Female, and Intersex in the Image of God* (Grand Rapids: Eerdmans, 2015), chap. 2, and pp. 204–8, where I argue for the freedom of eunuchs to marry as the corollary to the freedom of males and females not to marry.

Choice or Biology?

The language of "adopting a homosexual or transgender self-conception" in the Nashville Statement appears to suggest that people choose their sexual orientation and/or gender identity. This raises the question: When do cisgender (i.e., nontransgender) people choose to identify with their "reproductive structures"? As children we are told that we are girls or boys, identities reinforced by clothing, toys, and treatment by caregivers, teachers, and so forth. For most people, gender identity matches biological sex, which makes the idea of gender identity as a separate concept difficult for many to fathom. Only those who experience a disconnect between their sense of self and their bodily sex (and how others treat them because of that body) question what they hear—something many transgender children do long before they acquire the cognitive and linguistic skills to understand and explain how they feel. When our experience matches the experiences and/or expectations of the majority, we are often unaware of, and struggle to understand, those whose experiences differ.[11]

The question of choosing one's gender identity is even more complicated when "reproductive structures" (which article 6 insists determine bodily sex) do not match. For example, a person with Complete Androgen Insensitivity Syndrome (CAIS) is born with XY chromosomes, internal testes, no uterus, and no cervix but a short vagina and genitals that look typically female. At puberty they develop breasts and typical female skeletal structure but do not menstruate. With which reproductive structures should they identify?

What we learn from studying intersex and other bodily variations is just how often gender identity doesn't match chromosomes or genital shape or upbringing. For example, in Cloacal Exstrophy the abdomen doesn't fully close and the genitals don't form. Despite the fact that some of these babies are born with XY chromosomes (typical male pattern), they have historically been castrated, given feminizing genital surgery to form a vagina, and raised as girls. Yet doctors have found that a majority of these children end up choosing to identify and live as boys.[12] With CAIS (described above) the body doesn't respond to androgens. Although they also have XY chromosomes, these children consistently identify as girls.[13] These examples point toward the influence of biology on gender identity.

11. For example, Caucasians in the United States often think of "race" as something that pertains to people of color, rather than recognizing "whiteness" as a racial perspective.

12. William G. Reiner and John P. Gearhart, "Discordant Sexual Identity in Some Genetic Males with Cloacal Exstrophy Assigned to Female Sex at Birth," *New England Journal of Medicine* 350 (January 22, 2004): 333–41.

13. Denny Burk, one of the primary authors of the Nashville Statement, argues that "the presence of a Y chromosome indicates male sex and the absence of a Y chromosome seems to

Similarly, one should ask, When do heterosexuals choose to be straight? I think most of us woke up somewhere around adolescence feeling like our bodies were being taken over by aliens. Suddenly, our interests changed, seemingly "against our will." Remembering the budding of one's own sexuality is helpful because it reminds us that sexual desires are inherently connected to human biology. Why do middle schoolers start to become interested in the very activities that disgusted them a year earlier? Because their bodies are changing. (As a parent of young adolescents, I am watching this development unfold all over again, thankfully from a new vantage point.) Even if we cannot yet pinpoint the specific biological indicators of sexual orientation and gender identity, we know from experience that biology matters.

Kristina Olson, director of the TransYouth Project and associate professor of psychology at the University of Washington, summarized the current state of gender identity studies in a recent article in *Scientific American*. Describing the kinds of tests scientists run to explore the links between biology and gender identity, she recounts a study of forty-four sets of same-sex twins in which one twin within each set identified as transgender. "They found that in nine of the 23 identical twin pairs, both siblings were transgender, whereas in no case among the 21 same-sex fraternal twin pairs were both twins transgender, suggesting transgender identity has some genetic underpinning." Once again, the evidence points to biological influence, even though "which particular genetic variations are involved is an open question."[14]

Her explanation of the complexity of the science continues:

Similarly, although some neuroscience studies have shown that brain structures of trans people resemble those of individuals with the same gender identity, rather than people with the same sex at birth, these findings have often involved small samples and have not yet been replicated. Further complicating interpretation of neuroscience results is the fact that brains change in response to experience, so even when differences appear, scientists do not know whether structural or functional brain differences *cause* the experience of a particular

---

indicate female—despite ambiguities in secondary sex characteristics and whether the child has procreative ability." "Transgender Teen Named Homecoming Queen," September 23, 2013, reply to James Bradshaw, http://www.dennyburk.com/transgender-teen-named-homecoming-queen/. However, people with CAIS identify overwhelmingly as female, and it is this consistency in gender identity that has led doctors to follow gender identity rather than the Y chromosome in assigning them female at birth. In their case, the body's ability to process hormones is a more powerful indicator of gender identity than chromosome pattern. Amy B. Wisniewski, Stephen D. Chernausek, and Bradley P. Kropp, *Disorders of Sex Development: A Guide for Parents and Physicians* (Baltimore: Johns Hopkins University Press, 2012), 55.

14. Kristina Olson, "When Sex and Gender Collide," *Scientific American* 317, no. 3 (September 2017): 48.

gender identity or *reflect* the experience of gender identity. Muddying the already murky waters, neuroscientists continue to debate whether even among people who are not transgender, there are reliable sex (or gender) differences in brains. Thus . . . definitive conclusions about genetic and neural correlates of gender identity remain elusive.[15]

Too many Christians who make a distinction between intersex people as "born this way" and transgender people as those who "choose" their identity fail to remember that the brain is a part of the body; the brain is "sexed" both in the womb and throughout the lifetime. Transgender people may someday be identified as those with "intersex brains," but it is too early to tell.

Why Science Matters

As the Nashville Statement illustrates, it seems that if scientists could pinpoint physical causes for transgender identity, then transgender people would fall under the umbrella of those with "differences of sex development" and thus be included (at least by adherents of the statement) as those who "are created in the image of God and have dignity and worth equal to all other image-bearers." Instead of rejection, they would hear, "With all others they are welcome as faithful followers of Jesus Christ" and find encouragement in hearing that they are not "incapable of living a fruitful life in joyful obedience to Christ."[16]

Given the current state of scientific study, it is not far-fetched to imagine the discovery of biological causes for transgender identification. Nevertheless, the welcome of transgender people in the church should not hang on research being conducted in laboratories around the globe, nor can it wait for this.

While Christians wait for scientific answers and debate theological ethics, transgender people continue to suffer at the hands of others and at their own hands at alarming rates. Fifty-seven percent have family members who refuse to speak to them, 50–54 percent experience harassment at school, 60 percent have been refused health care by physicians, 64–65 percent have suffered physical or sexual violence, 57–70 percent have been discriminated against and/or victimized by law enforcement, and 69 percent have experienced homelessness.[17] Even more harrowing are the suicide rates. In the general population, the 4.6 percent rate of suicide attempts is deeply troubling, but this rate is

15. Olson, "When Sex and Gender Collide," 48. On the debate over sex/gender markers in the brain, see Lydia Denworth, "Is There a Female Brain?," *Scientific American* 317, no. 3 (September 2017): 38–43.

16. Nashville Statement, art. 6.

17. Ann P. Haas, Philip L. Rodgers, and Jody L. Herman, "Suicide Attempts among Transgender and Gender Non-conforming Adults: Findings of the National Transgender Discrimination

more than double (10–20 percent) for lesbian, gay, and bisexual persons, and it skyrockets to 41–46 percent for transgender and gender nonconforming people. For gender nonconforming and transgender people of color, the rate is terrifyingly high: 54–56 percent.[18] What should be of particular concern to Christians is how many of these harms result directly from teachings such as the Nashville Statement. Donovan Ackley III lost his job as professor of systematic theology at Azusa Pacific University after coming out as transgender.[19] He went on to work on suicide prevention as the director of training and curriculum at Trans Lifeline. Ackley observed, "Since The Council on Biblical Manhood and Womanhood published the Nashville Statement just before Labor Day 2017, more intersex and trans people in my work and social networks are in crisis—being disowned by families, harassed and threatened in schools and everyday social interactions, often with direct or overheard explanations that 'my pastor' or 'the Bible' says 'people like you are wrong.'"[20]

There is no neutral place to stand in the current conversation. Either we are adding to the trauma of transgender people by supporting or failing to challenge teachings like the Nashville Statement, or we are working for the care and protection of these children of God. Given the urgency, the lives at risk, let us now turn to examine "God's holy purposes in creation and redemption as revealed in Scripture" as they relate to this debate.[21]

The Role of Scripture in Moral Reasoning

The Bible Doesn't Mention Gender Identity

One of the major challenges to providing a "biblical perspective" on transgender people is that the Bible doesn't say anything about gender identity. In the English language, the distinction between biological "sex" and "gender role" wasn't articulated until 1955; "gender identity" was introduced as a separate concept in 1963.[22] This does not mean that transgender people did

---

Survey," January 2014, 2, http://williamsinstitute.law.ucla.edu/wp-content/uploads/AFSP-Williams-Suicide-Report-Final.pdf.

18. Haas, Rodgers, and Herman, "Suicide Attempts."

19. For a time after his transition, Dr. Ackley went by Heath Adam. He later took the name his parents would have given him had his gender been clear at birth.

20. Donovan Ackley III, "'And It Was Good': Pushing Back against the Nashville Statement and Christian Aggression," *Huffington Post*, October 14, 2017, https://www.huffingtonpost.com/entry/59e29505e4b09e31db9759a8.

21. Nashville Statement, art. 7.

22. John Money differentiated "gender role" from biological sex in 1955 in "Hermaphroditism, Gender and Precocity in Hyperadrenocorticism: Psychologic Findings," *Bulletin of the Johns Hopkins Hospital* 96 (1955): 253–64. Stoller and Greenson introduced the term "gender

not exist until the '60s (despite arguments I have heard, which trace the roots of our debate to the sexual revolution and feminist movements); rather, in the English-speaking West our understanding was limited by the language available to us. Other cultures have acknowledged transgender people for millennia.[23]

Article 7 of the Nashville Statement declares, "Self-conception as male or female should be defined by God's holy purposes in creation and redemption as revealed in Scripture." It is unclear why the authors avoid the term "gender identity" and replace it with the cumbersome "self-conception as male or female"; either way, they appear to be importing contemporary concepts back into ancient texts that do not consider such distinctions. Biblical authors speak of biological sex (the creation of male and female), record stories about men and women, and describe gender expectations in various ancient contexts; they do not distinguish instances when gender identity does not match apparent biological sex. Only a few passages speak to those who fall in between the categories of male and female, whom Jesus calls "eunuchs" in Matthew 19:12, but none mentions gender identity.

Does this mean that gender identity isn't "real" because it isn't mentioned in the Bible? No. Many advances in human understanding are not reflected in Scripture. At numerous times in history, scientific discoveries have appeared to run counter to the world described by biblical authors. They write of an Earth that has corners and does not move and (closer to our current topic) speak of human reproduction in antiquated terms. In Scripture barrenness is attributed to the mother whose womb is "closed" (1 Sam. 1:5–6); today we know that infertility is sometimes caused by the male. The biblical presentation of human reproductive structures (those very structures deemed essential for gender identity, according to the Nashville

---

identity" in 1963: "For Stoller '*gender identity* starts with the knowledge and awareness, whether conscious or unconscious, that one belongs to one sex and not the other. . . . *Gender role* is the overt behavior one displays in society, the role which he plays, especially with other people.'" David Haig, "The Inexorable Rise of Gender and the Decline of Sex: Social Change in Academic Titles, 1945–2001," *Archives of Sexual Behavior* 33, no. 2 (April 2004): 87–96, quoting Robert Stoller, *Sex and Gender,* vol. 1, *The Development of Masculinity and Femininity* (New York: J. Aronson, 1974), 10.

23. The Bugis of Indonesia acknowledge five sexes relatively comparable to male, female, transgender man, transgender woman, and hermaphrodite. Sharyn Graham Davies, *Challenging Gender Norms: Five Genders among Bugis in Indonesia* (Belmont, CA: Thomson Wadsworth, 2007). For millennia India has recognized transgender men, known as Hijras, who fulfill specific roles in the culture. A number of First Nations peoples in the Americas have also made space in their culture for transgender people, sometimes called "Two-Spirits." See part 2 of Gilbert Herdt, ed., *Third Sex, Third Gender: Beyond Sexual Dimorphism in Culture and History* (New York: Zone Books, 1996).

Statement) reflects ancient perspectives that have been improved through scientific research.[24]

Even if one agrees "that self-conception as male or female should be defined by God's holy purposes in creation and redemption as revealed in Scripture," we must concede that outside Jesus's acknowledgment of "eunuchs from birth" in Matthew 19, the Bible doesn't give much to go on to "define God's holy purposes" for those who fall outside the majority male/female pattern—or so I thought when I began my research. It was the apparent tension between God's good creation of humankind as male and female (in Genesis) *and* the acknowledgment by Jesus of those born outside this pattern (in Matthew) that drove me back to the Bible to see whether there were other scriptural clues to make sense of both passages and their place in God's story.

Genesis 1–2 and Matthew 19

> So God created humankind in his image, . . .
>   male and female he created them.
>
> (Gen. 1:27)

There is no doubt that Genesis describes a male/female pattern for humankind, but the question remains—what of those who do not fit this pattern? As I did earlier in my academic career, many Christians turn quickly to the idea of the fall, concluding that somehow those who do not fit the "creational pattern" must be a result of sin.[25] Their differences are likened to diseases—human life as it is *not* meant to be—differences that will be "healed" in the resurrection.

The first clue that led me to think I might need to reconsider this theological approach came not merely from the *fact* that Jesus identifies other kinds of people in Matthew 19:12 but from the *way* he talks about them. After being asked to weigh in on a debate about divorce, Jesus quotes Genesis 1 and 2 to make his argument: "He answered, 'Have you not read that the one who made them at the beginning "made them male and female," and said, "For this reason a man shall leave his father and mother and be joined to his wife, and the two shall become one flesh"? So they are no longer two, but one

---

24. Many ancients believed that the father provided the soul of the child while the mother provided the matter. (The Latin word for mother is *mater*, from which we get "matter" in English.) Thus, some ancient authors believed all human souls were literally "in Adam," participating in his sin and its consequences. DeFranza, *Sex Difference*, 113.

25. Dennis P. Hollinger, *The Meaning of Sex: Christian Ethics and the Moral Life* (Grand Rapids: Baker Academic, 2009), 84.

flesh. Therefore what God has joined together, let no one separate'" (Matt. 19:4–6). He names an exception in the case of adultery (vv. 8–9). Considering this stricter rule, his disciples surmise that (in a culture where one's spouse was often chosen by others) "it is better not to marry" (v. 10). Jesus does not applaud their deduction but admits, "Not everyone can accept this teaching, but only those to whom it is given. For there are eunuchs who have been so from birth, and there are eunuchs who have been made eunuchs by others, and there are eunuchs who have made themselves eunuchs for the sake of the kingdom of heaven. Let anyone accept this who can" (vv. 11–12).

Jesus names eunuchs as those who do not fit the pattern of male and female found in the passages from Genesis 1 and 2 that he quotes. Even more significantly, the Messiah does not speak of eunuchs as proof of the fall or as people in need of healing. Of all those healed in his ministry, we have no record of Jesus healing a eunuch. On the contrary, the Messiah recommends that his disciples learn from eunuchs and indicates that some people even "make themselves eunuchs for the sake of the kingdom of heaven." Christians debated for many centuries how to interpret this puzzling passage. Although later Christians would conclude Jesus was commending celibacy for single-minded service to God (like Paul's recommendation in 1 Cor. 7:32–35), this does not explain why he would employ the enigmatic figure of the eunuch to make this point. Simple celibacy was certainly not the only way early Christians interpreted his teaching.

First-century Jews spoke of babies born with ambiguous or differently formed genitals as "naturally born eunuchs."[26] Later rabbinic literature names three other categories for those who did not fit the male/female pattern at birth.[27] A number of intersex variations would have fallen under the ancient category of "eunuch." Even so, for the purposes of Jesus's audience, no one could make themselves a "naturally born eunuch"; thus, many early Christians

---

26. Julius Preuss, *Biblical and Talmudic Medicine*, trans. Fred Rosner (New York: Hebrew Publishing Company, 1978), 224–25. See also W. D. Davies and Dale C. Allison Jr., *A Critical and Exegetical Commentary on the Gospel according to Saint Matthew*, vol. 3 (Edinburgh: T&T Clark), 1997), 22; Ulrich Luz, *Matthew 8–20: A Commentary*, trans. James E. Crouch, ed. Helmut Koester (Minneapolis: Fortress, 2001), 501; Alfred Cohen, "Tumtum and Androgynous," *Journal of Halacha and Contemporary Society* 38 (1999): 74; and Kathryn M. Ringrose, *The Perfect Servant: Eunuchs and the Social Construction of Gender in Byzantium* (Chicago: University of Chicago Press, 2004), 15.

27. Those three categories are the *aylonith* (persons with underdeveloped genitalia that nevertheless appear more feminine than masculine), the *androgynos* (who appeared equally male and female), and *tumtum* (whose sex is unclear but believed to become clear in time). See John Hare, "Hermaphrodites, Eunuchs, and Intersex People: The Witness of Medical Science in Biblical Times and Today," in *Intersex, Theology, and the Bible: Troubling Bodies in Church, Text and Society*, ed. Susannah Cornwall (New York: Palgrave, 2015), 83–87.

looked to the second type of eunuch, those "made eunuchs by others," to find the meaning of the Messiah's words.

In the Roman Empire castrated eunuchs were most often found in three contexts: (1) as priests who emasculated themselves in service of the Great Mother Goddess, (2) as high-priced slaves who served imperial and aristocratic households, and (3) as exotic sex slaves (persons enslaved to individuals or pimps).[28]

Ritual castration was a part of some fertility cults.[29] We do not know to what extent, if at all, sacred prostitution (involving female priestesses and eunuch priests) was a part of their rituals. Evidence is unclear, but accusations abound, especially in Christian sources.[30] Augustine complains not only about the paganism and sexual sins of these priests but also about their gender transgressions. He calls them "effeminates [*molles*, literally "soft-ones"] consecrated to the Great Mother, who violate every canon of decency in men and women," visible "in the streets and squares of Carthage with their pomaded hair and powdered faces, gliding along with womanish languor."[31] According to Augustine, a eunuch priest was "neither changed into a woman nor allowed to remain a man."[32] Indeed, castrated men were often treated as a legal category separate from men and women.[33]

While these priests altered their own bodies, most eunuchs were castrated against their will as babies or children when they were kidnapped or sold into slavery. Many Roman emperors and aristocrats depended on enslaved, mutilated men to manage their households.[34] "Even in Judaea, where the practice of castration was frowned upon and outlawed, Herod the Great (37 BCE–AD 4) found it impossible, as Josephus Flavius (AD 37–95) relates, to manage his affairs without eunuchs."[35]

28. See DeFranza, *Sex Difference*, 73–90, on castrated eunuchs, and the whole of chap. 2 for the history of the interpretation of Matt. 19:12.

29. Piotr O. Scholz, *Eunuchs and Castrati: A Cultural History*, trans. John A. Broadwin and Shelley L. Frisch (Princeton: Markus Weiner, 2001), 93–94.

30. Matthew Kuefler, *The Manly Eunuch: Masculinity, Gender Ambiguity, and Christian Ideology in Late Antiquity* (Chicago: University of Chicago Press, 2001), 250–52.

31. Kuefler, *Manly Eunuch*, 253, quoting Augustine, *City of God* 7.26.

32. Kuefler, *Manly Eunuch*, 249, quoting Augustine, *City of God* 7.24.

33. Both "testify" (as when one testifies in court) and "testament" (as when one creates a last will and testament) are etymologically dependent on "testis," the male organ. Gen. 24:9 and 47:29 recount the practice of placing one hand on the male genitals (euphemistically translated "under the thigh") when taking an oath. In some ancient perspectives, eunuchs and women did not have the anatomical equipment to make promises, bear witness, or issue bequests. Scholz, *Eunuchs and Castrati*, 78–79.

34. Scholz, *Eunuchs and Castrati*, 112–23. See also Kuefler, *Manly Eunuch*, 61.

35. Scholz, *Eunuchs and Castrati*, 83.

Castrated slaves handled everything from powerful administrative functions and military command to cup-bearing and guarding the intimate spaces of their masters and mistresses. Cut off from their families of origin, raised to see the family of their master as their own family, and prevented from fathering children of their own, eunuchs owed their entire identity, their complete loyalty, to their masters. Their inability to procreate barred them from claiming power in their own name and also from producing heirs who might challenge the dynastic authority of the sacred king or emperor.[36] Their gender ambiguity also enabled them to mediate between men and women, elite and public, sacred and secular—in pagan and Christian households and in the church.[37] Kathryn Ringrose aptly calls them "perfect servants."[38]

Given their familiarity with eunuchs in these contexts, it may be less difficult to see why some ancient Christians might have thought Jesus was recommending his followers castrate themselves for religious service to prove they were perfect servants of God. Matthew Kuefler explains, "In an age that idealized the willingness to shed one's own blood for the sake of religion in the glorification of martyrs, self-castration may not have seemed either too strange or too demanding. . . . Moreover, in the same way that martyrdom was admired by Christians because it showed courage greater than most were capable of and lent to those willing to suffer it a charismatic authority unequalled by others, men willing to castrate themselves might have been respected and obeyed precisely because their behavior was atypical."[39]

Some Christian men castrated themselves; others transgressed gendered hairstyles, dress, or comportment because they recognized that the eunuch suggested more than a simple renunciation of marriage, but also a renunciation of gender privilege in the ancient world. The choice not to marry was a choice not to fulfill the requirements of manhood in ancient Jewish and Greco-Roman culture or lay claim to the privileges of masculinity in a patriarchal culture.

Similarly, some early Christian women rejected not only marriage but feminine expectations. They removed their veils, the symbol of their femininity in its shame and subordination to all things masculine. They saw themselves as relinquishing their feminine identity for a new identity "in Christ."[40] Many ancient Christians believed that their new identity in Christ was more important than the gender expectations and behaviors of their culture.

36. Ringrose, *Perfect Servant*, 5; Scholz, *Manly Eunuch*, 115.
37. Ringrose, *Perfect Servant*, 82–85.
38. Ringrose, *Perfect Servant*, 202.
39. Kuefler, *Manly Eunuch*, 263–64.
40. DeFranza, *Sex Difference*, 81–85.

Leaders at the first ecumenical council at Nicaea in 325 discouraged self-castration by declaring that those who emasculated themselves would not be considered for ordination while those whose bodies were altered against their will would not, for that reason, be ineligible for ordination.[41] Despite this pronouncement, a number of early Christian men continued to castrate themselves, believing that by doing so they were leaving behind this world with its concerns about sex and gender and inaugurating the coming kingdom of God.[42]

Eventually, the views of those like Augustine won the day. This African bishop argued that the only positive value of the eunuch was as an exemplar of the virtue of virginity. Augustine insisted that gender distinctions were an essential part of life in the present order. As a good Roman, he believed a virtuous community was built on a hierarchically ordered household, within a hierarchically ordered city, overseen by a hierarchically ordered church. When confronted with Christian ascetics who called themselves "eunuchs for the sake of the kingdom" and wore their hair long to display their disregard for gender rules, Augustine responded vehemently: "How lamentably ridiculous is that other argument, if it can be called such, which they have brought forward in defense of their long hair. They say that the Apostle forbade men to wear their hair long, but, they argue, those who have castrated themselves for the sake of the kingdom of Heaven are no longer men. O astonishing madness!"[43] But these eunuchs for the kingdom countered, "We assume this disgrace, because of our sins."[44] Their identity in Christ supplied such a solid foundation for their sense of self that they didn't need to fear being "disgraced" by disregarding the gender rules of their day, including wearing long hair.

Augustine's ideas about the importance of gender roles and gender hierarchy won out over the views of other Christians who believed that giving up gender privileges inaugurated the freedom of the future kingdom of God. Kuefler speculates, "Notions of male superiority and female inferiority were too deeply embedded in Roman cultural values for a religious philosophy arguing for their eradication to have succeeded in the West, even if that eradication had roots in earliest Christianity. Admitting the possibility of gender

41. DeFranza, *Sex Difference*, 72.

42. DeFranza, *Sex Difference*, 89.

43. Kuefler, *Manly Eunuch*, 274n131, quoting Augustine, *Work of Monks* 32. Kuefler comments on this passage, saying, "We should not miss the fact that Augustine was opposing what was apparently a developed exegetical tradition. He complained that these long-haired monks also compared themselves to the men called Nazirites among the ancient Hebrews." *Manly Eunuch*, 274.

44. "Does not the very nature of things teach you that if a man has long hair, it is a disgrace to him?" (1 Cor. 11:14). Kuefler, *Manly Eunuch*, 275n132, quoting Augustine, *Work of Monks* 31.

ambiguity in the soul while condemning it in the body was a means of rendering the genderless ideal of earliest Christianity quaint but harmless."[45] In other words, gender ambiguity could remain a spiritual value so long as the bodies of women, eunuchs, children, slaves, and lower-class men remained subject to earthly, male rulers.

Learning from the Study of Eunuchs in Early Christianity

The debates described above illustrate early Christians' attempts to work out the meaning of Jesus's words in Matthew 19:12. Many saw Jesus calling them to a more perfect path, which included a rejection of sexuality and marriage. But in the rejection of marriage and sexuality some ancient Christians saw the distinctions between the sexes fall away.[46] Each was called to virginity, each was called to virtue. The hierarchy of the family was replaced by hierarchy within monastic communities, but the lives of monks and nuns were markedly similar. Each saw themselves as (members of) the "bride" of Christ, each saw themselves as "sons" of God, each made themselves "eunuchs for the kingdom of heaven." In other words, many early Christians did not see gender identity and gender roles as essential to their identity as Christians. They saw gender roles, with their inherent hierarchies, as worldly and believed that Christians could experience the kingdom of heaven as they left these behind to live out their identities as new creations "in Christ."

We must be careful to differentiate between castrated eunuchs and transgender people who choose surgical transition. Ancient slave boys were castrated against their will, as babies or children. They were not asked whether they wanted to live their life as a "third gender." Their slave owners, pimps, parents, and even the church decided for them. What is enlightening for our discussion is that the outrage many Christians today express over the surgical alteration of genitals, of castration, when done willingly by some transgender people was not shared by many of our Christian ancestors who saw service to God as a eunuch (in the imperial household or in the church) as having higher value than conformity to male gender.[47]

Some ancient Christians believed one's identity in Christ superseded gendered identity, leaving them free to disregard the gender expectations of their day. This is the exact opposite of what many conservative Christians today mean when they challenge transgender Christians to find their identity in

---

45. Kuefler, *Manly Eunuch*, 230.
46. DeFranza, *Sex Difference*, 81–85.
47. See DeFranza, *Sex Difference*, 97–106, on the perspectives of Christians in the Middle Byzantine period.

Christ and take up their "God-ordained" role by living out the gendered expectations of society based on the shape of their genitals.

Jesus's words about "those who make themselves eunuchs for the sake of the kingdom of heaven" have troubled Christians for centuries. Nevertheless, however one reads the Lord's instruction, it is noteworthy that eunuchs are not presented as a problem to be fixed in the coming kingdom; rather, they are held up as models of radical discipleship, as those who love God enough to give up their masculinity, their male privilege, *for the sake of* God's kingdom. While some rabbis ridiculed eunuchs for their inability to appear masculine (e.g., lack of beard) and perform according to masculine ideals (e.g., father children), Jesus—in a move paradigmatic of his ministry—sets up these out-siders as models of Christian discipleship.[48]

Like other teachings of Jesus, his word about eunuchs seemed to overturn centuries of Jewish tradition—tradition grounded in Scripture. Jesus was teaching his disciples something new, but it would take his followers quite some time to put the pieces together. Why? Because many passages in the Hebrew Bible indicated that the distinctions between male and female were of ultimate importance. How could Jesus be overturning God's Word?

Eunuchs under the Old Covenant

The Bible reveals changes in how eunuchs were viewed in the Old Testament and how they were treated under the new covenant. These changes parallel other biblical movement from the Old to the New Testament—laws about mixing things that should be distinct, laws guarding the boundaries of Israel's identity.

Torah

The outsider status of eunuchs is inscribed in Deuteronomy 23:1: "No one who has been emasculated by crushing or cutting may enter the assembly of the Lord" (NIV). The practice of ritual castration in the religions of some of Israel's neighbors and the prohibition of mixing with foreigners may have motivated the exclusion of cut eunuchs from the assembly.[49] Eunuchs,

---

48. See DeFranza, *Sex Difference*, 104–6.

49. This prohibition comes right before laws excluding from the assembly children born of forbidden marriages (Deut. 23:2) as well as Ammonites and Moabites (v. 3), and the descen-dants of both, to the tenth generation. Gordon McConville, "Deuteronomy," in *New Bible Commentary, 21st Century Edition*, ed. G. J. Wenham, J. A. Motyer, D. A. Carson, and R. T. France (Downers Grove, IL: InterVarsity, 1994), 221.

whose bodies blurred the lines between male and female, were considered foreign, and separation from foreigners is an important theme throughout the Old Testament. Deuteronomy records a number of laws that make little sense from our vantage point but that may have been issued to remind the ancient Israelites of God's call for them to separate themselves from other peoples. For example: "Do not plant two kinds of seed in your vineyard; if you do, not only the crops you plant but also the fruit of the vineyard will be defiled. Do not plow with an ox and a donkey yoked together. Do not wear clothes of wool and linen woven together" (Deut. 22:9–11 NIV). In the garden, in the field, and at the loom, God's people would be reminded not to mix with other people groups who might mix their religion with the worship of Yahweh.

In the same passage prohibiting polyblends and warning against defiling one's vineyard by planting with different varieties of seeds, we find the one passage that some Christians believe directly addresses transgender people: "A woman must not wear men's clothing, nor a man wear women's clothing, for the Lord your God detests anyone who does this" (Deut. 22:5 NIV). In addition to the possibility that this law is directed against transgender people transitioning, commentators have suggested it may have been established to guard against heterosexual acts outside marriage made possible by gaining entrance to single-sex spaces through cross-dressing or same-sex activities by pretending to be the "other" sex. Alternatively, like the laws prohibiting the mixing of seeds and fabrics, this could be another reminder of keeping things separate—laws that seem random from our point of view, and even counterproductive at times, but that may have been given to remind the ancient Hebrews at every turn of their call to be separate from all other nations.[50] (It is also helpful to remember that many Christians have cited this verse to prohibit women wearing pants.)

Many food laws also reinforced the message that mixed things—creatures of more than one category, children of more than one race—were unclean.

> Everything in the waters that has fins and scales, . . . you may eat. But anything in the seas or the streams that does not have fins and scales, . . . they are detestable to you and detestable they shall remain. . . .

50. Tigay admits that the rationale for prohibiting mixed cropping is "not clear," especially given its benefit in arid climates. Similarly counterintuitive is the prohibition of "pairing wool and linen" since it "made for a stronger fabric." Supporting the argument that these laws reinforced the message not to mix with foreigners, Tigay notes that "fragments of such fabric have been unearthed . . . in the Sinai Peninsula, where religiously heterodox inscriptions in Hebrew were also found, along with inscriptions in other languages." Jeffrey H. Tigay, *Deuteronomy*, JPS Torah Commentary (Philadelphia: Jewish Publication Society, 1996), 202.

All creatures that swarm upon the earth are detestable; they shall not be eaten. Whatever moves on its belly, and whatever moves on all fours, or whatever has many feet, all the creatures that swarm upon the earth, you shall not eat; for they are detestable. You shall not make yourselves detestable with any creature that swarms; you shall not defile yourselves with them, and so become unclean. For I am the LORD your God; sanctify yourselves therefore, and be holy, for I am holy. You shall not defile yourselves with any swarming creature that moves on the earth. For I am the LORD who brought you up from the land of Egypt, to be your God; you shall be holy, for I am holy. (Lev. 11:9–11, 41–45)

Many of the creatures named above as "detestable" are creatures that mix the categories of animals named in Genesis 1:28, where God says to the newly created humans, "Rule over the fish in the sea and the birds in the sky and over every living creature that moves on the ground" (NIV). In Leviticus, the fish in the sea (those with "fins and scales") are clean, but other sea creatures, like lobsters, which crawl instead of swim, are detestable. Creatures that swarm or crawl on their belly instead of walking, these too are detestable; eating them made God's people detestable, defiled, unclean.[51] "You shall therefore make a distinction between the clean animal and the unclean, and between the unclean bird and the clean; you shall not bring abomination on yourselves by animal or by bird or by anything with which the ground teems, which I have set apart for you to hold unclean. You shall be holy to me; for I the LORD am holy, and I have separated you from the other peoples to be mine" (Lev. 20:25–26).

In the early parts of God's story, separation equaled holiness. Mixing was detestable, an abomination. But like a great storyteller, the Master Author was writing a complicated plot, with surprises in store for which God's people were not prepared.

Isaiah

One can only imagine the difficulty eunuchs and foreigners must have experienced as members of the community. Deuteronomy forbade castrated eunuchs from worshiping with the assembly of Israel; foreigners were painted as unclean defilers of God's holy people. Later in the story, we find evidence of the anxiety some eunuchs and foreigners felt about their place among God's people.

Do not let the foreigner joined to the LORD say,
    "The LORD will surely separate me from his people";

51. Mary Douglas, *Purity and Danger: An Analysis of the Concepts of Pollution and Taboo* (1966; repr., London: ARK Paperbacks, 1984), 55–57.

and do not let the eunuch say,
  "I am just a dry tree."
For thus says the LORD:
To the eunuchs who keep my sabbaths,
  who choose the things that please me
  and hold fast my covenant,
I will give, in my house and within my walls,
  a monument and a name
  better than sons and daughters;
I will give them an everlasting name
  that shall not be cut off.

And the foreigners who join themselves to the LORD,
  to minister to him, to love the name of the LORD,
  and to be his servants,
all who keep the sabbath, and do not profane it,
  and hold fast my covenant—
these I will bring to my holy mountain,
  and make them joyful in my house of prayer;
their burnt-offerings and their sacrifices
  will be accepted on my altar;
for my house shall be called a house of prayer
  for all peoples.

                                                    (Isa. 56:3–7)

Despite all the marks against eunuchs and the suspicion of foreigners, God assures these outsiders of their place in the community; but God goes way beyond mere "inclusion." The Lord does not promise to heal eunuchs or restore them to one of the two categories established in the book of Genesis. Yahweh does not declare these "dry trees" fertile so that they can perpetuate their name as Jewish men did, by begetting sons who begat sons. The Lord does not seem concerned to restore these ambiguous bodies to some creational pattern or ideal. Rather, they are blessed *as eunuchs*. They are promised, not the same blessing as those given to Jewish men, but something "*better* than sons and daughters . . . an everlasting name that shall not be cut off" (v. 5).

The passage goes on to assure the foreigner that they too have a place in the community. These outsiders are no longer to be treated as outsiders. Instead of doing everything to separate God's people from others, Yahweh declares, "My house shall be called a house of prayer for all peoples" (v. 7). God was doing something new, something different than what God had done in earlier parts of the story.

Eunuchs under the New Covenant

The Gospels

If the ancient Hebrews were surprised by the prophecy of Isaiah, they were shocked by the ministry of the Messiah. Against the Levitical and Deuteronomic concerns about foods that make one an abomination to God, Jesus insisted, "Listen to me, everyone, and understand this. Nothing outside a person can defile them by going into them. Rather, it is what comes out of a person that defiles them" (Mark 7:14–15 NIV). Given the emphasis on clean and unclean foods in the Torah, his disciples struggled to believe him.

> "Are you so dull?" [Jesus] asked. "Don't you see that nothing that enters a person from the outside can defile them? For it doesn't go into their heart but into their stomach, and then out of the body." (In saying this, Jesus declared all foods clean.)
>
> He went on: "What comes out of a person is what defiles them. For it is from within, out of a person's heart, that evil thoughts come—sexual immorality, theft, murder, adultery, greed, malice, deceit, lewdness, envy, slander, arrogance and folly. All these evils come from inside and defile a person." (vv. 18–23 NIV)

The Messiah was revealing a twist in the plot. Some parts of the old law were to be left behind. Jesus declared as clean those animals that mixed creational categories and also spoke positively about humans who didn't fit the categories of male or female, naturally born eunuchs, in Matthew 19:12. Even more shocking, he uses the image of cut eunuchs—those not permitted to worship with the assembly of Israel—as icons of radical discipleship. Like the eunuchs in Isaiah who were promised that they would be judged not by their bodies or gendered performance but by their faithfulness to Yahweh, Jesus emphasized virtue, holiness of heart in place of the ancient notion of holiness as separation. It would still take some years for these lessons to sink in to the heads and hearts and practices of his disciples.

The Acts of the Apostles

It took several direct interventions from God, including an angelic visitation, to convince the early Christian community that God's story was taking a new turn. Acts 10 records a vision given to Peter of clean and unclean animals. A voice from heaven says,

"Get up, Peter. Kill and eat."

"Surely not, Lord!" Peter replied. "I have never eaten anything impure or unclean."

"Do not call anything impure that God has made clean." (vv. 14–15 NIV)

This vision prepared Peter to accept the invitation to the house of a gentile to share with him the gospel. Peter exclaims, "I now realize how true it is that God does not show favoritism but accepts from every nation the one who fears him and does what is right" (vv. 34–35 NIV).

Two chapters earlier, an angel of the Lord sent Philip to share the gospel with one very particular human who embodied the mixed, outsider status of those in Isaiah 56.

> Now an angel of the Lord said to Philip, "Go south to the road—the desert road—that goes down from Jerusalem to Gaza." So he started out, and on his way he met an Ethiopian eunuch, an important official in charge of all the treasury of the Kandake (which means "queen of the Ethiopians"). This man had gone to Jerusalem to worship, and on his way home was sitting in his chariot reading the Book of Isaiah the prophet. The Spirit told Philip, "Go to that chariot and stay near it."
>
> Then Philip ran up to the chariot and heard the man reading Isaiah the prophet. "Do you understand what you are reading?" Philip asked.
>
> "How can I," he said, "unless someone explains it to me?" So he invited Philip to come up and sit with him.
>
> . . . Then Philip began with that very passage of Scripture and told him the good news about Jesus.
>
> As they traveled along the road, they came to some water and the eunuch said, "Look, here is water. What can stand in the way of my being baptized?" (Acts 8:26–31, 35–36 NIV)

Here was an individual who fit the profile of eunuchs in the first century—a high-ranking slave to the queen of the Ethiopians. It was probably his high status that allowed him the freedom and funds to make the pilgrimage from Ethiopia to Jerusalem, a trek of over two thousand miles. If he was wealthy enough to have a copy of the scroll of Isaiah and devout enough to be reading it, he would certainly have also been familiar with the exclusion of eunuchs from the assembly in Deuteronomy 23:1. As a gentile, he would also have recently experienced the limitation that his foreigner status placed on his proximity to the holy of holies—surrounded by the court of men, then the court of women, and finally the court of gentiles.

Is it any wonder that, when he heard the good news about Jesus, he would ask, "What can stand in the way of my being baptized?" He may very well have been wondering what his status would be in this new community. Would he remain a second- or third-class citizen among God's people? Would his body continue to prevent him from coming as close to God as Jewish men or Jewish women could come? Could he also be conformed to the image of Jesus, or would the form of his body perpetuate his place as an outsider?

Sometimes I wonder whether Philip might have responded similarly to the apostle Paul, whose letter to the Galatians was also attempting to clarify the relationship of Christians to the old law. "All of you who were baptized into Christ have clothed yourselves with Christ. There is neither Jew nor Gentile, neither slave nor free, nor is there male and female, for you are all one in Christ Jesus. If you belong to Christ, then you are Abraham's seed, and heirs according to the promise" (Gal. 3:27–29 NIV). This Ethiopian knew only too well the divide between Jew and gentile, slave and free, male and female. While we are not told what Philip said in response, we know that someone "gave orders to stop the chariot. Then both Philip and the eunuch went down into the water and Philip baptized him. When they came up out of the water, the Spirit of the Lord suddenly took Philip away, and the eunuch did not see him again, but went on his way rejoicing" (Acts 8:38–39 NIV).

The early church struggled to understand the place of gentiles in the church and which parts of the law remained binding for the new community. Acts 15 records the debate between Paul and the Pharisees, who insisted that "the Gentiles must be circumcised and required to keep the law of Moses" (v. 5 NIV). The latter had the stronger argument from Scripture. God *had* said to Abraham, "My covenant in your flesh is to be an *everlasting covenant*" (Gen. 17:13 NIV); but Paul, Barnabas, and eventually Peter insisted that God was doing something new, something unexpected, in the outpouring of the Spirit on uncircumcised gentiles. In the end the council decided, "It seemed good to the Holy Spirit and to us not to burden you with anything beyond the following requirements: You are to abstain from food sacrificed to idols, from blood, from the meat of strangled animals and from sexual immorality. You will do well to avoid these things" (Acts 15:28–29 NIV).

God was doing something new.

Canonical Context or "The Big Picture"

Why have I taken so long to recount God's grand story from Genesis to the Acts of the Apostles? Because, as article 7 of the Nashville Statement states, our perspectives on sex differences "should be defined by God's holy purposes in creation and redemption as revealed in Scripture." As we saw above, the story of creation and redemption in Scripture is not a short story but a complex, compelling narrative taking its readers beyond their wildest dreams.

Interpreting God's holy purposes in creation and redemption requires attention to context, especially canonical context. We must ask, Where in the great story of creation and redemption does this particular passage fit? The Bible itself shows us that not every biblical passage remains binding for Christians. Each has its authoritative place in the plot, but it is only in the later chapters that we have the vantage point to assess the whole.[52]

Returning to Genesis with New Eyes

We started thinking about the significance of sex/gender difference in Genesis with the creation of male and female, but later parts of the canonical narrative complicate the simplicity of those first chapters. The inclusion of eunuchs in the story adds a new plotline—the exclusion of cut eunuchs from the assembly in Deuteronomy fits with early themes of separation, but the promise to eunuchs of a place in God's temple and a blessing "better than sons and daughters" in Isaiah turns the narrative in a surprising direction. This new trajectory is bolstered by Jesus's acknowledgment of those born with bodies that fall between male and female, and castrated men who were no longer viewed as men nor granted the privileges of masculinity in the Gospel of Matthew. The narrative climaxes in the baptism of the Ethiopian eunuch in the book of Acts. The story of eunuchs parallels the narrative of clean and unclean things (food, animals, woven cloth, plants). While somewhat inscrutable to contemporary Christians, many of these laws make sense as everyday reminders that God's people were to remain separate from all others. Israel had been set apart, not to remain separate forever but so that eventually "the blessing given to Abraham might come to the Gentiles through Christ Jesus, so that by faith we might receive the promise of the Spirit" (Gal. 3:14 NIV).

The theme of separation reverberates in the first creation account. "God separated the light from the darkness" (Gen. 1:4), then "the waters from the waters" (v. 6), climaxing in the creation of "humankind" (v. 26) separated into "male and female" (v. 27). Even the animals are named in separate categories: "the fish of the sea," "the birds of the air," and "every living thing that moves upon the earth" (v. 28).

---

52. For more on the interpretation of Scripture as narrative, see N. T. Wright, "How Can the New Testament Be Authoritative?," *Vox Evangelica* 21 (1991): 7–32. Also available at http://ntwrightpage.com/2016/07/12/how-can-the-bible-be-authoritative/.

While I have often heard the argument that people whose bodies fall in between the "creation categories of male and female" are a result of the fall or "not what God intended," I have never heard frogs or penguins or ostriches employed as proof of sin's effect on God's good creation since these creatures mix the categories outlined in Genesis 1:28. Even if one argues that some of these hybrid creatures are identified as "unclean" early in Hebrew history, the remainder of the canon shifts the focus from ritual symbols of separation (e.g., clean and unclean food, circumcision) to faith and virtue (e.g., circumcision of the heart; see Rom. 2:12–29). Pointedly, the Jerusalem Council would argue that people should not be judged by whether they had had an operation on their genitals but by their relationship with God—a relationship based on grace through faith.

How then should Christians read the theological significance of Adam and Eve?

- Are they the *pattern* that God established for all people or the first *parents*?
- Are they God's *best* or the *beginning* of the story?
- Are they the exclusive *model* for all humans or the statistical *majority*?

As the bell curves at the beginning of this chapter illustrated, most humans fit into the categories of male or female fairly adequately, just as many animals fit into one of the three categories named in Genesis 1:28. Could the author of Genesis simply have been painting the story of creation in broad brushstrokes rather than listing an exhaustive inventory of all God's good creatures?

The text does not tell us whether Adam and Eve represent the ideal *form* of masculinity and femininity to which we all must conform or the *fountainheads* of the beautiful variety of human beings who come after. These are theological lenses we bring to the Bible. Nevertheless, simply because Genesis does not answer the question for us doesn't mean we are left without clues for finding the answer.

Revelation

Genesis is the place where all good theological anthropology must begin, but it is not the end of the story. The apostle John reminds us that humanity is not to be found in some Edenic past but in God's eschatological future, a future that is breaking into this present age but is not yet fully revealed.[53] "Beloved, we are God's children now; what we will be has not yet been revealed. What we do know is this: when he is revealed, we will be like him, for we will

53. See DeFranza, *Sex Difference*, chap. 6.

see him as he is. And all who have this hope in him purify themselves, just as he is pure" (1 John 3:2–3).

We find some clues to the end in the last book of the canon. Revelation 7 describes "a great multitude that no one could count, from every nation, tribe, people, and language, standing before the throne and in front of the Lamb" (v. 9 NIV). This passage describes human identities that had no place in the garden of Eden. There was no diversity of nations, tribes, peoples, and languages in the garden, yet these differences are preserved at the End. Eunuchs are promised a place in God's house *as they are*, not after some kind of restoration to an Edenic pattern (Isa. 56:5).

The Christian story is not circular but linear. It does not end where it started. As God's revelation unfolds, more and more outsiders are brought in; and while this was a surprise to many followers of Jesus, it shouldn't have been. God had said long before, through the prophet Isaiah, "My house shall be called a house of prayer for all peoples" (Isa. 56:7).

Conformity to Gender or Conformity to Christ?

Reading Adam and Eve as the beginning of the story rather than as some masculine and feminine ideal against which we all fall short is good news, not only for transgender, gender nonbinary, and intersex people, but for everyone. Elsewhere I have detailed the relationship between ancient notions of virtue and masculinity in Greek and Roman philosophy and its toxic impact on Western Christian theology.[54] In Latin the words for "virtue" (*virtus*), "male" (*vir*), and "strength" (*vis*) share the same root.[55] To be "soft" or "effeminate" was understood as proof of weakness—physical and moral weakness—so much so that it was sometimes difficult for church fathers to believe women could become as virtuous as men. The maleness of Jesus was at one time considered proof of male superiority and the hierarchical scale of masculine perfection. Thankfully, women are no longer called to become masculine in their imitation of Christ.[56]

54. DeFranza, *Sex Difference*, esp. chaps. 3, 4, and 6; and Megan K. DeFranza, "Gender Is Not a Virtue," *Perspectives: A Journal of Reformed Thought*, September/October 2016, https://perspectivesjournal.org/blog/2015/09/01/gender-not-virtue/.

55. Lactantius, a fourth-century writer and tutor of Constantine I (who ruled the Roman Empire from 306 to 337), preserved "a well-known, if invented, etymology": "Thus man [*vir*] was so named because strength [*vis*] is greater in him than in woman; and from this, virtue [*virtus*] has received its name. Likewise, woman [*mulier*] . . . is from softness [*mollitia*], changed and shortened by a letter, as though it were softly [*mollier*]." Kuefler, *Manly Eunuch*, 21, quoting Lactantius, *Workmanship of God* 12.16–17.

56. Reading Genesis through Paul's instructions to restrict the teaching of women (1 Tim. 2:11–15), Chrysostom wrote, "Their sex is weak and given to levity. For it is said here of the

Christ Jesus is "the image of the invisible God" (Col. 1:15), and all Christians—male, female, intersex, transgender—are "being transformed into his image with ever-increasing glory, which comes from the Lord, who is the Spirit" (2 Cor. 3:18 NIV). All Christians receive his inheritance as sons (Gal. 3:26–4:7).[57] All Christians become his bride (Eph. 5:25–27). These mixed metaphors illustrate the universal call of conformity to Christ and challenge the ways in which Christians throughout history have attempted to reconcile the call of the gospel with culturally formed gender ideals.

Which Matters More: Gender Identity or Identity in Christ?

I often hear objections to gender transitioning from cisgender Christians who argue that gender identity shouldn't matter more than one's identity in Christ; thus, they insist transgender people look to their genitals to determine their role in the world. This study of gender in the ancient church shows how many early Christians came to the opposite conclusion. They believed identity in Christ superseded cultural gender ideals, so much so that one could even make oneself a eunuch in radical obedience to Christ. Ancient castrated eunuchs are not identical to transgender people, but the biblical account of eunuchs does teach us that conformity to masculinity and femininity is not what is required of Christians; rather, we are called to be conformed to Christ—a call that can challenge gendered cultural ideals.[58]

Identity in Christ and obedience to Christ are important to transgender Christians. Lianne Simon, my colleague at Intersex and Faith, explains how it was her desire to focus on her calling as a Christian that influenced her decision to transition from the sex she was assigned at birth. Lianne was assigned

---

whole nature. For he did not say that 'Eve' was deceived, but 'the woman,' which is a term for her sex in general." Frederick G. McLeod, SJ, *The Image of God in the Antiochene Tradition* (Washington, DC: Catholic University of America Press, 1999), 203, quoting Chrysostom, *Commentary on the First Letter to Timothy* 2.11 (*Patrologia graeca* 62:545). Early Christian men struggled to reconcile virtue in those who were not men. Melania the Younger was celebrated as one "who performed 'manly deeds' and was received by the Fathers of Nitria 'like a man': since 'she had surpassed the limits of her sex and taken on a mentality that was manly, or rather angelic.'" Gillian Cloke, *"This Female Man of God": Women and Spiritual Power in the Patristic Age, AD 350–450* (New York: Routledge, 1995), 214, quoting Gerontius, *Life of Melania the Younger*, prologue and 39.

57. While the NIV and NRSV use the more inclusive translation "children" rather than "sons," I believe the noninclusive translation ("sons") more correctly illustrates the gendered nature of inheritance in the time of the early church.

58. DeFranza, *Sex Difference*, 277–78.

male because that is how her body looked at birth; her intersex traits were discovered later, years after she began questioning her gender.

> So why did I switch from living as a boy to living as a girl? Did I one day decide to rebel against God's clear plan? No. I prayed about it. A lot. Did I have a desperate need to be a girl? Um. No. At times being a girl sucks. Like when a man won't listen to me because I'm a woman.
>
> So why did my gender matter so much? Because I was close enough to death to smell the lilies at my funeral. My life revolved around my inability to function socially as a boy to the satisfaction of those around me.
>
> I wanted a life. I wanted peace. I wanted to live for Jesus rather than die by my own foolishness. I wanted to honor God with the hand he'd dealt me. . . .
>
> Most of all I wanted people to leave me alone.
>
> My doctor said that with my face and demeanor I wouldn't have any trouble being accepted as a girl. He was right. The bullying stopped.
>
> For more than forty years I've been able to focus on things other than my gender, to be a productive member of society, or as Article VI says, to "live a fruitful life in joyful obedience to Christ."[59]

Another transgender friend describes the fruitfulness that comes not only from living as their authentic self but also from finding a church in which they need not hide.

> I found a church that accepted me for everything I am, and believes that I bring something essential to Christian witness. I began bringing my whole self to worship, rather than spending my time praying with one eye open, wondering who was going to find out that I didn't belong.
>
> And let me tell you—when you bring your whole self into God's house, you quickly find yourself wrapped up in the reconciling work that got you there in the first place. You get caught up in GOD'S reconciling work. God starts stirring up holy trouble in you, and calling you to stand with all kinds of other oppressed people—people who wrestle daily with racism and sexism and ableism and xenophobia. Becoming reconciled with one sibling leads to work for reconciliation with everyone else! . . . Those very labels which I was taught were a liability have turned out to be the greatest gift. I'm not saying that they've been EASY gifts to receive, but I have come to find myself in the midst of a life full of blessing that I'm called to pass on to others.[60]

59. Lianne Simon, "Intersex and the Nashville Statement," September 3, 2017, http://www .liannesimon.com/2017/09/03/intersex-and-the-nashville-statement/.

60. Austen Hartke, "'Reconciling'—A Sermon on Matthew 5:21–37," February 12, 2017, http://austenhartke.com/blog-1/2017/2/12/reconciling-a-sermon-on-matthew-521–37. See also

There is no single path for transgender Christians. Some may decide to transition socially, not changing their bodies but changing the way they live in the world. Others may decide to transition fully from one (binary) sex identity to the "other," changing their legal name and body through medical procedures. Some may want hormones or surgeries but can't afford them or opt against them because they aren't satisfied with current outcomes; so, they do the best they can to live authentically in the world. Others may choose to live in the middle, as a third gender or nonbinary gender (with or without hormones and/or surgeries). Each risks their own safety to speak the truth about their sense of self.

Christians must stop demonizing transgender people as rebellious against God and nature on account of the fact that their experience of themselves is

Austen Hartke, *Transforming: The Bible and the Lives of Transgender Christians* (Louisville: Westminster John Knox, 2018).

different from the majority. Many transgender people are devout Christians prayerfully working out their salvation with "fear and trembling" (Phil. 2:12). Cisgender Christians can add to that fear—fear of judgment, fear of harassment, fear of rejection, fear of suicide and homicide—or we can walk with one another as siblings in Christ, thinking, talking, and praying together for God's guidance as to how we can most healthfully live out our calling as children of God being conformed to the image of Christ.[61]

While most of God's children experience themselves according to the majority pattern of Adam and Eve, Jesus makes visible God's concern for all, not only those in the majority. Following the Good Shepherd, we must also care for those whose experiences are less common—like the eunuchs known by Jesus, baptized by Philip, and promised through the prophet Isaiah that they would be judged not by their genitals but by their faithfulness to God, a faithfulness rewarded by a blessing "better than sons and daughters . . . an everlasting name that shall not be cut off. . . . For my house shall be called a house of prayer for all peoples" (Isa. 56:5, 7). This is good news, indeed.

---

61. Given the limitations of space in this chapter, I recommend Justin Sabia-Tanis's work (in this volume and elsewhere) for a discussion of health factors related to hormonal and surgical transitioning.

Response to Megan K. DeFranza

Owen Strachan

Megan DeFranza has written an engaging and theologically literate chapter. It summons engagement for numerous reasons, as does DeFranza's broader work. Clearly, she is a fluent writer, a creative thinker, and a person who wishes to lend help to those who struggle. My disagreements with her stem not from any personal antipathy or lack of respect for her evident gifting but rather from the content of her arguments. In what follows, I will consider her views in terms of logic, hermeneutics, science, and textual assertions.

For starters, DeFranza seeks to wed her understanding of science with her understanding of Scripture to form a coherent vision of gender. Early on, she states that sex difference "falls on a continuum" (p. 152). This means that gender is flexible, but then she qualifies her contention, arguing that while we all fall somewhere on a continuum, we also observe in human physiology "a binary pattern" (pp. 152, 153). But the spectrum is not complete. Later in her chapter, she notes that some individuals can live as a "third gender" (p. 177). This seems to suggest that we adopt a "tri-gender" perspective rather than a binary one. The new gender theory seems not that dissimilar from the old, and we are left with the confusing conclusion that gender is at once both fluid and stable. Is the "third gender" fixed? If it is unfixed, is it fixed by its unfixedness? This apparently diversified-but-essentialist gender paradigm left me wondering.

The broader theological point is worth referencing here as well. The Scripture's literal testimony seems to apply to DeFranza's argument regarding the broader trajectory of the eunuch in the Bible, for example. We hear a great bit less, though, about the literal testimony of Scripture in, say, the Pauline Epistles. The explosive passage in 1 Corinthians 11, for example, which clearly calls men to look like men and women to look like women, draws no sustained attention. The teaching of Paul that women should be "silent" regarding preaching and teaching in the local church, teaching based on the order of creation, gets no coverage. The hermeneutic on display in DeFranza's chapter is a confusing one; the Bible seems to be speaking literally with regard to trajectory hermeneutics but not necessarily with regard to other matters.

Elsewhere, DeFranza suggests that there are some people "who are not strictly male or female in body or gender identity" (p. 152), but this confuses the matter. According to Genesis 1–2, we are all either a man or a woman (see chap. 1 for my handling of intersex). Our identity cannot be separated from our body. Men have the body of a man; women have the body of a woman. We may not *feel* as though we are a man or a woman, but if we base our conception of our identity on our feelings, we are left in theological and existential chaos. Without any attempt at humor, in this line of thought, I may *feel* like an eighty-eight-year-old Icelandic grandmother, though such identity has no basis in biology. Or, more controversially, I might assert the identity of a different race, and I might even claim certain privileges or kinship dependent on that identity. My feelings cannot be the basis of my identity; my body, on the other hand, almost always can.

To counter the above response, DeFranza suggests that science may soon prove the existence of an "intersex brain": "Too many Christians who make a distinction between intersex people as 'born this way' and transgender people as those who 'choose' their identity fail to remember that the brain is a part of the body; the brain is 'sexed' both in the womb and throughout the lifetime. Transgender people may someday be identified as those with 'intersex brains,' but it is too early to tell" (p. 156). Her argument, in other words, is that the adoption of a cross-gender identity may owe to brain wiring, not a conscious and ostensibly rebellious choice. But this response does not provide the horsepower that it might seem to offer. I may well have a genetic predisposition to anger. My brain, that is, may in some way be wired to get explosively angry when I am frustrated. If this is true, however, this scientific datum would do nothing to solve the matter of the inherent sinfulness of unrighteous anger. We are *all* predisposed to sin; because of Adam's historical fall, we are fallen, guilty, and ungodly. Some of the expression of our wickedness may owe to genetics, and some may owe to conditioning. But it is not the *source* of our sin that matters most; it is the biblical testimony on the matter.

I have already referenced my concern with DeFranza's biblical hermeneutic. Her handling of certain texts also gave me pause. For example, in a discussion of barrenness, DeFranza argues the following: "In Scripture barrenness is attributed to the mother whose womb is 'closed' (1 Sam. 1:5–6); today we know that infertility is sometimes caused by the male. The biblical presentation of human reproductive structures (those very structures deemed essential for gender identity, according to the Nashville Statement) reflects ancient perspectives that have been improved through scientific research" (pp. 158–59). This is not a sound characterization of the ancient record. Sure, the biblical text uses language in different ways. Here, with reference to the "closed" womb, DeFranza seems to be making the mistake of reading a figurative statement as a literal one. She also seems to think that the Bible is blaming the woman for the inability to conceive, a conclusion that is not warranted. Her mishandling of biblical language gives way to a still more troubling problem. Contra what she says here, there is no sense in which "scientific research" has corrected the "biblical presentation" of any matter. The "ancient perspectives" of the Bible are not outmoded. They do not need to be revised. DeFranza's chapter in general shows greater dependence on her understanding of "scientific research" than of "ancient" doctrinal instruction.

We come across similar problems in DeFranza's handling of eunuchs and "gender rules." After a section on the reasons behind ancient castration practices, we get the following conclusion: "Ancient castrated eunuchs are not identical to transgender people, but the biblical account of eunuchs does teach us that conformity to masculinity and femininity is not what is required of Christians; rather, we are called to be conformed to Christ—a call that can challenge gendered cultural ideals" (p. 175). This is not at all what the biblical portrait of eunuchs teaches us. Eunuchs may have undergone castration for a variety of reasons. Whatever their background, the repentant eunuch is not left out of the kingdom of God. This does not mean that Scripture in any way endorses personal castration; far from it. It does mean that grace is offered to all in Christ. Confession and repentance enable sinners of every kind to enter God's household as sons and daughters.

But this glorious truth in no way softens the New Testament material on the sexes. To the contrary, the apostles issue repeated calls to embrace biblical manhood and womanhood as men or women. A husband, for example, who is being "conformed to Christ" is called by the apostle Paul to a position of headship in his marriage, just as a wife who is being "conformed to Christ" is called to submission (Eph. 5:22–33). When God brings young men and women into our congregations, we do not train them in an amorphous, degendered Christianity. We think here of Titus 2, which explicitly distinguishes between the training and comportment of godly men and godly women: "In the same way, older women are to be reverent in behavior, not slanderers, not slaves to excessive drinking. They are to teach what is good, so that they may encourage the young women to love their husbands and to love their children, to be self-controlled, pure, workers at home, kind, and in submission to their husbands, so that God's word will not be slandered. In the same way, encourage the young men to be self-controlled in everything" (Titus 2:3–7 CSB). The biblical teaching on the sexes thus goes a different direction than DeFranza.

After a section that sets Augustine up as the bad guy—almost the crazy uncle—regarding long-haired eunuchs, DeFranza concludes that the eunuchs had "such a solid foundation for their sense of self that they didn't need to fear being 'disgraced' by disregarding the gender rules of their day, including wearing long hair" (p. 163). But for a Bible-following Christian, Augustine was right to challenge the androgyny of this group. He was doing little other than applying the apostle Paul's words in 1 Corinthians 11:3–16, which explicitly challenge men to differentiate themselves from women in how long they grow their hair.

Our gender-neutral society does not obey Paul's words. Increasingly, young men grow their hair longer than young women, while young women adopt hairstyles commonly reserved for the opposite sex. This should not surprise us, for our secularizing society recognizes no divine design of the cosmos, let alone of humanity. We are all a blank slate today. There is no *telos* in our frame. We owe no allegiance to any divine being. We have no script for our sexuality. We are evolved from dust. Our bodies tell us basically nothing about who we are. But the Bible, praise God, has a different and better word. Though we who live in an androgynous culture might feel odd about training boys not to grow their hair like girls, in truth we are only doing what is "natural" (to use another Pauline term that betrays belief in God's anthropological design). Augustine was right. Our young men should not look and act and talk like girls. Our young women should not look and act and talk like boys. What DeFranza calls "gender rules" are actually a code of flourishing, a biblical vision of men and women alive to God, happily embracing the gift of the body, and the beauty of manhood and womanhood.

The last matter that drew my attention in DeFranza's chapter was her strong language regarding traditional Christians. At one point, DeFranza says this of people who do not affirm "transgender Christianity": "Christians must stop demonizing transgender people as rebellious against God and nature on account of the fact that their experience of themselves is different from the majority. Many transgender people are devout Christians prayerfully working out their salvation with 'fear and trembling' (Phil. 2:12)" (pp. 177–78). This is strong language, and it does not help the conversation. No one is "demonizing" anyone; conservative, Bible-loving evangelicals are trying to help people recover a fully biblical sense of identity. We disagree over the issues at hand, even strongly. But DeFranza, who identifies herself as a "bridge builder," is here painting a certain group in an uncharitable light.[1]

1. Megan K. DeFranza, "Portfolio," https://www.megandefranza.com/offerings/.

Throughout her essay, DeFranza sharply critiques the Nashville Statement. But the Nashville Statement represents a theologically sound and pastorally wise approach to the matters at hand. The current anthropological revolution sweeping over our culture is going to leave many broken by its false promises. We weep to think, for example, of children who are buying the lie that they are a girl trapped in a boy's body, or vice versa. Yet transgender teaching encourages such thinking. DeFranza is right on this point: there is no neutral ground regarding such ideology. Either you accept it or you do not. Either you see it as good and part of human flourishing to embrace transgender teaching, or you do not. Many have sought a third way, a middle ground, on this broader issue. But there is no middle ground. We must either give speed to transgenderism or seek, in grace and in truth, to show struggling sinners just like us a better way.

For the sake of many who stand to suffer through their disobedience to God and his good design, we cannot fail to speak up. We love those who feel trapped in their body; we have great compassion for the child confused by their anatomy; we offer Christic hope and the joy of biblical clarity to all who sense—as their confusion deepens and their rejection of their God-given sex spirals out of control—that something is wrong, deeply wrong.

Response to Megan K. DeFranza

Mark A. Yarhouse and Julia Sadusky

D
r. Megan DeFranza opens her chapter with a moving account of her previous approach to discussions around gender dysphoria. She describes how she almost made the mistake of publishing a paper on an evangelical perspective on sex reassignment surgery long before she had known anyone who was transgender. That paper, which she is now grateful she never published, was organized around the four acts of the biblical drama. In it, Dr. DeFranza had concluded that transgender people were struggling with gender identity as a result of the fall. This account reflects elements of what we describe in our chapter as the integrity and disability lenses. Dr. DeFranza goes on to discuss how personal encounters with transgender people, along with further reflection on Scripture and science, led her to another conclusion. Hers is a very personal journey of relationships that have informed her experience of the topic.

She then goes into an account of the relationship between experience and emotion and moral reasoning. She references such a relationship to note how what she believed at the time was tied to emotional reasoning about the topic she admits she knew little about. She was left believing that all transgender people were deceptive. Her general discomfort and mistrust greatly shaped not only her reactions to those who are transgender but also her theological reasoning. This indicates how much the lens through which we see people matters. We agree that if these are the only grounds on which Christians raise concerns around transgender experiences, there is little foundation for their thoughts.

While acknowledging that emotion and moral reasoning can be linked for both liberals and conservatives, we are left wondering what moral conclusions are not at risk of being tied to our emotions and experiences, her most recent conclusions included. In other words, in what way have her current feelings and experiences guided her to the conclusions she now holds? Regardless of

184

whether we acknowledge the part they play, they inevitably have an impact on the conclusions we draw. She seems to say that feelings alone can often keep people from concluding what she ends up concluding. This may disregard the many people who base their perspectives on transgender experiences on more than feelings.

From what Dr. DeFranza has written here and elsewhere, emotional reasoning is not the sole precursor to her shift in understanding. It was also studying the science of differences of sex development that was particularly impactful. She concludes that "human sex is dimorphic" but "also falls on a continuum" (p. 152). For Dr. DeFranza, all humans are "complex mosaics of male and female characteristics," a fact that should keep us from seeing those with gender nonconforming behaviors as "troublesome aberrations" (p. 152). Her point demands that theology account for the experiences beyond the binary, specifically intersex conditions and other experiences that do not seem to follow the usual pattern. Her question becomes ours: "What of those who do not fit this pattern?" (p. 159).

She makes a good point here too, noting that "like all humans, they [transgender people] vary in the ways they live in the world—conservative or liberal, chaste or licentious" (p. 149). We agree that it is important to consider and respond to the unique ways in which people live their lives, not making assumptions about their decisions or virtue based on their experience of gender identity. At the same time, we would invite Dr. DeFranza to consider the wide array of experiences that fall under the transgender umbrella and whether anything attached to transgender experience is volitional, and to speak to the pastoral care that may differ in these cases.

She notes what we have observed as well: Christians "tend to respond differently to people with verifiable biological variations (intersex) than to people with gender differences (gender nonconforming behavior and/or transgender identities)" (p. 152). She goes on to make her case by responding to elements of the Nashville Statement that portray transgender people as willfully disobedient and as those whose identity needs to be forsaken for the sake of the gospel. Gender identity is treated as a chosen reality, whereas intersex conditions are treated as medical concerns for which the architects of the Nashville Statement appear to show more compassion. Dr. DeFranza pushes back on this notion of choosing gender identity, pointing to social construction as more relevant to gender identity development.

Although we may not conclude that gender identity is purely a result of social construction in childhood or that aspects of its consolidation are never chosen, what Dr. DeFranza describes as a double standard confuses us as well. This beckons those adhering to the perspective of the Nashville Statement to explain the rationale for this seeming inconsistency. She emphasizes how, "when our experience matches the experiences and/or expectations of the majority, we are often unaware of, and struggle to understand, those whose experiences differ" (p. 154). We would go further to say that when our experience matches that of the majority, we may not take many steps to really understand those whose experiences differ or consider how consistently we approach their experience. The inconsistency matters because it creates a dynamic wherein people navigating gender identity concerns feel uniquely isolated and estranged in their communities—as they face challenges it seems highly unlikely anyone would willfully choose. This is more difficult for those who solely see the glamorous portrayals of transgender experiences in media. We would highlight that, whatever the source of transgender experiences, they bring unique challenges, particularly for Christians navigating gender identity and faith.

We were particularly grateful for Dr. DeFranza's reminder that the "brain is a part of the body" (p. 156). While this may seem like an obvious statement, we believe it is often lost on people who discuss gender dysphoria as if people with this condition have chosen it out of willful disobedience. "Too many Christians who make a distinction between intersex people as 'born this way' and transgender people as those who 'choose' their identity fail to remember that the brain is a part of the body; the brain is 'sexed' both in the womb and throughout the lifetime" (p. 156). She raises the possibility that people with gender dysphoria may have what some refer to as an "intersex condition of the brain," a point we made in our chapter as well. This begs the question of how perspectives from those who represent the Nashville Statement would be different if gender dysphoria were found to be an intersex condition of the brain. We agree with Dr. DeFranza that it seems likely this would demand a shift in perspective from suspicion to grace and an honest acknowledgment that "biology matters" when it comes to gender identity. At the same time, to say an experience has biological causes is not the same as saying that experience is an aspect of diversity to be celebrated. Many experiences with biological causes are not celebrated by those who have them, in the case of disabilities of any kind. This is noteworthy, since what is present in the natural order is not untouched by the fall.

Although there isn't a lot of Scripture to go on with respect to gender identity, Dr. DeFranza does look at what it means to be a eunuch at the time Scripture was recorded. Jesus himself recognized that while eunuchs were "outsiders," they would be identified as "models of Christian discipleship." She is able to draw a helpful line from the prohibitions in the Old Testament through Jesus's recognition of eunuchs to the baptism of the Ethiopian eunuch as recorded in the book of Acts. She argues that such a trajectory might give us a new appreciation for how we ought to approach outsiders in light of this. It is helpful to take from this that we could better see transgender Christians as models of discipleship—although Christians may disagree as to what makes one a model in this way and how decisions made around gender identity either help or inhibit this modeling.

We appreciated how Dr. DeFranza grapples with questions related to Adam and Eve—that is, whether they are a *"pattern* that God established for all people"; whether they are "God's *best* or the *beginning* of the story"; and whether they are "the exclusive *model* for all humans or the statistical *majority*" (p. 173). These are the kinds of questions that can be helpful for theological reflection. They may also inform pastoral care, especially when it seems obvious that Adam and Eve being the pattern for "all people" would leave out those who experience gender identity concerns. We need not throw out the pattern; we are inclined to think that exceptions actually prove the rule. Still, what could the Genesis narrative offer those with experiences outside the pattern?

We also appreciated how Dr. DeFranza raises questions about the eschaton. Will those struggling with elements of their gendered selves be "as they are" in eternity, or will they return to what might be thought of as God's original intent from creation? It is noteworthy that Jesus himself returned after his resurrection and was known by the wounds he bore. So if gender dysphoria is a "wound," what would it mean for it to be healed in eternity? Does the healing result in being conformed to one's birth sex? Or could healing look different in light of what could be an intersex condition of the brain? This is difficult because it requires so much speculation, but it raises broader questions often discussed in theology-of-disability circles and questions that, again, are important for pastoral care.

We think Dr. DeFranza helpfully reminds us that, while much of her chapter engages the eunuch and draws on research on people with intersex conditions, "ancient castrated eunuchs are not identical to transgender people" (p. 175). We appreciate that her goal is not to offer proof texts or to indiscriminately superimpose passages on current experiences. What this kind of scholarship does, according to DeFranza, is to instruct us "that conformity to masculinity and femininity is not what is required of Christians; rather we are called to be conformed to Christ—a call that can challenge gendered cultural ideals" (p. 175). Things like hairstyles, clothing choices, or other aspects of one's public presentation seem to be unhelpful measures of the degree to which one conforms to Christ. We too have questioned the efficacy of pastoral care that draws from gender stereotypes to judge the degree of healing and holiness of a person whose experience of gender identity diverges from the norms for men and women. We have heard of cases where people have been scrutinized in churches for dressing in androgynous ways, as if wearing a skirt as a woman is the sign of virtue and embracing one's essential femaleness. The exploration of eunuchs could encourage transgender Christians to see that they are not alone in their lack of conforming to ideals of masculinity and femininity of the day. Service to God, more than pressure to conform to stereotypes, may be more important when offering pastoral care.

Yet conformity to Christ and the pathways for those with gender dysphoria to do this are important considerations nonetheless. Here we believe Dr. DeFranza is trying to get too much mileage from intersex persons and from the experiences of eunuchs. She does not appear to be following her own caution: an intersex person, for example, is not a transgender female; a eunuch in Scripture is not a gender-nonbinary teen. And this is precisely where thoughtful Christians may disagree. What does it mean to be conformed to Christ when one experiences gender dysphoria? More broadly, what does it mean to be conformed to Christ when one is transgender? Given the wide array of experiences contained therein, we imagine it could vary considerably. For those operating from the integrity lens, the answer is to restore what they hold to be God's creational intent—that is, alignment with one's biological sex. For those who operate from the disability lens, it may mean managing one's gender dysphoria as best one can when one is unable to align gender identity and biological sex. For those operating from a diversity lens, it means celebrating God's creative expression of gender diversity.

As we read Dr. DeFranza, we conclude she is more inclined to view experiences of gender dysphoria and experiences of being transgender and gender nonbinary through a diversity lens, as reflecting the diversity of creation. Rather than attribute these experiences to the effects of the fall on creation, her tendency is to challenge that view, to revisit Adam and Eve as simply representatives of the "statistical majority" and declare that our guide should be found in Jesus's and Philip's treatment of the eunuch (again, conflating the different experiences). While not necessarily the celebratory language one often reads from the diversity lens, it is certainly a departure from either the integrity or the disability lenses. We take seriously the effects of the fall on the gender identity of each one of us, especially in cases of gender dysphoria, and find this frame helpful in validating the sense of those with gender dysphoria that their deep pain and suffering is not intended by God.

We differ with Dr. DeFranza in terms of these theological conclusions. So too, in terms of pastoral care and clinical services, her conclusions will likely make it difficult to critically engage not only the transgender experience but also atypical trends in transgender and gender-nonbinary identification (particularly among natal females) and potential social influences that are just now being studied. Responding to these trends is important, and to merely describe them as part of God's creational intent goes further than we would.

One aspect of the parallel with the eunuchs that we might invite Dr. De-Franza to develop more is the notion that eunuchs were called "to a more perfect path, which included a rejection of sexuality and marriage" (p. 164). This implies that with the call comes a rejection. This is described as giving something up, as a call to virtue within that sacrifice. This could be important for pastoral care, even though it is an unpopular notion. Certainly, a range of transgender people can be "models of radical discipleship" to others, just as the eunuch seemed to be. Still, this does not resolve the direction of the paths for Christians navigating gender dysphoria. What, if anything, are they called to sacrifice? Much is left unsaid in this regard.

Some Christians with gender dysphoria could sacrifice options such as seeking reassignment surgeries. Others could potentially sacrifice the opportunity for children and marriage, similar to how eunuchs did. These are deeply personal considerations. For each person, there is an opportunity to seek out what God is inviting one to give up and the continual call to virtue therein. The notion of liberation from all pain, albeit desirable, is both impossible in this life and a missed opportunity to learn and teach others something valuable. Christian joy and obedience to Christ on this side of eternity do not hinge on alleviation of all pain. Still, whether a person has an intersex condition or gender dysphoria, we see the value of journeying alongside them, seeking a positive vision for their life and steps that can lead to greater wholeness on this side of eternity, in light of the fullness to come.

Response to Megan K. DeFranza

Justin Sabia-Tanis

Megan DeFranza's chapter highlights the critical difference it makes when we speak with and listen to transgender people. Reading this chapter, I began to wonder how different this volume might be if we had all gathered in the same place to write. What if we were not merely authors writing at our own desks in different places but instead authors wrestling together with the meaning of these texts and concepts? After all, it is relatively easy to conjure up stereotypes of transgender people, or of Christians for that matter; yet we are called to see one another as humans, as fellow believers, and that takes more work. And seeing one another—truly seeing—matters.

I acknowledge the courage that it takes to describe a change of heart, as Dr. DeFranza does at the beginning of her chapter. She ably and helpfully demonstrates how theological inquiry and study can move us from a place of uninformed judgment to one of informed belief. When our sense of theological certainty is based on false premises or simply a lack of knowledge we are not aware of, we may *feel* that we are on solid ground even though we are not. By thoughtfully engaging with transgender people, we can gain knowledge about gender identity that is not otherwise available to us. This allows us to think and act with compassion, reflecting God's great love for humanity. I appreciate the honesty and clarity of the journey that begins this chapter. It is a testimony to the transformative powers of faith.

This chapter reflects thoughtfully listening to the witness of transgender Christians. Dr. DeFranza models what it means to willingly be accountable to those she is speaking about. Disability and human rights advocates have popularized the idea, "Nothing about us without us." That is, decisions should never be made about a community without its input. This is critical for several reasons. First, to include those who are the topic of conversation in the discussion is essential for affirming their fundamental human dignity. To speak about people without including them can be patronizing and dehumanizing. This is counter to our Christian beliefs. Second, to be included in the discussion reflects the Golden Rule—it is treating others how we ourselves would wish to be treated. None of us wish to be excluded from conversations about us, particularly those that lead to decision making concerning our well-being. Third, the people who are the topic of the conversation have knowledge of the situation that others simply do not have because they have not lived it. In this case, transgender people will always know more about how it feels to live as a transgender person than those who are not transgender. That includes the ways in which we hear and experience the presence and blessings of God, which is critical information for a theological discussion.

Dr. DeFranza also models how to use scientific information to enhance our understandings of the world around us. We were given the gift of being able to observe and learn about the world around us, resulting in discoveries that enhance our knowledge of the creation. Science need not be seen in opposition to faith but as an avenue for greater appreciation of the complexities with which the universe is endowed. Gender is but one of the facets of this creation. Science and Scripture read in tandem open up even greater depths of understanding.

Dr. DeFranza, in my opinion, of all of us in the book, does the best job of articulating the connections between Jesus's sayings in Matthew 19, both his affirmation of the creation of male and female in Genesis (Matt. 19:4–6) and his statements about the eunuchs in verse 12. She reminds us, first, that the context for Jesus's statements had to do with the allowability of divorce. Her summary of the ways Christians through the ages have struggled to understand and live out these verses is helpful. It reminds us that this is not, in fact, a new conversation. I was unaware of some of the interesting history cited here, in which the rejection of gendered privilege and norms was how some early Christians expressed their new identity in Christ.

This history reminds us to consider the ways of developing a Christian identity that supersedes worldly categories—such as that articulated in Galatians 3:28: "There is no longer Jew or Greek, there is no longer slave or free, there is no longer male and female; for all of you are one in Christ Jesus." This was and is part of Christian faith and development. We are called not to be conformed to the norms of an age but to be faithful to Christ. As Dr. DeFranza points out in her consideration of Matthew 19, Christ is one who affirmed both the creation of male and female *and* the realities of those who do not fit these categories. This also reminds us that conformity to social mores is not necessarily a sign of holiness. In fact, being out of step with the wider culture can be a way to demonstrate our Christian identities. After all, there are many biblical stories of those who did not easily fit into their societies, including many of the prophets, John the Baptist, and, of course,

Jesus. It is through these differences, not despite them, that God's will was made manifest.

Another strength of this chapter is its emphasis on narrative, both personal and biblical. When I took homiletics in seminary (yes, it was long enough ago that the class was not yet called "preaching"), the professor emphasized the importance of not just reading the passage that we would be preaching on but also finding its place in the larger, longer story. He recommended studying the surrounding chapters when we were preparing our sermons but also rereading the entire book of the Bible that the passage came from! This turned out to be time consuming but incredibly valuable advice because it compels me, even now, to preach from the wider story. It fundamentally changes how I understand the Bible and what I preach from it.

Dr. DeFranza reminds us to do likewise, to read the whole of the Bible before drawing conclusions based only on a handful of passages. She writes, "The story of creation and redemption in Scripture is not a short story but a complex, compelling narrative taking its readers beyond their wildest dreams" (p. 172). I think it is very helpful to consider the ways in which the biblical narrative arc moves from the narrow and specific to the widely inclusive. The Bible tells of the revelation of God's infinite and ineffable love for humanity, beginning with a single nation and unfolding to include the entire world, starting in an ancient age and continuing to this day and beyond. If we select only one moment in the story, we miss the wider picture.

In this vein, I found particularly helpful a process of questioning posed by Dr. DeFranza: "How then should Christians read the theological significance of Adam and Eve?

- Are they the *pattern* that God established for all people or the first *parents*?
- Are they God's *best* or the *beginning* of the story?
- Are they the exclusive *model* for all humans or the statistical *majority*?" (p. 173)

These questions articulate a process through which we can consider this material. To understand the meaning of a particular passage—especially one as important to this conversation as the story of Adam and Eve—we see most fully when we consider how it fits within the larger narrative.

That story includes both the biblical accounts as well as Christian history as it has unfolded over more than two millennia. I appreciated Dr. DeFranza's fascinating description of this history and its implications for understanding the ways in which Christians have engaged the question of gender in different ways throughout that history, often in diverse and usually unknown ways.

Her closing question, "Which matters more: gender identity or identity in Christ?" is a critical one. On the one hand, I want to answer: "Why choose?" in order to acknowledge that we can, of course, be both Christian and transgender. However, I certainly agree with her conclusion: "[The ancient church] believed identity in Christ superseded cultural gender ideals, so much so that one could even make oneself a eunuch in radical obedience to Christ. Ancient castrated eunuchs are not identical to transgender people, but the biblical account of eunuchs does teach us that conformity to masculinity and femininity is not what is required of Christians; rather, we are called to be conformed to Christ—a call that can challenge gendered cultural ideals" (p. 175).

The modern church often mistakenly places the emphasis on genitals, as she points out, rather than on Christian values. The obsessive interest in sexuality and gender identity in much of the Christian church has obscured and diverted our focus from what Christ preached was important about human life—namely, loving God and loving our neighbor as ourselves. At the same time, we also fail to notice other important aspects of genitals and their use—not speaking out against sexual assault, on the one hand, or not acknowledging the pleasure and joy of sexual intimacy freely given and received, on the other. Our Christian witness should include these aspects of sexuality and gender as well. We have significant work to do collectively in order to develop a healthy understanding of the roles of sexuality, sex, and gender.

The question here is, How do our conversations about transgender people's genitals—or more broadly, our medical treatment—enhance or detract from our ability to develop our Christian identities? Does our exclusion or inclusion of transgender people better witness to God's love or serve Christ's purposes? Why are we focused so heavily on issues of genitals and hormone treatments? Why in this volume are we not addressing significantly the rates of poverty that transgender people face, for example, or the levels of violence experienced by transgender women of color? Jesus interceded in acts of violence. Jesus spoke more about hunger and poverty than about sex and gender, after all.

Finally, the stories that come at the end of Dr. DeFranza's chapter are beautiful statements about the spiritual integrity and growth that can come when we bring our full selves to worship and Christian life. What I particularly find helpful is that these stories remind us that transgender Christians approach the questions of identity and transition through prayer and deep spiritual consideration. What is often missing from Christian discussions of the topic is the witness of transgender Christians who feel very strongly the leading and blessing from God on this path to gender transition. When we experience the love and guidance of Christ in our lives, that is very good news.

4

Holy Creation, Wholly Creative

God's Intention for Gender Diversity

Justin Sabia-Tanis

Is Gender a Binary Phenomenon, or Is It a Continuum?

In this chapter, I describe how gender falls on a continuum of identities, reflecting a range of healthy human possibilities. The resulting variations in individual appearance, expression, and self-understanding are rooted in a complex set of biological, social, cultural, and behavioral factors. I would like to invite you, while reading this chapter, to consider that these differences are naturally occurring and thus can be seen theologically as part of God's plan for a diverse and wondrous creation. To deny the value and beauty of these differences may disrespect and devalue the imagination and intention of the Creator.

Creation in Genesis

While we have often been taught that the creation story in Genesis is one that sets out oppositional pairs, this interpretation falls short in considering the complexity and nuance that the verses describe. In fact, each of the days of the creation story adds another cyclical spectrum to the world.

Genesis tells us that God separated the day and the night, the two extremes of light and darkness by which we mark the passage of time. Day and night, however, are not sharply divided. Think for a moment about a time when you were awake before dawn. There comes a moment when you notice that the earth is becoming gray, not just dark. Birds begin to sing, and animals start to stir as the night begins to lift and the light becomes brighter. Finally, the sun peeks over the horizon, and day has begun. The process reverses itself at the end of the day as evening draws on and the day comes to a close. While we may record the times of sunrise and sunset in almanacs as the official moments at which day and night change, the actual process of day becoming night becoming day is much more natural. It is gradual and peaceful.

When I was a child living in the Netherlands, I was taken on a school field trip to an island in the North Sea where the tides came and went dramatically. At the end of the day, we stood on the earthen embankment and watched as the waves crashed against the seawall that marked an abrupt demarcation between land and sea. But this is not the natural order of things—that wall was made artificially, by human hands. In fact, the division between land and sea that seems so clear in Genesis is even more difficult to discern than the line between day and night. On a beach, the waves ride up over the land in continual motion. Some of the water returns to the sea immediately, while some of it percolates down through the wet sand. The land slopes down from the beach into the sea, forming a liminal zone before dropping further to the sea floor. There are places with cloudy water because of the particulates of sand and salt floating up from the earth's surface to be suspended in the water. All of this is natural and part of the good and created world. While land and sea mark the extremes, they come together on the beach, coexisting in the shore zone.

We can see the same patterns with living creatures. There are beings, like coral, that fall somewhere between our categories of plant and animal. God created egg-laying mammals that swim, like the platypus, a creature so outlandish that travelers from outside Australia initially did not believe in its existence. There are sea dragons that look like plants, massive blue whales, pygmy goats, and protozoa. The earth is filled with diverse and wondrous living things of every shape, size, color, and affect. Recognizing this diversity of life is part of honoring the imagination and miraculous, life-giving nature of the Creator. God made it and said that it was good.

When we consider human beings, we should see ourselves through the same lenses with which we read the rest of the creation story—that is, that we too are part of a marvelous story in which diversity and variation play a critical role. Human beings share more than 99 percent of our DNA; we have a lot in common. But we also exhibit tremendous differences in color, size, shape, outlook, features, and so on. This is part of God's plan. Gender is one more facet of this natural variation intended by God as a feature of life on earth. Male and female define two categories of humans, but they are not meant to be exclusive boxes that limit our individual expression. Like night and day, land and sea, plant and animal, they are descriptors that have liminal spaces between them where aspects of both elements are combined. How people express those spaces, those differences, is part of the beauty that makes up the human family, part of the goodness of God's creation.

Much of the research that has been done on sex and gender has sought to create broad categories in which everyone falls, with differences being relegated to the side as abnormalities or curiosities. This fails, however, to provide us with a positive view of difference. John Archer and Barbara Lloyd write in their book *Sex and Gender*, "Most research has been nomothetic in character, in that it has sought to establish generalisations about the categories 'men' and 'women,' with individual variation within each category being relegated to a minor role. Both social role and evolutionary explanations are of this type."[1]

We should consider, however, that while the divisions described in Genesis set broad parameters for the natural world, they in no way articulate its detail, just as Archer and Lloyd point out about studies of gender. The world is separated into lesser and greater waters, for example, but there is no mention of ponds, lakes, rivers, waterfalls, and wetlands. Likewise, the land is not described in terms of plains, mountains, deserts, steppes, and the many other terrains that exist, yet we know these are intrinsic aspects of the earth. There are aspects of the earth completely unknown to the biblical scribes, such as permafrost, fjords, and glacial moraines, which were outside of the known world at that time and are not mentioned in the Bible. Yet we are clearly able to understand that they are part of the overall creation. These variations compose the complexity and beauty of the natural world; they are not counter to God's creation but rather aspects of it. They stem from the imagination of the Creator, who intended our world to be this way.

The creation story also affirms that human beings were made in the image and likeness of God, as both male and female. This must mean that God's own being includes more than one gender, if that is reflected in humanity. The Bible includes multiple images for God, including feminine ones, such as Hosea 13:8 and Deuteronomy 32:11–12, where God is compared to mother animals; Deuteronomy 32:18, where God is said to have given birth to humanity; Luke 15:8–10, where Jesus compares God to a woman searching for her lost coin; and Matthew 23:37 and Luke 13:34, where Jesus says he longs to care for the people of Jerusalem as a mother hen cares for her young. Divinity, then,

1. John Archer and Barbara Lloyd, *Sex and Gender*, 2nd ed. (Cambridge: Cambridge University Press, 2002), 14.

encompasses both male and female within the Godhead, modeling similar possibilities for humanity.

Genesis 2, which repeats the creation narrative with some differences, tells of Eve being created from the rib of Adam. We note that the Hebrew *'adam* here is not initially used as a name but as a general noun meaning "earth being." This person existed prior to the creation of gender and was, apparently, God's original plan. The most critical thing to note about the division of the sexes is in Genesis 2:18, in which God describes the rationale for this division—not to create a separation of genders but rather to solve the problem of human loneliness. First, God attempts to address this through the animals. When this does not work, God chooses to create an additional human being. God's focus here is addressing the fundamental need that we have for companionship and friendship. We need one another to thrive; we are not meant to be alone or isolated.

Sex, Gender, and the Natural World

The natural world offers us tremendous evidence of God's imagination and zeal for differences. Telescopes show us awe-inspiring and beautiful galaxies that exist at staggering distances from us; microscopes show us the tiniest of creatures living among us. One part of this miraculous creation is the planet Earth, teeming with a mind-boggling variety of life. For all our scientific efforts, we have not even finished cataloging the variety that exists in the sea or on the land.[2] We can see the abundance of forms, colors, functions, environments, and so on as signs of God's love for creativity. Elizabeth Johnson writes, "Biodiversity in its own natural way manifests the goodness of God which goes beyond our imagination. Noting how this insight validates the importance of the diversity of the species, Denis Edwards notes that 'no one creature, not even the human can image God by itself. Only the diversity of life—huge soaring trees, the community of ants, the flashing colors of the parrot, the beauty of the wildflower along with the human—can give expression to the radical diversity and otherness of the Trinitarian God.'"[3] Looking at the world's diversity gives us insights and glimpses into the nature of God; this is not a world of staid conformity but one that is exuberant in difference. That same feature can be seen in the way the world's creatures are sexed.

2. Sarah Gibbens, "New Amazon Species Discovered Every Other Day," *National Geographic*, September 1, 2017, https://news.nationalgeographic.com/2017/08/amazon-brazil-new-species-discovered-spd/.

3. Elizabeth A. Johnson, *Ask the Beasts: Darwin and the God of Love* (London: Bloomsbury Continuum, 2014), 149, quoting Denis Edwards, *Ecology at the Heart of Faith* (Maryknoll, NY: Orbis, 2006), 78.

Consider plants, for example. Some species are hermaphroditic, having both male and female parts in the same plant, while others are dioecious, with each plant having only male or female flowers. Other plants are gynodioecious, in which hermaphroditic and female plants live together in one environment.[4] As if all that is not varied enough, a number of plants are able to change their sex, even season to season, and a recent study at the University of Lincoln found plants that change sex in response to alterations in their environment.[5]

Some plants experience protandry, meaning they start as a male plant that produces pollen and can change to female and produce seeds and fruit; others demonstrate the reverse, called protogyny. Many plants are capable of both pollen and seed production; some can fertilize themselves. Still others demonstrate sequential sexes, as in oil palms and corn plants. Thus, while we can identify male and female aspects of plants, they are not static categories but labile ones that alter in response to the plants' needs, environments, life cycle, and so on. All of this is a normal and natural part of the world that God called good.

We can see similar differences in the animal world. Several categories of fish, for example, experience either sequential hermaphroditism—meaning they begin as one sex and then change to another—or simultaneous hermaphroditism—meaning they have the characteristics of both sexes simultaneously. Clown fish, the small orange-and-white striped fish popularized by the movie *Finding Nemo*, begin life as male and may change to female. Each group of clown fish has a dominant male and dominant female who are the only breeding pair. All others are subordinate males. If the female dies or is removed, the dominant male becomes female, and the most dominant of the subordinate males becomes the breeding male. Other types of fish change sex during their lifespan, like the Indo-Pacific cleaner wrasse, which begins life as female and becomes male as it matures.[6] Other types of amphibians, sponges, worms, and reptiles exhibit similar patterns.[7]

In an article on the phenomenon of sex changes in the plant and animal kingdoms, David Policansky summarizes these differences, noting that "sex

---

4. Carine L. Collin and Jacqui A. Shykoff, "Outcrossing Rates in the Gynomonoecious-Gynodioecious Species *Dianthus sylvestris* (Caryophyllaceae)," *American Journal of Botany* 90, no. 4 (April 1, 2003): 579–85.

5. University of Lincoln, "New Research Sheds Light on Why Plants Change Sex," *ScienceDaily* (blog), January 10, 2017, https://www.sciencedaily.com/releases/2017/01/170110094606.htm.

6. "Sex Change in Fish Found Common," *New York Times*, December 4, 1984, http://www.nytimes.com/1984/12/04/science/sex-change-in-fish-found-common.html.

7. For examples of different species that change sex, see the various articles included under the theme "Phenotypic Plasticity and the Evolution of Gender," *Integrative and Comparative Biology* 53, no. 4 (October 2013).

change is widespread, and many examples remain to be described. Nonetheless a great majority of organisms do not change sex, and some of these are closely related to organisms that do."[8] Thus, while variations or alterations of sex over the course of a lifetime are not the typical pattern, they nonetheless are a significant part of the natural world.

This occurs, too, among mammals, although more rarely, such as when female hyenas develop scrotums.[9] There are also genetic differences among the animals, such as the platypus, which has five pairs of sex chromosomes rather than the usual pair that most mammals have.[10] Therefore, like our previous examples of the liminal spaces between day and night, when dawn and twilight are just one small part of the cycle between day and night, those species that change sex are a fraction of the larger picture. Nonetheless, they are part of the natural occurrences of sex, which God created and declared good.

Human beings likewise exhibit these variations and can have up to at least six different combinations of the X and Y chromosomes, not simply XX (female) and XY (male). Most people with differences, such as X, XXY, XYY, and XXXY, are not aware of them, since biological variations come to light only if the person is chromosomally tested. These conditions are more common than one might expect. The University of Utah estimates that 1 out of every 2,000 to 2,500 baby girls born has just one X chromosome, or has one full and one partial X chromosome. Klinefelter Syndrome, in which a person has XXY chromosomes, is even more common: 1 in 660 male births.[11]

In addition, there is a growing body of evidence that gender dysphoria—the incongruence between a person's physical characteristics of gender and their self-identity—has a biological basis.[12] This may be due to hormonal differences experienced in utero, or it may be the result of genetic variations or other

---

8. David Policansky, "Sex Change in Plants and Animals," *Annual Review of Ecology and Systematics* 13 (1982): 484.

9. Martin M. Muller and Richard Wrangham, "Sexual Mimicry in Hyenas," *Quarterly Review of Biology* 77, no. 1 (2002): 3–16.

10. Steve Connor, "After 200-Year Quest, Scientists Finally Unravel the Bizarre Origins of the Duck-Billed Platypus," *Independent*, May 7, 2008, http://www.independent.co.uk/news/science/after-200-year-quest-scientists-finally-unravel-the-bizarre-origins-of-the-duck-billed-platypus-822812.html.

11. Genetic Science Learning Center, University of Utah, http://learn.genetics.utah.edu/content/disorders/aneuploidy/.

12. Aruna Saraswat, Jamie Weinand, and Joshua Safer, "Evidence Supporting the Biologic Nature of Gender Identity," *Endocrine Practice* 21, no. 2 (February 2015): 199–204; and Kristina R. Olson, "Prepubescent Transgender Children: What We Do and Do Not Know," *Journal of the American Academy of Child and Adolescent Psychiatry* 55, no. 3 (2016): 155–56.

factors. Multiple studies have been conducted that demonstrate variations in the bodies and brains of transgender people whose physiology is atypical for their sex and either falls between the norms for male and female or matches their gender identity.

Researchers in the Netherlands have compared children referred to gender clinics with control groups of gender-typical Dutch children and found ways in which some physical characteristics of gender dysphoric children resemble the peers of their gender identity, not their birth gender, or fall somewhere between boys and girls.[13] What if these variations are simply an intended part of the diversity that God included in the natural order, just like the differences of plants and animals previously described? If we then condemn or attempt to eradicate these naturally occurring variations, we are working counter to the will of God for creation, which God has declared to be good.

Gender Differences in the Bible

Gender differences have been recognized since ancient times. The Bible recognizes and affirms these variations and even addresses them directly. Jesus says in Matthew 19:11–12, "Not everyone can accept this teaching, but only those to whom it is given. For there are eunuchs who have been so from birth, and there are eunuchs who have been made eunuchs by others, and there are eunuchs who have made themselves eunuchs for the sake of the kingdom of heaven. Let anyone accept this who can."

Eunuchs in the ancient world were castrated men who were set apart socially and professionally because of their difference in gender. While some have attempted to say that the term "eunuch" in the Bible can refer to a court official, rather than to a eunuch per se, there is plenty of evidence that the writers of the biblical texts meant exactly what they said. Sean Burke points out, for example, that there were many other words meaning "court official" that were used elsewhere in the Bible; it does not make sense that the writers would use the word for "eunuch" as a synonym in this confusing way.[14]

Throughout the span of human history and across the globe, people have had differing concepts of gender. Many human societies have had more than two categories for gender, recognizing that some people are born in bodies that reflect more than one sex, while others come to live in ways different than most of those who share their natal gender. These parallel Jesus's words on

13. Sarah Melanie Burke, "Coming of Age: Gender Identity, Sex Hormones and the Developing Brain" (PhD diss., Vrije Universiteit Amsterdam, 2014).

14. See Sean D. Burke, "The Meaning of Eunuch," chap. 1 in *Queering the Ethiopian Eunuch: Strategies of Ambiguity in Acts* (Minneapolis: Fortress, 2013), 19–38.

the subject in Matthew 19—that some people are born with less usual sexual characteristics while others alter their genders during their lifetime—and this perspective is affirmed by science.

Jesus states that some people are eunuchs because they are born that way, while others become eunuchs during the course of their lifetimes. We know that ancient peoples in the Mediterranean region were aware of intersex conditions[15] and therefore could categorize someone as a eunuch from birth. Eunuchs were, as a result of the prohibitions in Deuteronomy 23:1, forbidden from entering into the holy of holies and practicing some aspects of the Jewish religion that were reserved for men. They lived in a separate category because of their gender.

Yet it is not only Jesus who recognizes these differences; the prophet Isaiah had already declared words of God's overcoming these barriers to welcome even the eunuchs.

> Thus says the LORD:
>> Maintain justice, and do what is right,
> for soon my salvation will come,
>> and my deliverance be revealed.
>
> Happy is the mortal who does this,
>> the one who holds it fast,
> who keeps the sabbath, not profaning it,
>> and refrains from doing any evil.
>
> Do not let the foreigner joined to the LORD say,
>> "The LORD will surely separate me from his people";
> and do not let the eunuch say,
>> "I am just a dry tree."
> For thus says the LORD:
> To the eunuchs who keep my sabbaths,
>> who choose the things that please me
>> and hold fast my covenant,
> I will give, in my house and within my walls,
>> a monument and a name
>> better than sons and daughters;
> I will give them an everlasting name
>> that shall not be cut off.
>
>   (Isa. 56:1–5)

15. For a description of the awareness of eunuchs, see Brittany E. Wilson, "'Neither Male nor Female': The Ethiopian Eunuch in Acts 8.26–40," *New Testament Studies* 60, no. 3 (July 2014): 405–11.

God not only says that the eunuchs are not separated from God's people but also extends the welcome so far as to promise that they will be given a name *better* than sons and daughters, an everlasting name that will never be taken from them. Those who have been cast out because of their anatomical differences are declared beloved of God as a result of their faithfulness. Moreover, God goes on to declare that God's house is a house for all people (v. 7). This passage in Isaiah makes it clear that God is including those who are different because of their gender. This speaks to God's recognition and acceptance of an array of genders.

This expansive welcome of those outside the gender norms is also extended by the evangelist Philip in the book of Acts, with the story of the baptism of the Ethiopian eunuch. This eunuch is an outsider in almost every possible way: he is from another region; he is not a Jew, although he has been to the temple in Jerusalem to worship; he is culturally and racially different; and he is a eunuch. The fact that he is repeatedly referred to as a eunuch and separately called a court official strongly supports the idea that he is, in fact, a literal eunuch.[16]

Upon hearing the good news about Jesus from Philip in Acts 8, the eunuch immediately poses the question: "What is to prevent me from being baptized?" (v. 36). Philip responds in action, not in words, and baptizes him. There is nothing that prevents him from being baptized. This question may have arisen because his status as a eunuch had prevented him from participating fully in religious life in the past. But here we read that he can be baptized. This echoes the expansive welcome of God that we read in Isaiah: baptism—full recognition and inclusion within the community—is, like God's house, not to be limited but is open to all who believe. The apostle Paul goes on to remind us in Galatians 3:28: there is neither Jew nor Greek, neither slave nor free, and no longer male and female in Christ Jesus.

The Continuum God Created

The creation story in Genesis sets the broad parameters of the world, stating the poles of a series of continuums: day and night; earth and sky; land and sea; plant, animal, and human; male and female. But we are intended to bring to this text our knowledge of the rich variation of the natural world: the beauty of dawn and dusk, an appreciation of the varied terrain of the earth, and the colorful diversity of the plants and animals. These facts should be a source of awe for us, reflecting the imagination of our Creator. The same

16. Annette Weissenrieder, "Searching for the Middle Ground from the End of the Earth: The Embodiment of Space in Acts 8:26–40," *Neotestamentica* 48, no. 1 (2014): 135.

holds true for gender: male and female may be the extremes of a continuum, but there are many variations along the way. These differences are deeply personal and affect all people, not just those who are transgender or intersex. Each of us has our unique ways of expressing ourselves, including the ways we understand and live masculinity and femininity. We all deserve the freedom to craft our lives according to God's guidance within us, God's plan for our individual creation.

Being transgender or intersex is experienced by many of us as a gift from God, an opportunity to see life from more than one perspective, to understand the world through uncommon but holy lenses. We affirm the God who knit us together in our mother's womb and God's use of some novel or unusual stitches in the knitting. But that in no way means that God was not the knitter: only that God was being a creative needleworker in those moments. God displays the same creativity in some human bodies that we see reflected in the broader world of living things.

In other writings, I have described the many ways in which the discovery of our own gender identity parallels our understandings of vocation: that gender differences arise in response to our following of God's leading for our individual lives. God calls some people to go on a journey that may include a change of gender, a transformative pilgrimage. Personally, I find the growing body of scientific research that points to physiological differences in the bodies of transgender people to be compelling and convincing. But at the end of the day, that matters less to me than the surety that I have experienced, as have other transgender people, of God's calling to set out on a journey between and among genders. I certainly do not understand all the reasons for it, and it is not always easy, but I do know that what God has called good is blessed. When I look at my life, and the lives of my transgender and intersex siblings in Christ, and all of God's people, I see reflected there the tremendous, awe-inspiring diversity made by an imaginative, loving Creator.

And if we are not sure about how to treat those who are different because of their gender, the Bible is clear about that as well: those who keep God's Word will be given a holy name; God's house is a house of prayer for all people; there is nothing to prevent the baptism of one who believes; and in Christ there is no male and female.

Gender Transitioning

Christians with gender dysphoria have the right to pursue treatment that offers the greatest possibility for their health and well-being. For many transgender people, but certainly not all, this entails gender transition, which can take a variety of forms, including **hormone replacement therapy** (HRT) and gender confirmation surgeries. Moreover, I believe that our calling to compassion requires us to advocate for people's rights to make this decision and work to ensure equitable access to it.

There are many Christians, myself included, who have thoughtfully and prayerfully decided to undergo gender transition. There are also Christians and other people of faith who are health care professionals who have similarly and faithfully made the decision to provide medical and psychological treatment to transgender people, believing that they are living out their vocation as healers in doing so.

I would urge that any serious consideration of this question be done in dialogue with transgender people and with those professionals who work with us. It is unhelpful—and, I would argue, unjust—to speak about us but not with us. Yet religious people are less likely to know a transgender person than the average American. According to the Public Religion Research Institute, between 2011 and 2017 the number of Americans who report having a close friend or family member who is transgender has risen, almost doubling from 11 percent to 21 percent.[17]

Looking at these numbers through the lens of religion, the same study found that Catholics reported having a family member or close friend at a rate the same as the national average, with nonwhite Protestants just slightly lower at 20 percent, and mainline white Protestants at 15 percent. There may be many reasons for this, and I would suggest that one reason may be that family members and friends are not disclosing their transgender identity to those they feel may be uncomfortable with it or may react negatively. But it is also a sign of the divisions within our society and our lack of contact with others who are unlike us. This disconnect makes it more challenging, though certainly not impossible, to learn from and about transgender Christians.

Let me give you one perspective. For me, the decision to transition was absolutely life-affirming and life-giving. It has transformed my life physically, socially, and spiritually, allowing me to live in a body that I felt comfortable in for the first time in my life. I tried many ways to reconcile my feelings with my gender before this. Being raised as a girl in the 1960s and '70s, I knew I wanted to be a boy, but it seemed impossible. My mother punished me for playing with my brother's toys and wearing his clothing. That did not make

17. Robert P. Jones, Daniel Cox, Betsy Cooper, and Rachel Lienesch. "Majority of Americans Oppose Transgender Bathroom Restrictions," Public Religion Research Institute, 2017, http://www.prri.org/research/lgbt-transgender-bathroom-discrimination-religious-liberty/. Data from PRRI August 2011 Survey; PRRI February 2017 Survey.

my feelings go away; I just learned to hide them and not share them with others.[18]

I chose to attend a women's college in the hopes that I could find affirmation for my female self and outgrow these feelings of discomfort. I received a great education, but my sense of dysphoria only grew. In addition to years spent in therapy, I also worked with a spiritual director. I had a strong relationship, a good job, and a ministry that was affecting lives, but inside, I felt deeply unhappy and like there was something unnamable that was just "off" about who I saw in the mirror.

Finally, I met some transgender men and knew right away that this was something I needed to explore. I went back into therapy and came to realize that I was not going to be able to reconcile my emotions with my body that way. After months of evaluation and conversation, my therapist referred me to a physician who prescribed testosterone. I felt calmer and more at peace within weeks of starting the treatments. A year later, I had my first surgery, draining my savings accounts to pay for it since it was excluded from my insurance plan. This was more than twenty years ago. It has only been in the last few years that I had health insurance that covered gender confirming procedures. The medical process has, at times, been painful and awkward.

Here's what I can tell you about the impact of gender transition for me, and for most of the transgender people I've met as friends and who have sought me out for pastoral care: It eases the feelings of gender dysphoria and allows us to move on with our lives. It has been effective and helpful, a healing process facilitated by doctors, nurses, mental health professionals, physical therapists, voice coaches, and others, depending on our individual needs. I am more able to focus on others, a better minister and an effective colleague because I am less preoccupied with my internal struggles and more able to be fully present with others.

It is important as you consider this question to hear from those who have undergone this process. There are people for whom medical treatment is not the answer—either because they cannot undergo it (e.g., people who have had cancer diagnoses that would be exacerbated by hormonal treatment), because it runs counter to their beliefs, or because it simply is not right for

18. For a current perspective on this, I highly recommend Kimberly Shappley and Breanne Randall, "I Had 4 Boys—Until One of Them Told Me She Was Really a Girl," *Good Housekeeping*, April 13, 2017, http://www.goodhousekeeping.com/life/parenting/a43702/transgender-child-kimberly-shappley/. Shappley is a conservative Christian who movingly describes her attempts to prevent her child from displaying cross-gender behavior and her regrets at this course of action. She also clearly articulates the benefits her child experienced as a result of socially transitioning.

them. No one should be pressured to transition or undergo any treatments that are not right for them.

Some people, especially those who identify outside the gender binary, may not want medical treatment but simply seek to be respected for who they are, as they are. It is vital that we make space for and respect those for whom medical treatment is not wanted or is only needed in limited ways. I focus on medical treatment here because the question of transitioning was one of the two questions that each contributor was instructed to address; however, I want to be clear in asserting the rights of transgender and gender-variant people to not access medical transition and to still be respected and valued.

A very few people make the decision to medically transition and then feel that it was a mistake. Studies show that this is a small fraction.[19] However, it should be noted that not every medical treatment works or is appropriate for every patient. We would not conclude that kidney transplants, for example, should not be performed because some patients are not better afterward while many patients report improved health. The vast majority of transgender patients show a lessening of gender dysphoria[20] and an improvement in life following transition, which may or may not include medical treatment.

How Have People in the Past Answered These Questions?

Medical treatment for gender dysphoria is relatively new. There have been few theological responses to it at all, especially in the early pioneering years of the 1950s–1970s when it was simply considered a medical situation. Christians and pastors of varied theological perspectives and convictions have answered this question in various ways over these decades. In the late 1990s, when I was researching the spirituality of transgender people for my doctor of ministry degree, I found both conservative and liberal pastors who felt that gender transition was not at all a question of faith but rather a medical issue that was best resolved between people and their doctors; they were supportive of their congregants who undertook such procedures. I also found both liberal and conservative churches that rejected transgender people as too far outside the norm for their congregation. Twenty-five to thirty years ago, perspectives

19. Anne A. Lawrence, "Factors Associated with Satisfaction or Regret Following Male-to-Female Sex Reassignment Surgery," *Archives of Sexual Behavior* 32, no. 4 (August 1, 2003): 299–315.

20. Mohammad Hassan Murad, Mohamed B. Elamin, Magaly Zumaeta Garcia, et al., "Hormonal Therapy and Sex Reassignment: A Systematic Review and Meta-Analysis of Quality of Life and Psychosocial Outcomes," *Clinical Endocrinology* 72 (2010): 214–31.

were mixed and largely the result of the interactions between one transgender person, their church, and their pastor or chaplain.

In the last two decades the conversation has shifted from being primarily about pastoral and medical concerns to something described in terms of sinfulness. I believe this has occurred partly in response to the greatly increased visibility of transgender people, the ease of sharing perspectives, and the solidification of various views on the topics. However, this trend has not been helpful to us in determining ethical and pastoral responses to transgender people, and I advocate for a return to a more pastoral focus.

The Reverend Pat Robertson was asked on his television program in 1999 whether it was a sin to undergo gender transition. Robertson refocused the question, stating that what was important was the person's relationship with God, "not what your external organs are, one way or the other, whether it's male or female. The question is, where are you living? Are you living for God and yes, he forgives you and yes, he loves you and yes, he understands what's going on in your body."[21] Robertson made similar statements in 2013 when he reiterated that he did not think being transgender was a sin. This is not to say that Robertson is supportive of transgender people, but I believe he is correct to reorient the question from one of sinfulness to a focus on a person's relationship with God.

This is an important starting point for our conversation. Robertson here guides us to engage the right questions: Are we living for God? Are we in right relationship with God? Are we sure of God's love for us? Grounded in these answers, we can then consider how we should live as Christians. These questions should be central to our considerations.

What Is Health and Well-Being for Transgender People?

I would encourage us to focus our response on the essential well-being of transgender people. We can agree that, as Christians, we strive to live according to Jesus's teaching, seeking to treat others as we would want to be treated. But what does health and wholeness mean in this context? And how would we want to be treated?

The United Methodist Church's resolution on health and wholeness is, I think, helpful. It states,

> Health is the ultimate design of God for humanity. Though life often thwarts that design, the health we have is a good gift of God. . . . Among Jesus' statements on the purpose of his presence is the statement that he came that we

21. Pat Robertson, *The 700 Club*, October 5, 1999.

"could live life to the fullest" (John 10:10). Every account of Jesus' ministry documents how Jesus saw restoration to health as a sign of the kingdom of heaven becoming present amongst us. When John the elder wrote to Gaius (3 John 2), he wished for him physical health no less than spiritual. The biblical narrative is filled with stories of God's healing presence in the world. This includes spiritual, psychological, emotional, social, as well as physical healing.[22]

We see here an affirmation that Jesus was deeply concerned with acts of physical, emotional, *and* spiritual healing, as well as the restoration of people's place within the community.

Indeed, it is difficult and unhelpful as embodied beings to separate body, mind, and spirit. Hans Urs von Balthasar noted, "The soul is wholly incarnate in the heart, and, in the heart, the body wholly becomes the medium for the expression of the soul. At the same time, the New Testament adds an element of personhood: it is first in Christianity that the entire man—body and soul—becomes a unique person through God's call and, with his heart, orients towards God this uniqueness that is his."[23] Again, this echoes Robertson's focus above—that what matters is where our lives are focused. But it also matters that our body, mind, and soul are integrated.

Gender dysphoria represents a rupture in this sense of oneness between body, mind, and spirit. The goal of gender-related psychological and medical treatment is, therefore, congruence, the ability to experience an alignment of the physical, mental, and spiritual. When a patient is able to live in comfort with body, mind, and spirit, they experience a greater sense of well-being. The process by which they achieve that congruence can be defined as a healing one.

What Is Gender Dysphoria?

For those who have never experienced gender dysphoria, understanding it requires a willingness to see from another perspective and then consider how you yourself might want to be treated in these circumstances. To get just a glimpse of this, imagine waking up in the morning and having to wear the clothes you associate with the opposite sex: if you are a man, you must put on a skirt, pantyhose, a bra, makeup, and so on. If you don't conduct yourself in a feminine way, people will comment on that; you might even lose

22. United Methodist Church, "Book of Resolutions: Health and Wholeness," http://www.umc.org/what-we-believe/health-and-wholeness.

23. Hans Urs von Balthasar, *Heart of the World* (San Francisco: Ignatius, 1979), 14–15.

your job for failing to maintain the right appearance. You might be called names on the street, be accused of being a lesbian, or be hassled by men. If you are a woman, you must wear a suit or jeans and a men's shirt. You might have to "**butch** it up." If you act at all feminine at any point in the day, you might be called a sissy and told to "be a man." Other men might physically assault you or challenge you to prove your masculinity. All day long, you must conform to society's ideas of what it means to be a woman or a man.

Give yourself a moment to seriously imagine what this would be like—throughout your childhood, day after day as an adult, to feel this uncomfortable, like you were being forced into a gender role that doesn't fit you. This may give you a bit of an idea what it is like to have gender dysphoria.

After living in or imagining these circumstances, your response is likely to be that you want it to stop, that you want to be able to wear the right clothes, behave in a way that feels natural to you, and be allowed to go about your life without being subjected to violence and discrimination. That is what most transgender and gender-variant people want: the right to be ourselves, honestly, freely, and without threat. For many people with gender dysphoria, gender transition is vital in allowing us to live in ways that feel congruent, comfortable, healthy, and whole, resolving or moving toward resolution of the profound unease that gender dysphoria brings.

It is important to acknowledge that people with gender dysphoria generally do not have other underlying psychological issues. This is supported by a number of studies using different psychological testing instruments.[24] The majority of the patients in these studies are free of psychopathology and mirror the general population. However, transgender and gender-variant people do experience the pressures of gender dysphoria, leading to higher than normal levels of anxiety and depression.

Studies show a strong link between experiences of stigmatization and psychological distress;[25] transgender people who have been targeted by prejudice and discrimination are more likely to be depressed and anxious. Moreover, researchers have also shown a link between nonacceptance and negative health

24. E.g., see Esther Gómez-Gil, Fernando Gutiérrez, Silvia Cañizares, et al., "Temperament and Character in Transsexuals," *Psychiatry Research* 210, no. 3 (December 30, 2013): 969–74; Cecilia Dhejne, Roy Van Vlerken, Gunter Heylens, and Jon Arcelus, "Mental Health and Gender Dysphoria: A Review of the Literature," *International Review of Psychiatry* 28, no. 1 (January 2, 2016): 44–57; and Patricia P. Miach, Ellen F. Berah, James N. Butcher, and Steve Rouse, "Utility of the MMPI-2 in Assessing Gender Dysphoric Patients," *Journal of Personality Assessment* 75, no. 2 (2000): 268–79.

25. Darryl B. Hill and Brian L. B. Willoughby, "The Development and Validation of the Genderism and Transphobia Scale," *Sex Roles* 53, nos. 7–8 (October 2005): 531–44.

outcomes for transgender people.[26] This certainly matches my pastoral experiences, not only with transgender people but with anyone who is subjected to harassment, violence, and stigma. Being treated with hostility is anxiety producing and distressing for most people, as we might imagine. On the other hand, there is also solid research indicating that supportive social interactions lead to much better outcomes for individuals. Several studies indicate that family and social acceptance decrease negative outcomes and increase well-being.[27]

It is important to recognize that we are talking about people who are, in line with the general population, mentally healthy and without underlying psychopathologies, which means, among other things, people who are able to make informed, competent decisions about their health care.

Counseling and Gender Dysphoria

Counseling alone does not relieve the symptoms of gender dysphoria in many people. Qualified and competent mental health professionals working with people with gender dysphoria explore many options to relieve it. People who seek medical treatment are those for whom counseling alone does not work adequately. The World Professional Association for Transgender Health, a leading organization of those who specialize in the treatment of transgender patients, notes, "Often with the help of psychotherapy, some individuals integrate their trans- or cross-gender feelings into the gender role they were assigned at birth and do not feel the need to feminize or masculinize their body. For others, changes in gender role and expression are sufficient to alleviate gender dysphoria. Some patients may need hormones, a possible change in gender role, but not surgery; others may need a change in gender role along with surgery, but not hormones. In other words, treatment for gender dysphoria has become more individualized."[28] Thus, there are a variety of treatment options that are outlined in the World Professional Association

26. Walter O. Bockting, M. H. Miner, R. E. Swinburne Romine, A. Hamilton, and E. Coleman, "Stigma, Mental Health, and Resilience in an Online Sample of the US Transgender Population," *American Journal of Public Health* 103, no. 5 (May 2013): 943–51.

27. Brian Mustanski and Richard T. Liu, "A Longitudinal Study of Predictors of Suicide Attempts among Lesbian, Gay, Bisexual, and Transgender Youth," *Archives of Sexual Behavior* 42, no. 3 (April 2013): 437–48; and Andrea L. Roberts, M. Rosario, N. Slopen, J. P. Calzo, and S. B. Austin, "Childhood Gender Nonconformity, Bullying Victimization, and Depressive Symptoms across Adolescence and Early Adulthood: An 11-Year Longitudinal Study," *Journal of the American Academy of Child and Adolescent Psychiatry* 52, no. 2 (February 1, 2013): 143–52.

28. World Professional Association for Transgender Health, "Standards of Care for the Health of Transsexual, Transgender, and Gender Nonconforming People," 8–9, http://www.wpath.org/publications/soc.

for Transgender Health standards of care, guiding professionals and patients through the treatment process. These standards include documentation from a mental health professional to begin medical treatment.

Moreover, for patients for whom therapy alone has not worked, the organization states clearly, "Treatment aimed at trying to change a person's gender identity and lived gender expression to become more congruent with sex assigned at birth has been attempted in the past . . . , yet without success, particularly in the long-term. Such treatment is no longer considered ethical."[29] Those who advocate counseling alone, without medical interventions, should clearly recognize that this position is considered unethical by all of the major organizations of mental health professionals.[30] Encouraging people to pursue noneffective remedies requires patients to pay providers and pursue treatment that has been proven not to relieve their distress and, in fact, may exacerbate it.

Safety of Medical Treatments for Gender Dysphoria

Medical treatments with hormones and surgeries have proven to be effective and safe for those patients who need them. Treatments have become, as noted above, more individualized and more effective as physicians gain valuable information about doses and monitoring of hormone replacement therapy and learn new techniques for surgical procedures. Most medical and mental health providers are committed to providing excellent care for their transgender patients and following ethical guidelines to ensure that they are not doing harm and are improving the health of their patients.

Patients are cognizant of the risks and do not undertake these treatments lightly. To medically transition means experiencing the discomfort of going through puberty a second time, when hormone replacement is initiated, enduring the pains of surgical procedures and their follow-ups, time off work or away from one's family, and so on. Not all insurance companies cover these procedures, so they may involve years of working to save the necessary funds and great personal expense and hardship.[31] This requires a significant commitment on the part of the patient, which shows a determination to achieve a sense of wholeness and congruence.

29. E. Coleman, W. Bockting, M. Botzer, et al., "Standards of Care for the Health of Transsexual, Transgender, and Gender-Nonconforming People," version 7, *International Journal of Transgenderism* 13, no. 4 (2012): 175. In-text citations from the original article have been omitted here.

30. American Psychological Association, "Guidelines for Psychological Practice with Transgender and Gender Nonconforming People," *American Psychologist* 70, no. 9 (2015): 832–64.

31. Alyssa Jackson, "The High Cost of Being Transgender," *CNN*, July 31, 2015, http://www.cnn.com/2015/07/31/health/transgender-costs-irpt/index.html.

There are increasing numbers of studies that validate the safety of these procedures, including hormone treatments,[32] surgery,[33] and both.[34] It is important to recognize that recent studies reflect more effective medical procedures that have evolved over the past few decades. We should place more priority on the findings of recent studies, which reflect current practice, rather than on older ones.

However, if patients are denied access to appropriate medical care, they may seek treatment without medical monitoring. This can be extremely dangerous.[35] One reason to support access to medical treatment is to ensure that patients are seeing qualified professionals who are committed to their patients' health and well-being.

Effectiveness of Medical Treatments

In his chapter on values in bioethics, Diego Garcia notes that medicines in and of themselves have no inherent worth. The value they hold lies in their ability to restore health or prevent disease.[36] Thus, we must weigh the potential dangers and damage of hormones and other therapies against the demonstrated benefits to the patient.

An increasing number of studies demonstrate the effectiveness of these treatments in reducing gender dysphoria.[37] One summary, commissioned by the Endocrine Society, provides an overview of current research and concludes, "We found 28 studies with fairly long follow-up duration that demonstrated

32. H. Asscheman, E. J. Giltay, J. A. Megens, W. P. deRonde, M. A. van Trotsenburg, and L. J. Gooren, "A Long-Term Follow-Up Study of Mortality in Transsexuals Receiving Treatment with Cross-Sex Hormones," *European Journal of Endocrinology* 164, no. 4 (April 1, 2011): 635–42.

33. Jochen Hess, Roberto Rossi Neto, Leo Panic, Herbert Rübben, and Wolfgang Senf, "Satisfaction with Male-to-Female Gender Reassignment Surgery: Results of a Retrospective Analysis," *Deutsches Ärzteblatt International* 111 (2014): 795–801; and Jan Eldh, Agnes Berg, and Maria Gustafsson, "Long-Term Follow Up after Sex Reassignment Surgery," *Scandinavian Journal of Plastic and Reconstructive Surgery and Hand Surgery* 31, no. 1 (1997): 39–45.

34. Anirban Majumder and Debmalya Sanyal, "Outcome and Preferences in Female-to-Male Subjects with Gender Dysphoria: Experience from Eastern India," *Indian Journal of Endocrinology and Metabolism* 20, no. 3 (2016): 308–11; and Hess, Neto, Panic, Rübben, and Senf, "Satisfaction with Male-to-Female Gender Reassignment Surgery."

35. Vanderbilt University Medical Center, "Program for LGBTI Health: Key Transgender Health Concerns," https://www.vumc.org/lgbtq/key-transgender-health-concerns.

36. Diego Garcia, "Values and Bioethics," in *Bioethical Decision Making and Argumentation*, ed. Pedro Serna and José-Antonio Seoane (Switzerland: Springer International, 2016), 21.

37. Stacey L. Colton Meier, K. M. Fitzgerald, S. Pardo, and J. Babcock, "The Effects of Hormonal Gender Affirmation Treatment on Mental Health in Female-to-Male Transsexuals," *Journal of Gay and Lesbian Mental Health* 15, no. 3 (July 2011): 281–99; and Marco Colizzi, Rosalia Costa, and Orlando Todarello, "Transsexual Patients' Psychiatric Comorbidity and Positive Effect of Cross-Sex Hormonal Treatment on Mental Health: Results from a Longitudinal Study," *Psychoneuroendocrinology* 39 (January 2014): 65–73.

improvements in gender dysphoria, psychological functioning and comorbidities, lower suicide rates, higher sexual satisfaction and, overall, improvement in the quality of life."[38] This is paralleled in other overviews.[39]

Studies also show the converse: those who do not receive or have not yet received treatment experience elevated levels of anxiety and depression. For example, in a study of female-to-male transgender people, researchers concluded that "female-to-male transsexuals who receive testosterone have lower levels of depression, anxiety, and stress, and higher levels of social support and health related quality of life. Testosterone use was not related to problems with drugs, alcohol, or suicidality. Overall findings provide clear evidence that Hormone Replacement Therapy (HRT) is associated with improved mental health outcomes in female-to-male transsexuals."[40] The same pattern of improvement is shown in the US Transgender Survey.

> Respondents who had transitioned ten or more years prior to participating in the survey (24%) were substantially less likely to be currently experiencing serious psychological distress, in contrast to those who had transitioned within the past year (41%). While psychological distress was higher among those early in their transition, it was higher yet among those who have not transitioned but wanted to. Nearly half (49%) of those who have not transitioned but wanted to were currently experiencing serious psychological distress, compared with 36% of those who had transitioned at any time prior to taking the survey.[41]

Hormones are often associated with the potential for disruptive emotions; for example, estrogen can cause greater emotional volatility, while testosterone can lead to experiences of rage. Yet transgender patients reported *greater* emotional stability while on hormone therapy, meaning that the psychological benefits were strong enough to offset these potential problems.

Considerations for Christians

I want to conclude by considering several aspects of gender transition through a uniquely Christian lens: respect for self and others, suffering and compas-

38. Murad, Elamin, Garcia, et al., "Hormonal Therapy and Sex Reassignment," 229.

39. See, e.g., Rosalia Costa and Marco Colizzi, "The Effect of Cross-Sex Hormonal Treatment on Gender Dysphoria Individuals' Mental Health: A Systematic Review," *Neuropsychiatric Disease and Treatment* 12 (2016): 1953–66.

40. Meier, Fitzgerald, Pardo, and Babcock, "Effects of Hormonal Gender Affirmation Treatment," 281.

41. S. E. James, J. L. Herman, S. Rankin, M. Keisling, L. Mottet, and M. Anafi, *The Report of the 2015 US Transgender Survey* (Washington, DC: National Center for Transgender Equality, 2016), 107.

sion, and an orientation toward God's view of justice. I believe that these three components are necessary in formulating a clear and Christian viewpoint, one that we can all live with. As ethicist Lisa Sowle Cahill states in her article on the role of theology in public bioethical discourse, "Attempts to fashion a life together, a life that necessarily involves moral obligations and decisions, force us to arrive at some mutual understanding of what that would mean—especially in its practical results."[42]

Respect

First, decisions about the use of medical treatments must be grounded in respect. We can begin by affirming that because all people are created in the *imago Dei*, all deserve to be respected and treated as persons beloved of God. This is an absolute bottom line that cannot be dismissed.

Decisions about proceeding with medical transition, for those for whom it is the right course of action, should come from a place of deep respect for the body and the self. Whenever possible, I believe we should alter the body from a place of love and desire for wholeness in our lives, not out of a sense of hatred for our bodies. This is not possible for everyone, particularly those with an intense experience of gender dysphoria. The overall effect of changing the body should result in a great sense of bodily unity and a feeling of well-being and health. Reverend Jakob Hero, a pastor and palliative care chaplain, writes about this need to move to a perspective of flourishing, thinking of transition as a process of adding to well-being rather than of correcting deficits.[43]

Second, it is important to cultivate respect for the diversity of perspectives on this issue. In an article on bioethics, Tom Beauchamp states about principles in a diverse world, "Respect is owed to people of dissimilar but peaceful cultural traditions because it is unjust and disrespectful to marginalize, oppress, or dominate persons merely because they are of an unlike culture or subculture."[44] We cannot dismiss perspectives simply because they are different than our own; after all, Jesus's differing views on the world and on God were what set him apart from the religious authorities of his day.

Transgender people are often treated disrespectfully in our society; Christians have a responsibility to treat others as we wish to be treated. That includes

42. Lisa Sowle Cahill, "Can Theology Have a Role in 'Public' Bioethical Discourse?," *Hastings Center Report* 20, no. 4 (July 1990): 11.

43. Jakob Hero, "Toward a Queer Theology of Flourishing: Transsexual Embodiment, Subjectivity, and Moral Agency," in *The Bloomsbury Reader in Religion, Sexuality, and Gender*, ed. Donald L. Boisvert and Carly Daniel-Hughes (London: Bloomsbury Academic, 2017), 223.

44. Tom L. Beauchamp, "Principalism in Bioethics," in Serna and Seoane, *Bioethical Decision Making*, 14.

a fundamental respect for the personhood of others, recognizing that they are made in the image of God. Specifically, that includes referring to them by the names they wish to be called, not using pronouns such as "it" in speaking about them, and not using derogatory names.

We have a moral responsibility to treat the views of others with respect, and we cannot discount or marginalize their views simply because they are different from our own. This includes respecting that Christians who have decided to pursue medical transition are doing so prayerfully, thoughtfully, and with attention to their faith. Many of us testify that we feel that God has affirmed our decisions. I have been struck through the years by the number of narratives by transgender people that include a strong feeling of God's presence at times of crisis or decision making. People feel very strongly that God was with them at a crucial moment, encouraging them away from suicide or toward the courage to take the next step in transition. I encourage you to listen to these stories with an open heart, believing that God may be speaking through these lives. After all, the Bible is filled with unlikely people sharing God's word.

I can certainly say that one of the clearest aspects of my transition has been a strong sense of God's abiding presence throughout it all. There were times when I was first taking hormones when my body was changing so rapidly I could hardly recognize myself in the mirror, and people I knew walked right by me on the street without recognizing me. The greatest comfort I had was my certainty that God knew who I was at all times and was affirming me. God has been a tremendous comfort to me as I have faced the challenges of surgery and recovery. God remains faithful and present in the lives of transgender people who know, worship, and love God.

Third, it is important to respect the deep complexity of these matters. Ethical decisions on these questions involve many aspects. In medical situations, there are often competing factors that both health care professionals and patients must consider when deciding on a course of treatment—some treatments can cause harm but are undertaken because the overall impact is one of greater health. This is as true around gender transition as it is around any other medical treatment. In all surgeries, for example, we essentially harm the body by cutting it, yet the overarching reason for undertaking the procedure is healing.

Garcia continues in his discussion of bioethics, stating, "We can now systematize the way of making moral decisions, but the question is how to determine whether a decision is morally right or wrong. We know that our first moral duty is not to choose one of the values at stake, deleting all others, but to preserve and carry out all of them to the greatest extent possible. The question, however, is how to proceed in order to achieve this goal."[45] Thus, this decision involves acknowledging that more than one value is at stake in the conversation. We are called to use the best of our abilities to bring wholeness to individuals and communities, which means employing faith, reason, prayer, medical practice, compassion, and kindness.

Compassion

I would argue that one of the key values Christians should bring to this question is compassion for those who are suffering or are in distress. Compassion is not, however, a passive state; we cannot look on the suffering of others, feel pity for them, and ignore them. In his article on Christology and medical ethics, David Tolley writes about the power of Christ's gaze on the suffering, while, in contrast, "a gaze of denial keeps a sufferer out of community; it forces a person to bear their suffering alone."[46] Drawing on the work of Karl Barth and Margaret Farley, Tolley argues that suffering with another, gazing on them with compassion as Christ does, requires caregivers to act with selfless love, which he refers to with the Greek term *agape*. He concludes, "In this light, *agape* has something substantial to say to us regarding how we care for people who suffer. First of all, professionals must demonstrate general respect for persons; caregivers should treat patients as ends in themselves. Second, these professionals must work to alleviate suffering where possible."[47] It was this goal that led some European Christian hospitals to become leaders in offering gender-related care. They felt that because they could relieve suffering, they therefore should, as a result of their faith and their vocation as healers.

Gender dysphoria undoubtedly is a source of suffering for some people, and it is one that can be alleviated through appropriate medical interventions, with demonstrable, verifiable, and effective results. Compassion argues that we allow people to receive medical treatments that will alleviate their suffering. Conversely, withholding medical treatment when it has proven to be effective, advocating for the denial of medical treatment, or insisting that patients continue with ineffective treatments (such as counseling alone) deliberately and knowingly extends suffering. In addition, transgender people suffer as a result of intolerance and exclusion because of our gender identities. The rampant discrimination that people face, particularly those who experience

45. Garcia, "Values and Bioethics," in Serna and Seoane, *Bioethical Decision Making*, 24.
46. David C. Tolley, "Aesthetic Christology and Medical Ethics: The Status of Christ's Gaze in Care for the Suffering," *Scottish Journal of Theology* 61, no. 2 (May 2008): 13.
47. Tolley, "Aesthetic Christology and Medical Ethics," 14.

both racism and antitransgender bias, leads to depression, anxiety, and a decrease in health and wellness.

Christians should be deeply wary of theologies or arguments that allow one person to prescribe or condone suffering for someone else. When we say that preventable and undesired suffering is justifiable or even beneficial for that person, we are on dangerous ethical grounds. It is one thing to make a decision for yourself that may lead to your own suffering but another thing entirely to insist that another person suffer unnecessarily.

Michael Jensen, an evangelical Anglican, writes, "Suffering is an aberration—it has no value for its own sake and is not good in and of itself." He wisely cautions, "Though some Christians have glorified suffering for its own sake, this is a false trail. Truth and love are the nonnegotiables, not pain. In this regard, it is noteworthy that the final scene of the Book of Revelation depicts a world from which suffering and mourning and pain have been blessedly eliminated."[48] By this rationale, it is not appropriate to say that the suffering of those with gender dysphoria should remain untreated or that discrimination should be allowed to run unchecked or that these serve some wider purpose. This sort of unnecessary suffering is not good, character building, or any other platitude.

The Most Reverend J. S. Habgood, archbishop of York, writes on the question of suffering, "This is a subject on which Christians need to be cautious, because there have been times when Christianity has seemed to encourage an unhealthy resignation to suffering, and there is a sad history of Christian opposition to many pain-relieving techniques."[49] He goes on to say, "The doctrine of creation has often functioned as a restraining influence on too much interference with the way things are. But there is another side to the doctrine of creation, the affirmation of human creativeness, which can function in precisely the opposite direction, as an invitation to innovation."[50]

Neither of these writers is speaking specifically about gender dysphoria, but they are raising critical cautions about the ways in which Christians have approached suffering, especially the suffering of others. I believe we can apply these Christian writings to the question before us, stating a shared goal in the alleviation of suffering. This means we cannot ignore it or condone it for its own sake.

Christopher Tollefsen writes of suffering in general,

48. Michael P. Jensen in Scott J. Fitzpatrick, Ian H. Kerridge, Christopher F. C. Jordens, et al., "Religious Perspectives on Human Suffering: Implications for Medicine and Bioethics," *Journal of Religion and Health* 55, no. 1 (2016): 166.

49. J. S. Habgood, "Medical Ethics—A Christian View," *Journal of Medical Ethics* 11 (1985): 12.

50. Habgood, "Medical Ethics," 13.

Human beings are capable of recognising, in certain experiences, including some involving pain, that we are in one or another state of disharmony. . . . Thus, suffering involves an awareness on our part of a harmony that should exist, whether in our physical or mental being, or our moral being, or between loved ones, or between ourselves and God, and a further awareness that that harmony is currently being damaged, rent asunder. In consequence, suffering often includes feelings of alienation, of abandonment, of loss; we feel the absence of a wholeness that we know should characterise things, but does not.

He goes on to say that simply trying to cover up or ignore this rupture does not help: it "might alleviate suffering, but . . . at a great moral cost: an opportunity to repair what is broken is lost."[51] While he, again, is not addressing gender dysphoria specifically, his words are certainly applicable. What I find compelling about his statement is that there is a moral cost to ignoring suffering or failing to act, and that is the missed opportunity to fix what is broken. We do have the opportunities and knowledge to treat those who suffer from and experience gender dysphoria and societal alienation; to fail to act is to miss this opportunity for healing.

At the end of the day, I believe that as Christians we are called to extend mercy to others as mercy has been extended to us, to give compassion to others as it has been given to us, and to treat others as we would want to be treated by them. If you had a condition for which there was an effective treatment, would you not want that treatment extended to you? And do you not believe that Jesus, who sought the healing of so many in body, mind, and soul, would want you to have it as well?

Justice

Finally, I want to raise the issue of justice. Many, perhaps most, transgender people who seek to transition cannot afford to do so in the United States. While insurance is increasingly covering medical procedures, many people still have no coverage at all for transition-related care. These treatments are not equitably available. More than that, transgender people remain vulnerable to many forms of discrimination that threaten our health and well-being. This is a question of justice.

I was recently moved by a painting called *The Seven Works of Mercy* that is part of the collection of the Rijksmuseum in Amsterdam.[52] Dating from

---

51. Christopher Tollefsen in Fitzpatrick, Kerridge, Jordens, et al., "Religious Perspectives on Human Suffering," 163.
52. This painting can be viewed at https://www.rijksmuseum.nl/en/collection/SK-A-2815-1.

1504, it depicts the scenes described in Matthew 25:31–46 when Jesus states how he will separate the blessed from the accursed based on their actions toward the least among us. In the center panel of the painting, we see Christ in his glory, sitting above the world. Below him, the rest of the image shows hungry people being given bread, thirsty people receiving water, those in need being given clothing, the grieving being comforted, and so on. What is most arresting about this painting is that in almost all of these scenes, we also see Christ as one of those in need—he is waiting to receive bread, water, and clothing. It is a literal illustration of "truly I tell you, just as you did it to one of the least of these who are members of my family, you did it to me" (Matt. 25:40). His face in the heavens and his face among the people on earth are exactly the same.

In Matthew 25, Jesus describes who are the righteous, who will inherit God's realm, and who are accursed because they did not provide for those in need. In this passage, and in Luke 10, Jesus describes the criteria by which he will judge humanity. In response to the question, "What must I do to inherit eternal life?" (Luke 10:25), Jesus affirms the lawyer's answer that the law says, "You shall love the Lord your God with all your heart, and with all your soul, and with all your strength, and with all your mind; and your neighbor as yourself" (v. 27). Jesus replies, "You have given the right answer; do this, and you will live" (v. 28). These statements about loving God and our neighbor, and living out that love through concrete actions that benefit the least of these, are core to Jesus's message about eternal life. They are Jesus's words about what we need to do to be counted among the righteous and inherit the dominion of God.

I came across the painting *The Seven Works of Mercy* while I was writing this chapter, and it spoke clearly to me about Christ's priorities. First, there is nothing in either of the passages quoted here to suggest that, for Jesus, anything about an individual's identity or personal characteristics is even remotely related to the conditions for eternal life. There is certainly no mention of gender, sexuality, sex, or any other demographic characteristic. Jesus is not concerned about any of these factors. What matters, in Jesus's eyes and teachings, is the degree to which we love God and the manner in which we treat others. Transgender Christians strive for these goals, as do other believers.

As I prayed in front of the painting, I was moved to think of the ways in which transgender people are disproportionately likely in our society to be in positions of need. Nearly one-third (29 percent) of transgender people in the United States are living in poverty, more than twice the rate of the general population (14 percent), and nearly 30 percent have been homeless at some point in their lives.[53] In surveys like the National Transgender Discrimination Survey[54] and its follow-up, the US Transgender Survey,[55] respondents report discrimination in every aspect of life—including housing, employment, education, health care, and public accommodation. Many report multiple incidents of discrimination and harassment. These rates are significantly higher among communities of color.

For example, transgender people are four times more likely to be living in severe poverty at less than $10,000 per year of income. Much of this was due to workplace discrimination, reported by 78 percent of the respondents. Unemployment levels are double those of the general population; people of color, however, have even higher rates: African American transgender people reported an unemployment rate of 28 percent and American Indians of 24 percent. Similar patterns were found in other aspects of life, like housing, where 19 percent of respondents had been denied housing at some point in their lives due to their gender identity. This led to a 1.7 percent rate of current homelessness, which is twice that estimated by the National Coalition for the Homeless for the US population as a whole. Yet 13 percent of African American respondents said they were currently homeless, as well as 8 percent of American Indians, 5 percent of Latino/as, and 3 percent of multiracial respondents. These patterns of significantly higher rates of discrimination continue in every aspect of life, with people of color reporting rates even higher than the already alarming baseline.[56]

Yet transgender people are denied services from many Christian organizations. To give just one example, in April 2017, Isabella Red Cloud, a Christian transgender woman, was turned away from receiving breakfast at the Union Gospel Mission in Sioux Falls, South Dakota, and then later cited by the police for trespassing after she tried to attend a worship service.[57] The mission workers did not approve of her wearing women's clothing, but in expressing their disapproval, they failed to provide for Christ; after all, he says that when

53. James, Herman, Rankin, Keisling, Mottet, and Anafi, *Report of the 2015 US Transgender Survey*, 3.

54. Jaime Grant, Lisa Mottet, and Justin Tanis, with Jack Harrison, Jody L. Herman, and Mara Keisling, *Injustice at Every Turn: A Report of the National Transgender Discrimination Survey* (Washington, DC: National Center for Transgender Equality and National Gay and Lesbian Task Force, 2011). Note: the author of this chapter is one of the lead authors of this report.

55. James, Herman, Rankin, Keisling, Mottet, and Anafi, *Report of the 2015 US Transgender Survey*.

56. Grant, Mottet, and Tanis, with Harrison, Herman, and Keisling, *Injustice at Every Turn*.

57. Rebecca David, "Transgender Woman Speaks Out after Being Denied Service at Union Gospel Mission," KDLT News, April 24, 2017, http://www.kdlt.com/2017/04/24/transgender -woman-speaks-denied-service-union-gospel-mission/.

the hungry come and are given no food, "Truly I tell you, just as you did not do it to one of the least of these, you did not do it to me" (Matt. 25:45).

As Christians considering Jesus's words in Matthew 25, we should be deeply concerned about all of those who do not have food, water, clothing, or shelter. But we should bear in mind that transgender people, people of color, and other stigmatized minority groups are more likely to be among those in need. Jesus said that whenever we provide for one of the least of these, we do it for him. Can we see Jesus among the transgender people whom we are discussing?

Conclusion

There are many critical areas to consider around this topic, as with all ethical issues in medical care. I believe that Christians have a duty to support access to medical treatments that alleviate suffering and promote health and well-being. Medical treatment for gender dysphoria treats the condition, diminishing distress and allowing patients to live more fulfilling lives. Suffering for its own sake serves no useful purpose; compassion dictates that we should seek to end suffering and promote a sense of well-being and congruence. The medical data is clear that counseling alone fails to address the issue in many patients, while medical transition can be safe and effective.

Supporting the health and thriving of transgender people includes setting aside the prejudice that contributes to suffering. Much of the anxiety and distress that transgender people face is the result of intolerance and a lack of acceptance. People should have the right to make their own decisions about their health care, in consultation with their doctors, and to choose that which promotes their greatest health and flourishing. Medical treatments that affirm their identity and support their well-being are ethical and necessary.

Ultimately, it is not suffering that guides me in these questions; it is awe. God created a magnificent world filled with abundant diversity in every facet of creation. I marvel at the beauty of the differences between us and celebrate our common humanity. We were meant to live on this planet, honoring and worshiping God and treating one another as we would want to be treated. This is how Jesus summed up the Law and the Prophets, guiding us in life. I rejoice in the fantastic imagination of our Creator and the goodness with which all life has been bestowed.

Response to Justin Sabia-Tanis

Owen Strachan

I t is a pleasure to engage the reflective writing of Justin Sabia-Tanis. As will be immediately apparent, we disagree about a great deal, but the chapter in question displays relative graciousness of tone, a needed ingredient in this conversation. Further, my heart went out to Justin as I read his story; our fallen world and our own sinful hearts bring us all into much turmoil, chaos, and pain. Those who would seek to help us do not always know how to help us. I resonate with the pain expressed here, and I am sure it goes deeper than the printed page.

To begin, the definition of "gender" used in this article encompasses so much as to be unhelpful:

> Gender is one more facet of this natural variation intended by God as a feature of life on earth. Male and female define two categories of humans, but they are not meant to be exclusive boxes that limit our individual expression. Like night and day, land and sea, plant and animal, they are descriptors that have liminal spaces between them where aspects of both elements are combined. How people express those spaces, those differences, is part of the beauty that makes up the human family, part of the goodness of God's creation. (pp. 196–97)

All things exist, yes, and all things exist in the God-made world. We think here of an Edwardsean "chain of being" on this point. But it is the very limitation of a thing that makes it that thing.

Fundamentally, male and female are "exclusive" realities. To use Justin's own words, night is not day, land is not sea, and plant is not animal. There is no "liminal space" in which the land is only partially land. In the same way, there is no "liminal space" in which we are 75 percent male and 25 percent female. God made men, and God made women. The fall does corrupt our humanity to varying degrees, but this does not change divine making.

In addition, God took definitive steps in both the old and new covenants to "limit our individual expression" of our identity. I have covered several of these steps in my chapter and so will not spell them out exhaustively here, but at base, the apostles wanted men and women to dress and look differently, to conduct themselves differently in the home, and to adopt different positions in the church (1 Cor. 11:3–16; Eph. 5:22–33; 1 Tim. 2–3). The "expression" of our manly or womanly identity is definitely limited by God, and limited not for our suffering but for our flourishing. God is in the business of restoring men and women to the *telos* of his grand design. The Lord, as I have said elsewhere, loves to create structures in which we live out the beauty of "ordered love." The "human family," which Sabia-Tanis notes, is the first site—ground zero—of this principle. The Bible nowhere amends the natural order of the God-made family; the new covenant only expands on the vision initiated in Genesis 2, with husbands gaining far more direction about loving their wives, wives learning much more about the joy of submission, and children understanding more about their duties to their father and mother.

Sabia-Tanis also covers the image of God and suggests that the divine being is multigendered:

> The creation story also affirms that human beings were made in the image and likeness of God, as both male and female. This must mean that God's own being includes more than one gender, if that is reflected in humanity. The Bible includes multiple images for God, including feminine ones, such as Hosea 13:8 and Deuteronomy 32:11–12, where God is compared to mother animals; Deuteronomy 32:18, where God is said to have given birth to humanity; Luke 15:8–10, where Jesus compares God to a woman searching for her lost coin; and Matthew 23:37 and Luke 13:34, where Jesus says he longs to care for the people of Jerusalem as a mother hen cares for her young. Divinity, then, encompasses both male and female within the Godhead, modeling similar possibilities for humanity. (pp. 197–98)

With respect, this is not what the image of God signals in theological terms. The identity of God in the Bible is exclusively male. This does not mean that God has a male anatomy (though Christ surely did), but it does mean that the core identity of the first person of the Godhead is that of Father, an identity that begins with the exclusive relationship of Father and Son. God the Father is the covenantal head of the people of God, being Israel in the Old Testament and the "one new man" constituted in Christ per the New Testament.

The fact that mankind is male and female as God's image does not mean that God is male and female; this would contradict the plain teaching of the rest of Scripture. It does mean that mankind is a spiritual being, made to know God and take dominion of the earth according to his good plan. The metaphors used of God in the Bible are instructive, but they are just what we know them to be: metaphors. Jesus referring to himself as a mother hen no more speaks to his supposed femaleness than it does to his "henness."

We must also think carefully about Sabia-Tanis's presentation of marriage. We read as follows:

> Genesis 2, which repeats the creation narrative with some differences, tells of Eve being created from the rib of Adam. We note that the Hebrew *'adam* here is not initially used as a name but as a general noun meaning "earth being." This person existed prior to the creation of gender and was, apparently, God's original plan. The most critical thing to note about the division of the sexes is in Genesis 2:18, in which God describes the rationale for this division—not to create a separation of genders but rather to solve the problem of human loneliness. First, God attempts to address this through the animals. When this does not work, God chooses to create an additional human being. God's focus here is addressing the fundamental need that we have for companionship and friendship. We need one another to thrive; we are not meant to be alone or isolated. (p. 198)

Yet again we meet a false binary. No, the purpose of God making the sexes is not to create "separation" between them. Yes, God is solving "the problem of human loneliness." But here we are only beginning to capture the profound reality of the formation of the sexes. God wishes to give us a living framework for unity-in-diversity, the very concept that undergirds the central fact of biblical doctrine, the Holy Trinity. The man and the woman are equal in dignity and worth, of the same kind, but they are not the same. They are marvelously distinct from one another. That which Sabia-Tanis downplays, the text magnifies. We are not supposed to see the first man and woman in blurry terms here. Genesis 2 records the man's exultation in the woman—this *at last* is the one who is like him but also *not* like him. He is made for loving union with the woman. He is made to care for her, lead her, protect her, and provide for her, all of which Genesis 2–3 introduces in seed form. It is true that his "loneliness" ends, but it ends because of complementary marriage—covenantal union grounded in the holy distinctiveness of man and the holy distinctiveness of woman.

As in DeFranza's chapter, Sabia-Tanis finds in the biblical eunuch a forerunner of the transgender person. Of Isaiah 56:1–5, Sabia-Tanis writes, "God not only says that the eunuchs are not separated from God's people, but [God] extends the welcome so far as to promise that they will be given a name *better* than sons and daughters, an everlasting name that will never be taken from them. . . . This passage in Isaiah makes it clear that God is including those who are different because of their gender. This speaks to God's recognition and acceptance of an array of genders" (p. 203). This passage in Isaiah does not signal that God approves of eunuchism per se, let alone the ways in which people become eunuchs. Isaiah is quoting the Lord as saying that those who formerly saw themselves outside the grace of God now, through salvation, find themselves welcomed into the household of God. We know this is the case in this text because the Lord speaks also of the "foreigner," the one who once was far from the Lord and his will but who is now a member of the holy family (v. 5). Both "foreigner" and "eunuch" were alienated from God but now, through God's "salvation," are welcomed (v. 2). The Lord is no more approving of the eunuch than he is the natives of Babylon, born into sin and estranged from both the covenant Lord and the covenant people.

I think here of Paul's treatment of sinful identity in the new covenant. After listing an array of sinful identities the Corinthians formerly assumed, a list that includes effeminate male homosexuals, Paul writes some of the most beautiful words in Scripture: "Such were some of you" (1 Cor. 6:11 ESV). In other words, once you took on an ungodly personage and lived according to that self-conception. But now, in Christ, you are washed, and you no longer have that identity, just as you have broken with those sinful practices.

We see here, to extend the matter, that our belief in the *imago Dei* is not enough for our compassionate engagement of "transgender" individuals. Yes, every person is made in God's image, but sadly, we image-bearers hate God in our natural state. Just because we recognize that every person in some diminished way reflects the likeness of God does not mean that we can affirm their lifestyle, their predilections, their self-conception. The man who cheats on his wife is an image-bearer, but the fact of his image-bearing in no way allows me to overlook or affirm his adultery. So it is with every sinful behavior and self-conception.

First Corinthians 6, mentioned above, helps greatly here. Although it does not speak directly to the matter at hand, it does show us that God nowhere approves of a disobedient Christian or an intermingled identity. As I seek to show in chapter 1, we cannot act against our body, which is to act against our nature (see Rom. 1:18–32). We may only glorify the Lord when we embrace our body and live in accordance with divine design. Our bodies are not lying to us; in conversion, God helps us say yes to the gift of the body and yes to the bodily identity he has established.

Ironically, Sabia-Tanis and I come very close to agreeing on this point. We read this, for example, in his chapter: "Gender dysphoria represents a rupture in this sense of oneness between body, mind, and spirit. The goal of gender-related psychological and medical treatment is, therefore, congruence, the ability to experience an alignment of the physical, mental, and spiritual. When a patient is able to live in comfort with body, mind, and spirit, they experience a greater sense of well-being" (p. 209). I agree with this formulation. But I do not agree that we should in any way "align" ourselves with an identity that counters our body, our divinely formed self. For a variety of reasons, we may not feel as though our body matches who we are. But we must see that God's best for us is not to live in confusion. This is what the gospel does, in part: it awakens us to love the body God has given us, to become the man or woman God made us to be, and to know the joy that comes through fidelity to the natural and spiritual goodness of God.

But we will not know truly God-honoring "well-being" through transitioning, surgical and chemical alteration, or cross-dressing. We might think we know this well-being; we might be utterly convinced of this fact. But this is not the case. We are not living in the will of God; we are not honoring God; we are dishonoring the Lord and willfully sinning against him. We are placing ourselves under the real threat of divine judgment. It is terrible to type these words, but the Bible offers the straying sinner, the one rejecting God's promises, no comfort. We can understand the profound distress individuals who battle gender dysphoria experience; not only can we understand, but we can empathize. We can—and should—love such individuals. But we cannot affirm their decision to break with God's holy will. The Israelites were prohibited in the strongest possible terms from "bending their gender," as my chapter shows, a prohibition that is in no way softened in the new covenant, but upheld.

The love we offer those who struggle in this way, then, is not a cultural love that only accepts and affirms. It is instead a costly love, a self-denying love, a transformative love powered by the very grace that raised Christ Jesus from the dead. If God can raise Christ, he can restore the sinner, however troubled, however confused, however isolated they may feel.

Response to Justin Sabia-Tanis

Mark A. Yarhouse and Julia Sadusky

D
r. Justin Sabia-Tanis opens his chapter with accounts of the creation that challenge what are usually portrayed as clearly demarcated differences. That is, in addition to night and day, we have dusk and dawn. In addition to land and sea, we have marshes and lagoons. When we extend this thinking to human beings, he says, we of course are told of male and female categories, but these categories are not exhaustive, and we should expect to see variations that occur in nature. For Dr. Sabia-Tanis, these variations should not be thought of in moral categories (as though a person chooses gender diversity) or as a result of the fall (as though the variations resulted in human beings whose gender was "tainted" by the fall).

Dr. Sabia-Tanis identifies companionship as the primary purpose of the male/female relationship: "God's focus here is addressing the fundamental need that we have for companionship and friendship. We need one another to thrive; we are not meant to be alone or isolated" (p. 198). He goes on to discuss biodiversity, especially plant life and the fact that some plants are hermaphroditic, dioecious, and gynodioecious. We suspect the value of these distinctions is likely related to how one views the connection between plants and human beings. For Dr. Sabia-Tanis, the connection is most accessible through intersex experiences, which are "biological variations" perhaps more so than medical conditions. This brings Dr. Sabia-Tanis to gender dysphoria, which he notes may indeed have a biological basis: "What if these variations are simply an intended part of the diversity that God included in the natural order, just like the differences of plants and animals previously described?" (p. 201). This is important for pastoral care, he says: "If we then condemn or attempt to eradicate these naturally occurring variations, we are working counter to the will of God for creation, which God has declared to be good" (p. 201).

We agree with Dr. Sabia-Tanis that something like what we today refer to as gender dysphoria has existed across cultures and throughout history. What are we to make of this? How do we conceptualize it? Does its presence across time and space prove a biological source? How do we think about the moral implications of a natural occurrence?

Dr. Sabia-Tanis refers to eunuchs in his considerations as well. Jesus does reference eunuchs in Matthew 19—that some are born so, some made so, and some choose to be so. We aren't certain this is quite the same as "some people are born with less usual sexual characteristics while others alter their gender during their lifetime" (p. 202). Apart from those who were made eunuchs (or those whose testicles were removed) and those who choose to live as eunuchs (probably renouncing marriage), we read Jesus as indicating that some people who were referred to as eunuchs (by birth) had diminished sexual capacity or may have had ambiguous genitalia, although it is difficult to speculate beyond that.

Again, we seem to move toward speculation in claiming that "God is including those who are different because of their gender" and that it "speaks to God's recognition and acceptance of an array of genders" (p. 203). These are conclusions we are not prepared to make from Isaiah 56:1–5. Given that the instruction is also to "choose the things that please [God]," it is unclear all that is entailed in this when discussing gender identity. There is a sense in which the inclusion of the Ethiopian eunuch is encouraging to many people who experience their sex or gender differently than those in the majority, and in that sense God's love and grace and mercy are indeed "expansive." But the degree to which the parallel between gender-diverse experience and eunuchs covers every aspect of the variety of experiences is another consideration.

We appreciated the questions Dr. Sabia-Tanis raised about vocation. We see this as moving in a helpful direction insofar as it is a call for wisdom, discernment, and further discussion. Dr. Sabia-Tanis portrays how people discern vocation as a parallel to the discovery of one's gender identity. We are not prepared to make that same claim, but for Dr. Sabia-Tanis, "Gender differences arise in response to our following of God's leading for our individual lives. God calls some people to go on a journey that may include a change of gender, a transformative pilgrimage" (p. 204). Dr. Sabia-Tanis describes a "surety" in God's calling and provision in this area of life. "When I look at my life, and the lives of my transgender and intersex siblings in Christ, and all of God's people, I see reflected there the tremendous, awe-inspiring diversity made by an imaginative, loving Creator" (p. 204). These conclusions, in our typology, reflect what we referred to as the diversity lens. Within this, diverse gender experiences reflect God's creativity and imagination and are to be understood neither in moral categories of sin and repentance (integrity lens) nor in terms of disability or dysfunction (disability lens). This appeals to the need for purpose in one's gender identity and gives meaning that has spiritual significance.

We agree that questions about how best to proceed with one's gender identity should be considered with the people who are facing such decisions, as Dr. Sabia-Tanis says: "I would urge that any serious consideration of this question [whether to undergo gender transition] be done in dialogue with transgender people and with those professionals who work with us" (p. 205). This helps us stay in touch with the implications of various decisions on the lives of real people. It is too easy to make bold statements without regard for the implications of taking various options off the table. This also stresses the importance of interaction with the medical and psychological community that can inform those decisions, especially as people of faith journey with their faith community and receive pastoral care.

Dr. Sabia-Tanis shared his own journey and decision to transition. We too have seen clients respond very well to cross-sex hormones, and we think it is a mistake to misrepresent those times when clients have reported such actions to be beneficial to their well-being. Dr. Sabia-Tanis acknowledges that this path is not right for everyone: "There are people for whom medical treatment is not the answer—either because they cannot undergo it . . . , because it runs counter to their beliefs, or because it simply is not right for them" (pp. 206–7). Is the decision to transition, then, to be thought of more as a gray area, a wisdom issue, subject to the discernment of the person and those who provide that person with spiritual advice or oversight?

We do wonder whether the current cultural climate sets a different expectation for what "the answer" is for transgender persons, and we have written elsewhere about how this may affect the likelihood that individuals would choose alternatives to transitioning. Dr. Sabia-Tanis articulates that "there are a variety of treatment options that are outlined in the World Professional Association for Transgender Health standards of care, guiding professionals and patients through the treatment process. These standards include documentation from a mental health professional to begin medical treatment" (pp. 211–12). We also see a trend toward removing mental health professionals from the process, as they are seen by some in the transgender community as a barrier to the access to care for transgender persons. We are wary of an informed consent model of care (as opposed to a comprehensive mental health evaluation) because of the greater potential for some to pursue more invasive interventions when they may have been better off addressing their concerns through other strategies.

The parallel made by Dr. Sabia-Tanis to kidney transplants is worth considering but somewhat problematic, in our view. Of course, kidney transplants do not work or are not appropriate for every patient. At the same time, the challenge with bringing forward medical conditions is that it draws on the disability lens for an argument that is really steeped in a diversity framework. A kidney transplant is viewed as a medically necessary procedure precisely because of end-stage kidney disease caused by diabetes, polycystic kidney disease, or other conditions. The parallel is fitting only insofar as one thinks of their gender dysphoria in a similar way—that is, as a disease or disorder, rather than as a natural occurrence to be celebrated and not treated.

Some of the history Dr. Sabia-Tanis shares, in terms of how people have responded to what we today call gender dysphoria, is in line with our own experiences as practitioners. We too have seen responses that treat gender dysphoria more like a medical issue (disability lens), while other responses have framed this as sin in need of repentance (integrity lens).

Certainly there is value in raising questions about spiritual and physical health. To be human is to care for body, mind, and soul. Where disagreements arise tends to have to do with what is healthy for a person, how we measure health, and what we make of suffering. In light of biblical teachings on the subject, Christians have a particularly unique relationship with pain and suffering, and we want to think through what it may mean to identify our suffering with the passion of Christ. To make the aim freedom from suffering is, in some ways, a departure from the historic appreciation for the redemptive value of suffering. This is certainly provocative today, and it could be an untapped resource for the person navigating gender dysphoria.

The claim that "people with gender dysphoria generally do not have other underlying psychological issues" (p. 210) was surprising to us, especially in light of the research showing that there are in fact many comorbidities. For instance, the *DSM-5* notes that children referred with gender dysphoria have higher rates of anxiety, impulse-control, and depressive disorders. The older a child gets, the more emotional and behavioral concerns there often are. At the same time, these comorbidities are often understood as being tied to the lack of acceptance of gender-variant behavior, accounted for by the minority stress model. Comorbidities among adolescents and adults diagnosed with gender dysphoria are many, with anxiety and depressive disorders being of particular concern.

It is also noteworthy that Dr. Sabia-Tanis references the use of therapy for resolution with one's birth sex as unethical. If some people have used therapy, as Dr. Sabia-Tanis also claims, and were able to "integrate their trans- or cross-gender feelings into the gender role they were assigned at birth or do not feel the need to feminize or masculinize their body" (p. 211), then at what point do we move to the conclusion that continuing such practices is unethical?

When do we stop trying? Does a practice such as therapy become unethical after it has been tried but has failed? These are questions that warrant further reflection among those who have their clients' best interests in view, especially if we can agree that there are particular challenges to taking irreversible steps. We certainly agree that applying therapies that are ineffective for resolution of gender identity ought to be cautioned against. Still, could therapy that is identity-focused but has no fixed outcome be beneficial? If so, what would it take for this to be maintained as the standard approach?

Our experience has been that, historically, clients consider a range of options and coping strategies in a step-wise manner, often through trial and error. Very few tend to take such steps lightly. At the same time, in the past two years we have seen an increase in atypical presentations that are much more complicated. Here we are particularly thinking of late-onset cases among natal females who are requesting some of the most invasive procedures, such as chest reconstruction. While it's true that they meet the criteria for gender dysphoria in the *DSM-5*—which only requires that they have two of the six diagnostic criteria—they are atypical in that they are late-onset and natal females, which is the reverse of what has been seen in specialty clinics for many, many years. We know little in the form of research on the impact of these decisions because it differs from the more gradual, step-wise approach to transitioning that has historically been taken. With this comes much less confidence that all clients will continue to approach requests for invasive procedures in quite the same measured manner. Further, how should a clinical approach and a pastoral approach be different when a person seems to be taking such decisions lightly, dismissing the apparent risks? This is not common, to be sure. But when it occurs, we wonder what is the best approach.

We agree that "we must weigh the potential dangers and damage of hormones and other therapies against the demonstrated benefits to the patient" (p. 213). At the same time, when these dangers and damages have been identified, particularly when applied to natal females and to an adolescent pursuing puberty blockers (and the likely subsequent use of cross-sex hormones), it seems that more recently the model has become informed consent, rather than a more nuanced mental health assessment, careful consideration of what constitutes medical necessity, and a corresponding model of care. There is certainly reason for this shift, especially since it reflects a shift within the medical field as a whole. At the same time, we have concern about the potential dangers of pursuing hormones and other therapies when the benefits are less clear but the patient insists on this path. It is difficult to appreciate at the age of fourteen the experience of lifelong infertility or other challenges.

We agree that pursuing suffering for its own sake would be a mistake and not good pastoral guidance. However, we view a Christian response to suffering as more rich and complicated than that. We want to say that suffering is for the purpose of sanctification insofar as God uses our circumstances and our pain to make us more Christlike. Thus, suffering, for the Christian, is not for its own sake but for the sake of love for God and neighbor. For the mother who wakes up in the middle of the night to nurse a hungry baby, suffering is not to be avoided but embraced out of radical love—love that someone who is not a parent may find hard to comprehend.

The difficult question that arises with viewing suffering as purposeful is how to know the circumstances in which to embrace suffering and the circumstances that would call us to alleviate suffering. After all, we treat many medical conditions under the assumption that living with the condition would not be God's will for a person, all things being equal. When has "innovation" been used as an avoidance of the purification that some suffering certainly brings? Seeking healing is in keeping with Christian principles, but disagreements will remain when it comes to the avenues for healing and whether there is room for nuance in these conversations regarding the moral implications of different pathways.

Another question remains as to what can be gleaned from suffering. If it is not meant to be taken up for its own sake, for what sake ought it be taken up? Not all people would look to Jesus as a model for life, but for Christians he offers a perfect model for responding to suffering. In some moments, this meant radical alleviation of burdens few would offer to relieve. In other moments, and in the most significant moments of his life, he chose suffering, even while praying, "Father, if you are willing, take this cup from me; yet not my will, but yours be done" (Luke 22:42 NIV). Within this prayer is both the desire to be relieved from suffering and the acceptance of God's will when it includes the most unbearable pain a human could ever face. Where does that leave the Christian with gender dysphoria?

Response to Justin Sabia-Tanis

Megan K. DeFranza

am grateful to Dr. Justin Sabia-Tanis for his willingness to participate in this book project. He has offered readers an invaluable resource for thinking Christianly about transgender identities, despite the personal cost of interacting with those who may question not only his arguments and personal choices but even his membership in the body of Christ. We are indebted to him, and to other transgender Christians who extend themselves to help cisgender people try to think outside of our own experiences and read the Bible through a new set of lenses.

The first half of Dr. Sabia-Tanis's chapter reads more like a hymn than an academic argument. It resounds as a song of praise to the genius and playfulness of the Creator, whose creations push the boundaries of our imaginations. Where I write about how amphibians and penguins blend the categories of creatures we find in Genesis 1 (land animals, birds that fly, and fish of the sea), Dr. Sabia-Tanis takes us through example after example illustrating just how many of God's creations fall on the boundaries between light and dark, land and sea, male and female. I continue to marvel at how biblical scholars who do not speak of dawn and dusk, deltas and marshes, seahorses and hyenas as being "results of the fall," because of how these things blur the lines of separation we find in the first verses of the Bible, can all the while insist that humans who find themselves between male and female cannot be God's intent. Still, I shouldn't be too hard on them since I myself made these arguments before I took the time to study the matter with a more open mind and to listen more attentively to the voices of transgender Christians. Now it seems so obvious to me that the categories in Genesis 1 could never be reasonably read as an exhaustive list of God's good creations such that anything that doesn't fit these categories must be understood through the lens of creation's fallenness into sin. But it wasn't obvious to me then. I had to reconsider not what the Bible said but the assumptions, the theological lenses, through which I was interpreting these verses, including assumptions from my own experiences as a cisgender female theologian.

The second half of the chapter reads very differently as Dr. Sabia-Tanis describes the experience of gender dysphoria and calls Christians to move from judgmentalism to compassion. Citing numerous studies, he documents the relief most transgender people experience when they transition to living as the gender with which they identify, begin hormone replacement, or undergo gender affirmation surgeries, relief that may sound counterintuitive. "Hormones are often associated with the potential for disruptive emotions; for example, estrogen can cause greater emotional volatility, while testosterone can lead to experiences of rage. Yet transgender patients reported *greater* emotional stability while on hormone therapy, meaning that the psychological benefits were strong enough to offset these potential problems" (p. 214). Given the positive outcomes that so many transgender people describe, readers are asked to consider whether we would deny access to medical care to people whose pain could be similarly alleviated through surgeries or medications, even when those interventions come with health risks and unknown long-term effects.

When my mother was diagnosed with a type of brain cancer for which there was no known cure, my family was faced with the difficulties of weighing the dangers of brain surgery and the risks of experimental drugs. Our churches prayed for her healing and for wisdom, but no one argued that considering risky trials was a failure to trust in God or accept God's providence. They did not pile onto our struggles the extra burden of questioning our faith in God when faced with such painful choices. Yet many Christians are quick to add to the stress of transgender people seeking medical care the pain of judgment, abandonment, excommunication, and even harassment. Just as we must ask ourselves whether we are being logically consistent in our assessment of creatures who blur the lines of demarcation in Genesis 1, we must consider whether we are being consistent in our judgments of those willing to accept the risks of transgender medical treatments, many of which have higher rates of success than new drugs for cancer.

To be fair, I must also note that I harbor my own worries about the health risks being assumed not only by transgender adults but now also by transgender teens. I cannot imagine the weight that must burden the parents of transgender kids as they consider the unknown outcomes of puberty blockers and long-term hormone replacement therapy for their transgender child. As a parent, it is difficult to imagine my teenager having the maturity and perspective to be able to make such an irreversible decision, and yet I also empathize with the concern to act before natural hormones induce secondary sex characteristics at odds with the gender identity of the child, which are also irreversible. I am grateful for those who, like Dr. Kristina Olson of the TransYouth Project, are making it their life's work to track the health outcomes of this generation of transgender children so that future children and parents will have more data to aid their own decision making.[1]

The comparison between the risks of medical treatments for gender dysphoria and other illnesses is very helpful, but it does lead me to a question that I hope Dr. Sabia-Tanis will address at some point. Should the experiences of transgender people be viewed as diversity to be celebrated or as challenges that should elicit our compassion? The first half of his chapter seems to employ what Dr. Yarhouse and Dr. Sadusky have helpfully labeled the diversity framework, while the second half of the chapter (minus the last paragraph) seems to be interpreting transgender experiences through the lens of the disability framework. The disability framework seems to be at play in the following paragraph:

> At the end of the day, I believe that as Christians we are called to extend mercy to others as mercy has been extended to us, to give compassion to others as it has been given to us, and to treat others as we would want to be treated by them. If you had a condition for which there was an effective treatment, would you not want that treatment extended to you? And do you not believe that Jesus, who sought the healing of so many in body, mind, and soul, would want you to have it as well? (p. 219)

The tension between these frameworks leaves me with a number of questions for Dr. Sabia-Tanis. Do the experiences of transgender people differ enough from one to another so that some may prefer the diversity framework while others view their experiences through the framework of disability? Should we see gender dysphoria as a morally neutral illness for which we now have better medicine—as we have for bacterial infections or depression or other differences in endocrine function? Is the suffering that often accompanies gender dysphoria inherent to the trans experience, or do transgender people suffer solely because they live in a world where a strict binary is expected, where transgressing gender expectations and performance is punished through harassment, violence, abandonment, and even murder? Can a society be envisioned in which transgender and gender nonconforming people are valued for the ways they expand our vision of God's creative genius in such a way that gender affirmation surgeries and hormone therapies fall by the wayside or are seen as medically unnecessary, elective enhancements? Is the

---

1. Social Cognitive Development Lab, "TransYouth Project and Gender Development," http://depts.washington.edu/scdlab/research/transyouth-project-gender-development/.

disability lens necessary simply because of the harm experienced by those who are different in a society that privileges and rewards binary ideals (against which most transgender and many cisgender people fall short)? If our culture venerated transgender people for their unique insights, as do a number of cultures around the globe, would gender dysphoria become a thing of the past? Have we created this so-called disability, as we have created anorexia and bulimia, by our unrealistic expectations?

It seems to me that the diversity framework offers us a broader view of gender that would benefit everyone. It calls us to question the narrow, unrealistic, culturally designed and enforced ideals of gendered beauty that undermine the health and well-being of transgender and cisgender people alike. It invites us to let go of our fear, freeing us to expend our time and energy pursuing the activities that mattered most to Jesus. As Dr. Sabia-Tanis reminds us, "What matters, in Jesus's eyes and teachings, is the degree to which we love God and the manner in which we treat others. Transgender Christians strive for these goals, as do other believers" (p. 220).[2]

As cisgender Christians strive to love God and our transgender neighbors as ourselves, we would do well to think carefully about the story, which Dr. Sabia-Tanis recounts, of a First Nations transgender woman who was denied food and admittance to the worship service at the Union Gospel Mission in Sioux Falls, South Dakota, because she dressed as a woman (pp. 221–22). The account is a damning indictment of the way transgender people are too often being treated by many who call themselves Christians and recalls only too clearly the parable of the sheep and the goats told by our Lord in Matthew 25:31–46. We must take Christ's warning to heart, lest we find ourselves as surprised by the verdict as those to whom Jesus said, "Truly I tell you, just as you did not do it to one of the least of these, you did not do it to me" (v. 45).

"Whoever has ears, let them hear" (Matt. 13:9, 43 NIV).

---

2. Referencing the greatest commandments, which Jesus names in John 13:34–35.

Glossary

The following terms and definitions have been informed by a range of sources. It should be noted that many of these concepts are still evolving and that precise definitions are often a matter of debate.

AFAB/AMAB (assigned female/male at birth)—see **assigned sex; birth sex**.

agender—refers to a person who does not identify with any gender.

androgyne (lit. Greek for "male-female")—a person appearing as neither a man nor a woman; expressing either a mixed or neutral gender.

androphilia—sexual attraction to men and/or masculinity.

assigned sex—the sex category (i.e., male, female, intersex) that an infant is identified with by medical professionals and parents. See also **birth sex**.

autogynephilia—the phenomenon of a man being sexually attracted to the thought of himself as a female. Associated with Ray Blanchard's controversial theory concerning male-to-female transsexuals.

berdache—see **Two-Spirit**.

bigender—refers to a person who identifies as both man and woman.

biological sex—see **birth sex; sex**.

birth sex (also "natal sex")—the biological sex that one is born as (i.e., male, female, intersex), as determined by such things as chromosomes, hormones, gonads, and genitals.

body dysmorphic disorder (BDD)—a condition involving obsessive thoughts about one's bodily flaws or defects, whether real or imagined.

body integrity identity disorder (BIID)—a condition in which a person perceives a part of their body (typically a limb) as alien to them, which can lead to seeking elective amputation.

butch—refers to a masculine-appearing person (e.g., a masculine lesbian).

cis/cisgender/cissexual (from the Latin *cis*, meaning "on the same side of")—coined by trans activists in the 1990s, these terms refer to individuals whose gender identity aligns with their birth sex (i.e., a nontransgender person).

cisnormativity—the belief that all humans are, or at least should be, cisgender.

cross-dresser/cross-dressing (also/formerly "transvestite")—someone who regularly dresses in attire associated with the other gender, whether for sexual excitement, emotional release, or performance art. Any individual can do this, but statistically, most cross-dressers are heterosexual men with no desire to surgically modify their bodies.

detransition—the process by which a person returns to living in alignment with their birth sex after having transitioned to living as the opposite sex/gender.

differences/disorders of sex development (DSDs)—see intersex.

drag king—a male-emulating female. Often the cross-dressing element is for entertainment purposes rather than sexual arousal.

drag queen—typically a gay, female-emulating male (usually in a "campy" style). Often the cross-dressing element is for entertainment purposes rather than sexual arousal.

essentialism—as used with regard to issues of sexuality, the belief that categories of human sex (i.e., male and female) and/or gender (i.e., man and woman) have a fixed, definable essence rooted in the physical realities of nature, etc.

femme—refers to a feminine-appearing person (e.g., a feminine lesbian).

fetish—see paraphilia.

FtM/F2M (female-to-male)—a person who has transitioned from living as female to living as male.

gender—usage depends on context but most often refers to the common traits (e.g., inner sense of self, attitudes, feelings, behaviors, role expectations, etc.) associated with being a man/masculine, a woman/feminine, or some gender-variant alternative, within a given sociocultural context.

gender-affirming hormone therapy—the use of hormones to facilitate the development of secondary sex characteristics as part of the process of transitioning. Typically involves the use of testosterone by those transitioning from female to male, and the use of estrogen and/or androgen blockers by those transitioning from male to female. See also hormone replacement therapy.

gender-affirming/confirmation surgery—various surgical procedures that serve to transition one's body to align with one's gender identity. Common procedures include chest surgeries (e.g., breast augmentation or mastectomy), removal of gonads, and various genital surgeries. Also known as sex reassignment surgery.

gender atypical—see gender nonconformity.

gender dysphoria—a condition where one's transgender experience leads to psychological/emotional distress. Used as a diagnostic category in the current edition of the Diagnostic and Statistical Manual of Mental Disorders (DSM-5).

gender expansive (also "gender creative," "gender explorative," "gender variant"; formerly "tomboys" or "sissies")—typically refers to children who do not conform to cultural gender expectations. Transgender is included within gender expansiveness, but not all gender expansive children are necessarily transgender.

gender expression—an individual's chosen outward expression of gender (via behavior, dress, and/or other culturally recognized signals).

genderfluid—a person whose gender identity and/or expression is highly flexible and capable of changing from day to day.

gender identity—one's own internal sense of being a man/male, a woman/female, or in some sense genderfluid or gender variant/nonconforming.

gender minority—individuals whose gender identity differs from their birth sex and/or whose gender expression varies from their culture's gender norms and expectations.

gender nonconformity—gender behavior, expression, or experience that does not match cultural gender norms, roles, and expectations regarding the categories of man/masculine and woman/feminine.

gender norms/normative—a culture's expectations, roles, and social scripts regarding men/masculinity and women/femininity and the appropriate expressions, behaviors, and dress that align with them.

genderqueer (also "nonbinary," "gender bending," "genderfluid," etc.)—various expressions of gender variance/nonconformity.

gender reassignment surgery—see **sex reassignment surgery**.

gender role—a culture's expected norms, social scripts, and behaviors associated with men/masculinity and women/femininity.

gender transition—see **transition**.

gender variance—gender behavior, expression, or experience that does not match a culture's gender roles and norms.

gynephilia—sexual attraction to women and/or femininity.

hermaphrodite—see **intersex**.

hormone replacement therapy (HRT)—the use of hormones to facilitate the development of secondary sex characteristics as part of the process of transitioning. Typically involves the use of testosterone by those transitioning from female to male and the use of estrogen and/or androgen blockers by those transitioning from male to female. Trans activists prefer the term "gender-affirming hormone therapy."

intersex (formerly "hermaphrodite")—refers to persons born with atypical physical sex characteristics such that their chromosomes, hormones, internal reproductive organs, and/or genitals do not align with typical male or female characteristics.

misgendering—the experience of being labeled by others as having a gender other than that with which one identifies.

MtF/M2F (male-to-female)—a person who has transitioned from living as male to living as female.

natal sex—see **birth sex**.

nonbinary (also "genderqueer")—refers to a person who doesn't identify as either male/man or female/woman.

pangender (from the Greek prefix *pan*, meaning "all")—refers to a person who identifies with a gender beyond the binary of male or female. The person may consider themself to be a member of a third gender or of all genders.

paraphilia—a pattern of sexual desires, preferences, fantasies, and/or behaviors that focus on unusual acts, situations, persons, or objects. Examples include exhibitionism, necrophilia, objectophilia, pedophilia, and zoophilia.

postgender—refers to a sociopolitical vision that considers all gender categories to be arbitrary and oppressive social constructs, and in response, calls for the dismantling of all fixed gender categories so that each person is free to choose their own unique expressions of sex/gender.

queer—can be used either more broadly to refer to anyone who identifies with the LGBTQ+ community or other sexual minority groups or more narrowly to refer specifically to lesbian, gay, and bisexual persons.

queer theory—a critical theory that emerged in the 1990s from the confluence of several academic disciplines including French poststructuralism, feminist thought, and gay and lesbian studies. Focuses on the deconstruction of seemingly stable, "natural" categories such as sex, gender, and sexuality by emphasizing their thoroughly socially/linguistically constructed nature.

sex—commonly refers to the biological categories of male and female, based on chromosomes, hormones, gonads, and/or genitals. Alternatively, can be used to refer to engaging in sexual acts.

sex reassignment surgery (SRS)—various surgical procedures that serve to change one's body to align with one's gender identity. Common procedures include chest surgeries (i.e., breast augmentation or mastectomy), removal of gonads, and various genital surgeries. Also known as gender-affirming/confirmation surgery.

sexual orientation—refers to the sex/gender of the persons to whom one is sexually/romantically attracted.

sexuality—can be used generally to refer to issues related to human sexuality or more specifically to refer to one's focus of sexual desire (i.e., sexual orientation).

social constructionism—as used with regard to issues of sexuality, the belief that human gender (i.e., man and woman) and sex (i.e., male and female) are socially constructed categories that reflect contingent, unstable cultural sensibilities, not fixed, stable realities rooted in the nature of things.

SRS—see sex reassignment surgery.

TGNC—transgender and gender nonconforming.

third gender/sex—refers to a person who does not identify as either a man or woman, but rather a third option.

trans/trans-/trans*—abbreviations for "transgender," sometimes used with specific nuances in certain contexts.

transgender—most commonly used as an umbrella term that refers to many types of people whose expression of gender, in one way or another, does not match their birth sex, including cross-dressers, transsexuals, and other gender-variant/nonconforming people. Sometimes used more specifically to refer to a person who consistently lives as a gender other than that which correlates with their birth sex but who chooses not to undergo sex reassignment surgery.

transgender studies—a subfield of LGBTQ+ studies that arose as an academic discipline in the 1990s, is typically aligned methodologically with poststructuralist thought and queer theory, and focuses on a wide array of issues related to transgender experience(s).

transition—the process a transgender person experiences as they turn from living in alignment with their birth sex to living in alignment with their gender identity. Can include many phases and dimensions, such as social transitioning (i.e., living publicly as one's gender identity on a daily basis), physical transitioning (i.e., hormone replacement therapy, sex reassignment surgery), and legal transitioning (i.e., legally changing one's name and sex).

transition regret—the regret that some transgender/transsexual people experience after transitioning to living as the other sex/gender.

transman—a person whose birth sex is female but whose gender expression is male.

transsexual—a transgender person who permanently transitions to living as the sex/gender they identify with. Often involves medical interventions, such as hormone replacement therapy and sex reassignment surgery.

transvestite—see **cross-dresser/ cross-dressing**.

transwoman—a person whose birth sex is male but whose gender expression is female.

Two-Spirit (formerly "berdache")— traditionally refers to people who fulfilled a third-gender or gender-variant role within indigenous North American cultures. Today, some LGBTQ+ American Indian and Alaska indigenous people identify as Two-Spirit.

Contributors

James K. Beilby (PhD, Marquette University) is professor of systematic and philosophical theology at Bethel University (St. Paul, MN). He is the author, editor, or coeditor of twelve books, including *Understanding Spiritual Warfare: Four Views* (Baker Academic, 2012), *Thinking about Christian Apologetics: What It Is and Why We Do It* (InterVarsity, 2011), *The Routledge Companion to Modern Theology* (Routledge, 2013), and *The Historical Jesus: Five Views* (InterVarsity, 2009). He has also published nearly forty articles or essays in journals such as *Faith and Philosophy*, *International Journal for Philosophy of Religion*, and *Religious Studies*.

Megan K. DeFranza (PhD, Marquette University) is a research associate at the Center for Mind and Culture (Boston) and a visiting researcher at Boston University School of Theology. She is the author of *Sex Difference in Christian Theology* (Eerdmans, 2015) and a contributing author to a number of books and articles, including *Two Views on Homosexuality, the Bible, and the Church* (Zondervan, 2016), *Intersex, Theology, and the Bible* (Palgrave MacMillan, 2015), and *Evangelical Postcolonial Conversations* (InterVarsity, 2014). With Lianne Simon, she cofounded the nonprofit Intersex and Faith, and together with Paul Van Ness, she recently completed the documentary film *Stories of Intersex and Faith*. Find out more at www.megandefranza.com and www.intersexandfaith.org, and follow her on Twitter: @MKDeFranza and @intersexfaith.

Paul Rhodes Eddy (PhD, Marquette University) is professor of biblical and theological studies at Bethel University and a teaching pastor at Woodland Hills Church (St. Paul, MN). He has authored, coauthored, or coedited a dozen books, including *The Jesus Legend: A Case for the Historical Reliability* *of the Synoptic Jesus Tradition* (Baker Academic, 2007), *The Historical Jesus: Five Views* (InterVarsity, 2009), *Across the Spectrum: Understanding Issues in Evangelical Theology*, 2nd ed. (Baker Academic, 2009), and *John Hick's Pluralist Philosophy of World Religions* (Wipf & Stock, 2015). He has also authored a number of articles and essays related to the theology of religions and the historical study of Jesus.

Justin Sabia-Tanis (PhD, Graduate Theological Union; DMin, San Francisco Theological Seminary) is assistant professor and director of the Social Transformation Program at United Theological Seminary of the Twin Cities. His career includes pastoral ministry and nonprofit work. He is the author of *Trans-gendered: Theology, Ministry, and Communities of Faith* (Pilgrim, 2003) and has contributed chapters to *The Queer Bible Commentary* (SCM, 2015) and *Take Back the Word: A Queer Reading of the Bible* (Pilgrim, 2000).

Julia Sadusky (PsyD, Regent University, Virginia) is a postdoctoral fellow at EDCare in Denver, Colorado. At Regent Univeresity she served as research assistant in the Institute for the Study of Sexual Identity and provided services through the Sexual and Gender Identity Clinic, offering individual, family, couples, and group therapy for those navigating sexual and gender identity concerns. She also works as a youth and ministry educator, offering trainings and consultations related to sexuality, gender, and theology. Recent publications with Dr. Mark Yarhouse include *Approaching Gender Dysphoria* published through Grove Ethics and *A Christian View of Sex Reassignment Surgery and Hormone Therapy* published through the Center for Faith, Sexuality, and Gender.

Owen Strachan (PhD, Trinity Evangelical Divinity School) is associate professor of Christian theology at Midwestern Baptist Theological Seminary. He is the director of the Center for Public Theology and hosts the City of God podcast. At the administrative level, Strachan is director of The Residency, Midwestern Seminary's residential PhD program. He is also the former president and current fellow of the Council on Biblical Manhood and Womanhood and a fellow of the Ethics and Religious Liberty Commission and of Reformanda Ministries. Strachan has published fourteen books, including *Reenchanting Humanity* (B&H Academic, 2019). He has written articles for *Themelios*, *Trinity Journal*, and the *Midwestern Journal of Theology*.

Mark A. Yarhouse (PsyD, Wheaton College Graduate School) is the Dr. Arthur P. Rech and Mrs. Jean May Rech Chair in Psychology at Wheaton College. He is the author or coauthor of twelve books, including *Understanding Gender Dysphoria: Navigating Transgender Issues in a Changing*

Culture (IVP Academic, 2015) and *Listening to Sexual Minorities: A Study of Sexual Identity and Faith on Christian College Campuses* (IVP Academic, 2018). He has also published over eighty peer-reviewed articles in journals such as *Professional Psychology: Research and Practice*, *Psychotherapy*, and *Journal of Pastoral Care and Counseling*.

Scripture Index

Subject Index

251